Walking a I

Michael Shearer

ISBN-13: 978-1722279486

Chapter 1.

Novices

My son, Kes, was always a canny kid.

I remember an incident from when he was about six. I'd finished marking (I'm a teacher) about half an hour before closing time at my local pub and wearily pushed it all aside to nip down the road for a swift pint. I'd only reached our front door, when there was a wail from the bedroom.

"Da-ad!"

The two syllables are always a bad sign. I went up.

"Can you tell me a story, Dad, one of *your* ones."

"No, Kes, I've got to go out."

"One from a book then. Ple-ase."

"OK, OK. But it will have to be short."

I reached down Kipling's 'Just So Stories' and flicked through to find the shortest; less than one page. I read it out and shut the book with a dramatic snatch.

"Is that it?"

"Yep."

"A bit short."

"Some stories are long, Kes, some stories are short."

"Can I have another one then?"

"No, Kes. I have to go out urgently."

"Where you going?"

"I'm going where flamingos fly, where pelicans breed, where mermaids swim in the warm surf and blow kisses no man can ever forget."

"Oh, right."

I moved towards the door.

" Dad."

"Yes, Kes?"

"While you're there?"

"Yes, Kes?"

"Could you buy me a packet of crisps?"

Smart arse.

Kes had always been precocious in conversation. I suppose it's what you might expect of the son of a philosopher brought up in a house containing 10,000 books and where the main activities are reading and talking (we have no television). I remember him at seven addressing a group of visiting undergraduates, late, the students fresh back from the pub, on the subject of the existence of God; and shutting them all up.

"But if you haven't got something which explains everything," he said, "then you haven't got anything which is explained."

Leibnitz said something similar.

Kes was nine when we did this walk across Spain. We hitch-hiked from our home in Essex, through France until we got to the French side of the Pyrenees, then we walked, over the mountains and then more or less West.

As we walked through Angouleme, down in the South West of France, we reached a river.

"How about a break?" said Kes hopefully.

All day it had been oppressively dull and humid but the world had shed its weight with a recent shower. The very air had lightened, the sun's rays tingled with a fragile delicacy. The river was overhung with foliage and its flow was a living green. Everything seemed airy and fresh, and each shade of green had acquired a sunlit tinge of lemon. The scene felt like a gift. We went down to the river, eased off our packs, and brewed up some tea.

We were sitting quietly, contented, when a Vision appeared straight out of a painting. Round the bend in the river came a young woman in a row boat. She was exquisitely beautiful and seemed to focus the qualities of fragility and delicacy in the light and the landscape. She embodied the moment. She had long, dark, Pre-Raphaelite tresses and wore a dress of white lace, and rowed with such grace and gentleness the mystery was how such kissing touches of the blades of the oars could possibly impel the boat forward. She stroked the river and, in gratitude, it carried her along like some exotic, lacy white leaf. We stared in admiration.

Then, round the bend behind her, another boat. This time a burly young man, stripped to the waist, muscles everywhere. He whacked the boat along as if his intention was to assault the water. He didn't so much propel the boat forward with his oars, as heave the entire river backwards. A great, sweaty hulk of a man, covered in tattoos. We watched the two and their contrasting styles.

"Don't think much of your one," said Kes quietly.

"It's all right for you, Kes," I said mournfully. "I shall have none of that sort of thing for weeks."

"It's all right for you," said Kes firmly, "I've had none of that sort of thing for nine years."

We watched the vision of lace and delicate curves pursued by muscle and tattoos.

"I feel, Kes, that this may be the moment to broach Certain Subjects which a father ought to speak about with his growing son."

"Oh, yeah?" said Kes suspiciously, stirring his tea.

"You haven't heard any unusual noises from the living-room from your mother and I on occasion?"

"Once or twice."

"Well, we have learned to do it quietly. Perhaps you will have noticed the splodges on the wallpaper and ceiling?"

"Yeah?"

"This, Kes, is a result of the practice of Tea Bag Hurling."

"Tea Bag Hurling?"

"Exactly. Allow me to demonstrate."

I scooped out the tea bag from my green enamel mug and held it on the spoon at arm's length behind me. It fell off.

"That's very impressive, Dad."

"No, no, that's not it," I said quickly, retrieving the tea bag, placing it on the spoon and flicking it out about twenty feet towards the river.

"There. You try."

Kes hooked out his tea bag, and in one fluid movement, cast it out over the river bank and far out into the river.

"Well, it just shows you what a little instruction can do."

How we found ourselves sitting by a French river heading towards the Spanish border is a small story in itself.

When it all began is a moot point, but certainly a significant moment was the day I noticed a sketch of Northern Spain pinned up on a board at the college where I work. It had an unsteady red line wiggling across it, like a very thin snake, or a trace of someone with a very bad heart. "Lecture," it said, "Pilgrimage on the Camino de Santiago." It pulled somewhere inside.

Imagine, to get out of all this work and go fishing, fix my over-stressed heart, now that would be something like. The yearning bred instant daydreams. I stood before the poster with my mind in a disengaged limbo. What was I to do with this feeling? Just a fantasy surely, which escaped into the air in a regretful sigh. I had a class to teach, tedious admin to complete. Some other time maybe, I'd come back to that hankering, sort it out, explore what it contained. Not now. The here and now hoovered back my straying imagination. I pulled away from the map like a magnet from metal, hurried on, and forgot all about it.

Some weeks later I was wandering around the college trying not to think of marking, when I saw the map had "TODAY" scrawled diagonally across it. An echo of the earlier feeling, a foretaste of its content, wafted through me like seeing a rosebud and anticipating its scent. And besides, I thought, almost anything is better than marking, so I went along.

In the hall, I sat next to Roger, the Careers Officer; a large & ungainly man, like a friendly bear.

An hour later my feelings were more disturbing. As the lecture had progressed and the colourful slides flicked onto the screen, an uneasiness grew and strengthened into a feeling I did not recognise.

Feelings are like tastes. Can I convey the taste of pomegranates if you've never tasted one? Or a soup; a bit of this, a nuance of that?

Still, in the soup of my feelings one bit, like a lump of chicken, was clearly identifiable: I knew that I was going to walk across Spain. No, stronger than that; it was already true that I had walked across Spain, in the future. I knew something I could not logically know, and, as a teacher of Logic and Philosophy, I found this upsetting. I had a memory of the future.

I turned to Roger to see his eyes sparkling. "I'm going to do this walk," he stated firmly.

"Me too," I replied.

That evening I announced to the family, over dinner, that I was going to walk across Spain in the summer.

I've always walked. I've done many of the well-known named walks in England, walked in Wales, in Scotland, in Northern France and the wonderful but difficult G10, across the grain of the landscape in the French Pyrenees; a walk which permanently damaged my ankles.

"Can I come?" said Kes, over the dinner table.

"No, Kes. It's a long way, over five hundred miles."

Kes was still only eight at this time, and skinny, and short for his

4

age.

"I'm not sure *I* can make it," I continued. "I'm overweight, nearly thirty-nine, and not very fit. I very much doubt that *you* could do it."

Kes responded with a child's grief. He raised a spoon to his lips slowly, with a hopeless distaste, as if it were full of maggots. I'd never seen him so swiftly and completely down. I felt guilty.

"I'll tell you what," I said, to make myself feel better, "if you can prove to me that you can walk five hundred miles, I'll take you."

"How can I do that?"

"Well, I'll have to get fitter, so I'll do some practice walks. You'll have to do them too. Long walks. If you make it, I'll take you. OK.?"

Kes brightened.

I didn't want to take him. Getting myself along would be hard enough, I didn't want the responsibility of coping with a child as well. I thought that on the first long walk together he'd realise that he didn't want to go after all and he'd voluntarily back out. I wouldn't have vetoed the thing, he would see for himself that he couldn't do it.

So, the next Easter found the pair of us, kitted out with gear from jumble sales and army surplus stores, and walking from the outermost edge of London to Canterbury. I don't recall much about the three-day trip (unlike the Camino itself, I didn't keep a diary) except that the weather was foul. It was blustery cold, with frequent driving rain that slapped into our faces. The paths were muddy and we slipped and slid our way along, heads down, ploughing into the wind. We walked hand in hand where we could, and every few minutes I'd have Kes dangling on the end of my arm as he lost his footing and started to splat into the mud, yet again. We tried to give up, twice. The first time that we dismally admitted to each other that we'd had enough, we found a clear patch in a bleak copse with tangled ivy over stumps of trees, which we could use as a windbreak, and brewed up a last cup of tea. Kes drooped himself over the stove to keep warm, and silently cried.

No Spain now.

Then a young woman came around the corner cheerfully playing an Irish jig on a tin whistle. She joined us for tea, and soon we were up and walking with her.

Then later, after Ruth had walked ahead, we lapsed once more and gave up in earnest where the path reached a road, and started to hitch the rest of the way. A Jaguar stopped and the driver put our rucksacks into the boot.

"Out walking, eh?" he said, as we drove off.

"Sure."

"Where are you going?"

"Canterbury."

"Oh, fine."

And after about half a mile he stopped.

"That's the path you want," he said, gesturing.

"But..."

He was out of the car already, unpacking our rucksacks.

"Good luck," he said, shook my hand and was off.

We looked at our rucksacks dismally. Couldn't we even give up successfully? A group of walkers appeared from nowhere and I explained that Kes was having a bit of trouble.

"No problem," said one, who looked like a shaved grizzly, and he picked up Kes' rucksack with one hand and strode off down the path. We hurried after him.

Thus we reached Canterbury.

At the next holiday we walked out of our front door together to walk to Kings Lynn, a hundred miles North. A week later we arrived, foot-sore but triumphant, and I was honour-bound to take Kes to Spain.

Chapter 2.

Ingatestone to St.Jean

So it was that, one July evening, tired after the hassle of packing, we went down to the Community Club bar in Ingatestone, Essex on the eve of our trip.

I stared into my beer trying to read the future in the settling froth.

"I see a passionate Spanish senorita," I said hopefully," with jet black hair and flashing eyes. What do you see in yours, Kes?"

"I see blackcurrant and lemonade and two bits of ice," he replied factually.

"No, no."

I waved my hands over my glass expressively, doing my gypsy clairvoyant impression.

"It's getting clearer now. Good God! I think it's two senoritas! Now come on, Kes, you see how to do it. Try harder. Concentrate."

He gazed seriously into his drink.

"I see blackcurrant and lemonade and two smaller bits of ice," he said.

"You have no soul, Kes."

"Soul?"

"Sex is just the visible manifestation of an amalgamation of souls, Kes."

"Oh, yeah?"

"Or maybe the other way round."

He looked puzzled, then grinned.

After two long walks together, we had got closer. I had discovered his strengths, he had found some of my weaknesses. We were easy in each other's company.

On the great day of departure we were up early, posed for posterity by our privet while our photo was taken, and set off to hitch to Southern France. In a couple of hours we were at the coast sharing the 'Pride of Dover' with four ton of assorted youth and a lot of Japanese with brown corduroy baseball caps with 'YAMAHA' printed on them. The Japanese were plainly bound together as a group. There was much shared concern when a younger employee leaned too far over the rail. It looked like a large family outing rather than a

Company; they had a group loyalty and regard which contrasted markedly with the spiky individualism of the English school parties ranging round the ship like fluid packs of hyenas.

Kes had never been abroad before. I'd given him long lectures on walking in Spain in August and its difficulties.

"The heat will be our biggest problem, I expect. The sun will be our enemy."

About half way across the Channel I found Kes in the stern of the boat, gazing wistfully at the broad, dead-straight, sun-speckled wake behind us.

"Can't feel it getting hotter, Dad," he said distrustfully.

"Have faith, Kes," I replied.

At Boulogne I decided to teach Kes a little patience, and while everyone else competitively clattered and battered their way off the quay and through a narrow gate into the wide world, I took a break and smoked a cigarette, cool and superior, sitting on a bollard. The bollard, I soon discovered, was covered with a rich, glutinous, oil like chewing-gum, which stuck to my trousers like the residue of some embarrassing lapse, and stayed there for weeks afterwards.

Feeling nervous we walked through the town and alongside a stinking river, southwards.

"Hitching is an art-form, Kes."

"Oh, yeah."

"Yes, indeed. We must find a suitable spot. Success in hitching, like interior decorating and sex, is all in the preparation."

"Right, Dad."

But there wasn't a good spot until we had walked right out of town, and then we waited for hours.

"Art-form, eh?"

"I'm a little rusty, give me time."

"I dread to think what your decorating is like," said Kes archly.

Eventually we got a lift in an ancient lorry. The driver was ancient too, and unshaven. He had a lump the size of an orange on his elbow and wheezed a lot. The lorry was equally decrepit. He had to hold the gear stick in position while he drove, and had to pull the choke out to get the thing up the slightest hill.

Still, we arrived at Montreuil (about twenty miles from the coast) where the citadelle was a youth-hostel. Kes insisted on dragging me round the ramparts to see the view. It was peacefully rural except for a group of scouts, in bright red scarves, rolling full length on the ground down the slope towards the river. Mosquitoes zipped about. Kes rushed off to the dungeons or something, and he soon appeared far below me. I waved.

"I think I can see a goldcrest," I shouted down.

"There's two beetles mating down here," he yelled back.

"Naturally, this is France, Kes," I explained, "everything does it all the time here."

In the evening I wrote up my diary, as I did most nights. I kept a notebook handy in a breast pocket during the day and jotted down anything which grabbed my attention: thoughts and feelings, facts and remarks, outlines of conversation, quotes.

In the night I was plagued by mosquitoes and acquired a 3-D map of our route on my back.

"OK. if we get lost, Dad," said Kes, consolingly, the next morning, "we can just whip up your shirt and ask someone to point out exactly where we are."

"Yes, but I couldn't see where they pointed and your geography stops at Thurrock."

After a long wait hitching, a young woman stopped and we climbed into a car filled with dirty washing. She dropped us at Saint Maixent; one of those French villages with a perfectly straight road coming from the horizon going into it, and a mirror image going to the horizon coming out of it.

"We're gonna be here a long time, Kes."

Cars whipped through this place as if it were the straight at Indianapolis. So we hitched and hitched and sucked mints and repacked the bags, and threw stones at a post for three hours until finally getting a lift to Rouen. Only eighty miles, but it had taken all day.

In the evening we went for a walk down the cobbled roads by the river and watched the huge, flat, industrial barges, and the screaming swifts swooping over the town, in the evening light. As we unwound in the twilight a huge barge, like a small oil tanker, quietly turned mid-river, and slowly drifted towards us. The mind took on the pace of the movement, the boat inched in, heavy and easy; I felt calm and unburdened. There was a couple (and a dog) on board. The man handled the five-foot wheel with a casual ease, wafting the massive boat up to a huddle of moored vessels just close enough for his wife to throw a rope over a bollard but without the hull touching the quay. I sat and enjoyed the quiet grace.

The great secret of the novelist, well, some of them anyway, is that the world works like a novel. It has plot and structure, symbols and metaphors. It is organised according to meaning.

By the river I could have found myself concerned with any of a myriad of other features which were available: the lights of the town, the night sky, the water's flow. I could have found myself indifferent to the scene and turning to Kes in need of speech or contact. But no, the ease of this berthing was self-selected: that this man should turn his wheel of fortune and so delicately achieve a temporary home-coming. This embodied, summed-up, and foretold my greatest need; and I knew it.

The world provides such frequent and inter-connected instances of a person's themes and symbols. Synchronicity, meaningful coincidence, is not a weird rarity, it is common and frequent.

A symbol is a part of the puzzle, a piece which implies the whole. We get the word 'symbol' from the Ancient Greek 'symbolon.' A 'symbolon' was a single coin or token; a circle, a oneness complete in its wholeness. When friends or lovers parted, a symbolon might be broken in two. Each kept one part, in witness of the whole that had been lost and which might one day be retrieved. The jagged edge of the cleft symbolon was therefore a reminder of lost love and a broken heart, and of a promise of possible healing. Only once unity is shattered does proper symbolism begin.

There's a special sort of feeling which goes with encountering this sort of symbol. Something happens which electrically grabs your attention, something apparently trivial, but maybe the back of your neck tingles. It's like a personal message saying something like: this is really important to you. Pay attention to this, but note that it is symbolic, and just a part of something bigger which you'll have to find out about for yourself.

The man and his boat was like that.

This trip was riddled with such events.

****

The next day we walked out of Rouen to find the route to Tours.
"Can I hitch, Dad?"

"No, Kes, it's a difficult art which takes many years to perfect.
When I've taught you some more, perhaps, you might try a little. The
important thing is not to get discouraged."

But we did, hitching another two hours.

"Just let me try once," said Kes, waving his arm in
demonstration.

There was a screech of brakes and a sleek, silver sports car
driven by a beautiful brunette appeared.

"Jeez, Kes," I gasped.

She seemed flustered and had plainly stopped completely on
impulse. I began to realise that Kes was a major asset. With his
startlingly blond hair and his sweet, cherubic face he seemed to catch
the eye of women.

She dropped us off at Tours.

Tours is a big town and we walked a long way to go through and
get out of it. Women kept stopping and offering us lifts even when
we weren't hitching. So we were soon speeding on towards
Angouleme, as the warm weather turned to rain.

Beyond Angouleme, a slim, young woman stopped in a Citroen
and beamed at Kes with something approaching worship. We got in.
There was a baby on the back seat. Kes got in beside it and the car
roared off.

"I just adore children," cooed the woman in French, staring in
devotion at Kes over her shoulder and driving fast through thick
traffic, apparently solely by intuition. She seemed to regard the whole
thing as an honour to have temporary contact with the adorable Kes.
She took us to the edge of town and onto the Bordeaux road. With
her eyes brimful of a gushing and enveloping love, she reluctantly
bade us adieux, just as a big British truck shuddered to a halt. He
took us to Bordeaux.

Bordeaux is an impressive looking city. Spires and bridges and a
wide river. Down that spacious river was the rest of the world. It held
promise of other countries. That's not the only promise it held. As
we got out of the truck a scrawny young woman leered at us.

"What's she doing, Dad?"

"Advertising, I think, Kes. Anyway, " I changed the subject,
swiftly, "not a bad day, maybe 360 miles. Lets find somewhere to

stay."

We walked through the back streets looking for the youth-hostel. This part of town was decidedly seedy. Odours like decomposing lizards oozed from the drains. We passed a pornographic cinema. Tattoo parlours showed pictures of women with elaborate decorations in astonishing places. Kes was fascinated. I got the distinct impression that there were diseases to be caught in Bordeaux that science had yet to discover.

Eventually we found the youth-hostel and it was very full. There were literally people hanging out of the windows. We went in and found the warden; a big, sullen chap with all the flesh on his face seeking the floor.

"Full, full," he intoned, "no room here."

"Is there anywhere else we can go?" I asked.

"Nowhere. The whole of Bordeaux is full."

"Surely there's somewhere."

"Nowhere. Don't you know what day it is?"

"No."

"The Tour de France arrives here tomorrow. All beds taken."

"Well, we didn't know."

"Are you members?" he asked, apparently to have a good reason to turn us away.

"Yes, of course."

He suddenly looked very guilty.

"I will see what I can find," he said, in a shifty manner.

Forty minutes later he returned and told us he'd found us two beds.

I had a bed next to a cycling journalist. Kes had a bed next to a cycling journalist. The place was all press men. It became clear that the warden had filled the hostel with people who would pay over the odds and was making a few bob.

The very idea of racing to a place, a competition, felt like a kind of insanity. You couldn't get much further from my conception of a pilgrimage than the Tour de France: a journey of pain to determine a victor. The strongest wins, all else are losers.

'Pilgrim' and 'pilgrimage' are odd words in English. Anyone who uses them positively is a bit suspect. As if they might, at any moment, ask you if Jesus has come into your life. The pilgrim is cranky and slightly worse than train-spotters, bird-watchers and stamp-collectors.

I blame Henry VIII.

Pilgrimage is a universal phenomenon. Every part of the globe has its sacred places and its traditions of walking to them. In some religions, like Islam, it is central to the entire practice. Native Americans, Tibetans, Poles and Peruvians, all have their holy journeys. Even England, to Canterbury and Walsingham, to Glastonbury and Holy Island, and many more.

Things got tricky with Henry VIII. When he broke with Rome, all things Catholic became not only banned but suspect, even treasonous. Pilgrimage was associated with the Catholic. Henry even sent spies into continental Europe to discover whether any English were taking part in foreign pilgrimages. No wonder the words fell into disrepute and became dubious.

We left early the following day and got a bus out of town and, from there, hitched easily, through endless dreary forest to Bayonne.

We wandered the streets in the old quarter trying to find somewhere cheap enough to stay. No youth hostel. At our third attempt we found a room in the Bar Basque with its bullfighting posters and murals of Basque men in traditional red berets. It was a sordid little room at the top of a cliff-like house. Outside our window were willows below and swooping swifts. The plumbing played popular classics on kazoos while I sorted out some bread and a tin of mackerel in white wine that my father had brought over for Christmas and nobody would eat. It had simmered in the rucksack and was warm. It stunk like runny cheese and tasted odd. We ate it anyway. In the morning the room reeked like some exotic brothel. We paid the bill and slunk away, before they found out, leaving all the windows wide open.

We crossed the wide, seven-arched bridge, where people were fishing beneath flags of the nations, and made for the station. In the booking hall I fiddled with our rucksacks nervously.

"Shouldn't we get some tickets, Dad?"

"Yeah, but I'm a bit anxious about my terrible French, and besides, I can't remember the French for ticket. You don't know the French for ticket by any chance?"

"Teekay?"

"Don't think that's right. Still, here goes."

And I strode to the ticket office and faced the pretty, pert, Parisian-looking, young lady behind the glass.

"Bonjour."

"Bonjour, monsieur."

"St. Jean?"

"Oui?"

"St. Jean Pied de Port?"

"Oui?"

Then, thankfully, the Gods came to my rescue and I recalled the French for ticket.

"Deux bidets, s'il vous plait."

Seventeen different emotions appeared to contest for supremacy over the muscles of her face.

"Deux bidets!?" she said, beaming.

"Wee," I replied, smiling back.

I soon secured my tickets and returned to Kes in triumph.

"No trouble at all," I said, waving the tickets.

"Well, you seem to be a smash hit at the ticket office."

I turned to see the young woman talking in an animated way to a friend and gesticulating in our direction. Both seemed in a very good mood. They saw us watching and waved. We waved back.

"Women, Kes," I informed him, "are traditionally renowned for their intuition. She has probably some subtle awareness of my skills as a Tea-Bag Hurler."

"Tea-bag hurler?" said Kes, doubtfully.

"Just so."

We hefted our rucksacks and went to board the train.

The short rail trip from Bayonne to St.Jean was a pleasure; such a pretty line, with the foothills of the Pyrenees, coped with cloud, looming over all like a serious old age. I looked up at those dark, deep-violet cones and thought, sombrely, that tomorrow we would be up there, on foot at last, crossing those mountains.

Landscape broods. In a vast mass, like mountains, this is easy to feel and can be intimidating. They seemed to be waiting, waiting to be looked at properly. I gazed at them awhile, felt their call.

We got on the train. The carriage was packed with school kids with small rucksacks and they flitted with excitement from one side of the compartment to the other, vying with each other to spot something and to share it with the others. The carriage filled with whoops and giggles and cries of wonder. The train curved around the town and over the wide river and plunged into a peculiar world which seemed to be a series of echoes of other countries: Austrian chalets, Mexican names for stations, farms like haciendas, patches of thorough French cultivation. There were stands of wild Buddleia, deep cuttings filled with ferns. Then a sudden tunnel which made the ears pop, and a station like somewhere desperate in Bolivia where nothing had moved for at least a decade. The station names were like stopping places on the way to Xanadu: Jatxou, Itxassou, Behereharta. I jotted them down like a reporter.

Amid a carpet of thick-pile maize, like crowds of waving, green children, lay a sleepy white farm with matt-brown shutters and a dozing donkey by a well. The line began to follow a lively, fast-flowing river, crossing it sometimes and back again. We got glimpses, like snapshots, of river-bank, cliffs of tumbled rock, the water flowing strongly, sometimes with children standing on rocks ready to dive, who waved and shouted to our kids on board. We plunged into more tunnels and out suddenly like a gasp of air. Plane trees, and oak and horse-chestnut brushed close. In the harvested fields, piles of grass like gnomes' huts. Onward the train weaved, around vast pyramids of wooded hills. There was the river again, the colour of cold, green slate, till we arrived at the bare, quiet station of St.Jean.

Chapter 3.

St.Jean

We walked through deserted, peaceful, residential roads and uphill to the main street; a motley of hotels and bars and souvenir shops with the wooded mountains apparently just outside of town. The Pyrenees felt like a backdrop, something to make the town more pretty. It was a picturesque place with old bridges over the docile River Nive flanked by the white walls of the backs of houses with wooden balconies and brown shutters.

Our first task was to find somewhere to stay and we were directed by the tourist office to the house of Madame Dubril in the steep and cobbled Rue de la Citadelle. We knocked tentatively and were greeted by a formidable and crusty, late middle-aged woman who admitted us reluctantly into her cluttered, book-lined office. Here she grilled and humiliated us, and Kes turned off and went into screen-saver mode. She disbelieved we were pilgrims, doubted our sincerity, plainly thought we were not serious and were merely disguised motorists. She tutted a great deal, sighed in dismissive disapproval and ridiculed my limping French.

"You are pilgrims?" she sneered sarcastically.

"Yes," I replied, submissive.

"Hmm," she sniffed critically, "and walking?"

"Yes."

And so it went on. It was like something out of Kafka. We were plainly impostors and deeply guilty, though of what exactly was unclear. I had to argue and convince and justify; solve the riddle without knowing what it was.

"Do you have a passport?"

"Yes," and I awkwardly rummaged for my British passport.

"Not that thing," she complained cuttingly, "your pilgrims' passport."

I'd heard of these. With this document you could get free or cheap accommodation all the way along.

"No, we'll get those in Roncesvalles."

"No passports!" she spat, apparently scandalised.

On and on it went for ages with constant tutting, as if she were sucking a sweet.

Eventually, she filled out our details in a large ledger and took us to a refuge, our dormitory accommodation, further up the hill. At long last, after searching the place for illicit intruders, she left, to our relief.

"What a cow!" said Kes succinctly.

Brooding over the experience, I came to a different view of this ordeal.

"She's like a guardian of the Way, I think, Kes. It's like a test of resolve. You have to pass muster. She's like the dog..."

"Bitch," interrupted Kes.

"... the bitch with eyes as big as saucers. Or the Sphinx. Give the wrong answer and you're devoured on the spot. And she teaches humility."

"She teaches resentment," said Kes, unconvinced.

"Well, maybe, but there we were, thinking we were Special, about to walk 500 miles, and she brought us down."

"She does that, all right."

"Undermines the pride and makes you beg. A suitably humble attitude for pilgrims. She starts you off on the right foot."

"She just likes insulting people," said Kes simply.

Still, we dumped our rucksacks and went off to explore.

There were lots of locals crossing the river and climbing a hill the other side. We followed an amateur band and found a "Festival de Force Basque." In we went and sat around a simple sports field and watched short, burly men competing in trials of strength. It was like a primary-school sports day solely for adult males. We watched races where they carried heavy sacks, wood chopping contests, a competition involving hauling bales of hay up on a pulley and endless tug-of-war heats. There was no running or jumping whatsoever.

The Olympics emerged from an essentially military tradition, a development of army training, a citizen's duty to ready themselves for the defence of their city. It can be useful in battle to be able to run and jump, throw your spear, wrestle. The ancient Greeks ran in their amour in the Olympics, held weights when jumping. But here, in St.Jean, was an alternative; a rural Olympics. You don't run and jump, or wrestle, or throw spears, much, on a farm. These agricultural athletes pulled and hefted, lifted and pushed, demonstrated their prowess in shifting awkward things about; like hay bales and farm carts. The finale involved lifting one end of a heavy cart and walking around in a circle with it. Muscles ruled here, and the emphasis was on efficient bulk and tensile sinew. Biceps bulged like marrows and veins stood out like pods of runner-beans, and the crowd of lesser men, plus maidens, potential wives, loved it.

Afterwards we bought a bottle of wine, some bread, cheese and eggs and took a quiet path by the river side, passed a pair of lovers, crossed a wooden footbridge and found a picnic site by the river. Backed by an ancient wall was a sloping half-moon of poor grass going down to a stony beach. Tall trees flanked the opposite bank and the old pilgrims' church, Notre Dame du Bout du Pont, was down river, to our left. I opened the wine and put the bottle to cool in the river, boiled up the eggs on my trusty, old stove, and we settled down to a slow and leisurely meal.

The air felt exotically sultry, but spangled with the sound of the continuously variegated tinkling of running water. Fish jumped beneath bankside shrubs. A lacing lattice of swallows swooped low over the stream for the first few early evening gnats.

"It's the early gnat that catches the bird, Kes," I observed, lazily pointing, relaxed, swigging cheap red wine out of my chipped enamel mug, laying back, gloriously at my ease.

"Still a bit hot though," I continued.

"Aah," said Kes, raising one finger, "I have something for the heat."

He produced a small, plastic fan like a fat sausage with propeller blades at one end. He raised it to his face and grinned.

18

"Turn it on then."

"It is on," said Kes.

"Doesn't it work?"

"Oh, yes, it works."

"It isn't working now."

"No, no, not now."

He moved his face around the fan as if receiving a cooling breeze.

"Why doesn't it work now, Kes?"

"No batteries."

"Well, put them in then."

"Didn't bring any. Have to save weight, you said."

He closed his eyes and enjoyed the imaginary cooling.

"Let me get this right. You brought a portable fan to keep you cool but left the batteries to save weight?"

"All in the mind, man," he said smugly.

I cracked and peeled a hard-boiled egg, put the shell in a paper bag, spread the egg on some bread and bit deep.

"What do you think of this pilgrimage lark, Kes?"

"It's an adventure."

"Surely, but nothing more? You don't feel as if you were a pilgrim?"

"No, do you?"

"Yes......" I paused to let my mind come up with some insight as to what I was doing here. I found only an amorphous feeling of confident expectation. '*Have patience*,' it whispered, '*slow down and have a little patience*.'

"I'm here for a purpose, but I don't know what it is. Maybe, with luck, I'll find out why I'm doing it, on the Way."

He nodded and drank his wine.

Eventually we packed up and retraced our steps, over the footbridge, and past the lovers, still sitting in an agonised tension of togetherness and separation, to the old pilgrims' church. Just on the river bank, with its south-west tower forming a gateway to the bridge and the whole Way, it is a marker of an intention. The colour of the stone arrests and chills. It is a sombre, steely mauve; cold and serious. I went in and lit a candle just because it felt right, though I am neither Catholic nor Christian, and found myself suffused with an emotional ache of loss that seeped out in tears. My shoulders felt hunched and heavy and I became convinced that something awful would happen. I shrugged off the mood as silly.

On the way to the refuge we heard English voices from a crowd of a dozen or so outside the tourist office. They were being filmed by a Spanish television crew. A pretty young woman with frizzy red hair like a child's toy and tiny, delicate hands, wearing a deep-blue p.v.c. anorak, one of the crew, explained to me that they were making a film of the Way with a Spanish astrologer from Valencia as the principal figure. They were waiting for him to arrive. Angel, the director, a bustling, stocky man with constantly flickering, bright eyes, asked me to stand amid the group and keep looking at my watch. I borrowed his watch and obliged, while the camera rolled. Then the astrologer appeared. He was a tall, thin man, sun-browned, wearing a khaki shirt and shorts, and sandals with no socks. He had a long pilgrim's staff and a black, bushy beard. He wore a hat like a pith-helmet but of woven straw. He walked up with slow and measured strides, as if it were a meditation exercise. He stopped and posed for the camera, leaning on his staff with both hands. Then he took off his hat and wiped his brow; he was quite bald.

"What a Pratt," I thought.

****

Kes, tired, turned in early. I updated my diary, studied our sketch-maps for the next day and took a glance at the one-page map of the whole route. A wriggling red line snaked across the whole width of Northern Spain. 500 miles. More than twice the longest distance I'd ever walked in one go. Just walking, no more hitching now, walking every day. It didn't seem possible that we could do it.

That night my parent-alarm went off about 3.00 a.m. Kes wasn't breathing properly. Thin little gasps of wheezy air came from his bunk. It didn't sound enough, and it was much too fast. I lay awake till dawn, listening, anxious

****

"Sleep all right last night?" I inquired, packing.

"Yeah, why shouldn't I? Fine. Except for the cat."

"What cat?"

"The one that came and sat on my chest, and fell asleep. Bloody thing snored all night."

Chapter 4.

Into Spain

The morning was misty and damp. As we began to descend the narrow, cobbled street we could see the mountains high ahead with warm, soft tints of orange on the tops.

Down by the church we filled our water bottles at the tap outside and looked up at the figure of St.James in a niche in the church tower over the gateway to the bridge. He looked like some theatrical figure in a cinematic epic, apparently dressed in a skin, like Hercules, brandishing his pilgrim's staff as if it were a cudgel. James is Iago in Spanish. So Saint James is Sant-Iago, where we were bound & where he is supposed to be buried.

Through the gate & over the bridge; our entrance to pilgrimage, we climbed the Rue d'Espagne. I felt that a band should play and someone should wave us off, but St.Jean Pied de Port just went about its business, setting up market stalls, people buying baguettes. We bought some bread and bacon and ascended the curving road.

No more hitching now. Just walking, walking.

"Let's play a game," said Kes.

"What do you mean, a game?"

"A game. As we walk. Something to pass the time. I'm bored."

"Bored! We've only been going half an hour and there's 500 miles to go! What do you mean, 'bored'?"

"Well, I'm bored."

So we played 'I spy' and I racked my brains for all those games parents invent on long car journeys. We played all those I could remember; several times.

A swathed figure in a white beany-hat caught us up. She carried a huge rucksack and was having some trouble getting along, as she grew closer we could see that she was sweating profusely. Still, she was young and fit, and going at about twice our pace. She turned out to be a young Australian woman although she scarcely stayed long enough to say 'G'day' before belting ahead as if Santiago were just over the ridge. Pilgrims caught and passed us about once every twenty minutes. We were slow; this was going to be a long day.

We passed farmhouses like chalets, with what looked like lush bananas as garden plants and courgettes in the ditches. Great sleek, fat, black slugs reminded us of our pace.

One farmhouse had a notice which announced 'AGUA' (water), our first Spanish word, and we sat on their garden bench and smelt fresh bread and garlic-soused cooking. The vegetable garden was a tilth of reddish soil, like dried blood, with vigorous tomatoes like tennis balls. Everything spoke of a comfortable, domestic, well-fed French life.

Traditionally, until recently, English culture had a deep hue of Puritanism, imbuing experience with a serious tone of fact, responsibility and self-control. Viewed from behind the white cliffs, France seems a land of racy freedom and self-indulgence. In England enjoyment is always rather vulgar and dubious; in France it is an art-form. Somehow this simple, yet lush and well-appointed, French garden represented and embodied an entire way of life: settled, secure in the anticipation of pleasure. It was all of this that we turned our backs on, and climbed.

We soon got beyond roads and all around were the ponderous dark green ridges of monstrous mountains like lump-backed shoals of huge fish. Mother nature; immense, powerful and implacable. Sheep bells tinkled like a wandering, melodious river, over the unfathomable silence. The air smelt musty, like hypericon or fox. I felt immersed in the landscape and we grew silent in respect.

As we climbed it grew hotter as the day advanced. We climbed out of the trees, and beyond the farms, and vegetation became simpler and more patchy.

Eventually, we reached a high point, near a cross-roads, where a small statue of the Virgin was niched by bare rocks. Quick green lizards scuttled about and the earth curved over a lip and plunged to the deep valley below. Eagles and vultures and red kite soared around, magnificently. Here were short low walls about breast high, the ground nearby littered with spent cartridges.

Onward, climbing on springy grass now, surrounded by bracken, past huge, handsome cardboard-brown cows. Well, handsome at the front end, rather bony and mucky round the back.

"Curious things, cows, Kes."

"What do you mean?"

"Quite handsome up the front. Serious errors of design at the back."

"Maybe God did the back and his son did the front," said Kes.

Gradually, the grass grew rarer. The cows became sheep; soon there was only sparse grass under a hot sun in a vast, powder-blue sky. Unused to rationing, we ran out of water.

The Pratt, Claudio, in the pith helmet caught us up, he had slept late. He seemed concerned at our pace, and slowed and talked and almost shepherded us along. He seemed proud of being an astrologer. I'd associated the role with charlatans preying on the gullible, issuing vague, irrefutable predictions. This guy had dignity, and seemed a cross between a philosopher and a doctor. He spoke good English (and French) and had been many years at university studying (it seemed) more or less everything. And the Spanish were making a T.V. programme about him.

We talked of astrology and science, of logic and Aristotle, of mysticism and peanuts and the habits of slugs. And we played 'I spy' and all the games he could recall. Not a Pratt at all.

Kes had been complaining about his feet for some time. A look showed raw areas of rubbing and blisters. His new, expensive boots were doing him no good at all. He changed to a pair of battered, old trainers and we looked at the shiny, dapper boots as if they were enemies. After some discussion, we left the heavy boots in the landscape, prominent by the path, hoping some needy traveller would find them; and walked on. It was as if the Camino was teaching us our first little lesson: if thine possessions are nothing but a lumber, impeding your purpose, shake free and dump them. No point in carrying something you can't use. I looked back on them, nestling in the short grass, like a temptation rejected.

Seeing our problems were eased, Claudio, the astrologer, walked on alone.

We walked through, and emerged above, the clouds, into the sun.

A flock of sheep sunned-bathed warily ahead.

"You see those sheep, Kes?"

"Yere," he answered, suspicious.

"You see some of them are lying down?"

"Yere."

"Do you know why some of them are lying down?"

"Yere."

"Why?"

"They've got no legs."

"Correct!"

But one lone sheep wasn't lying down, or starring at us, chewing but vigilant, it rushed round and round, over the lumpy ground, in small circles.

"Look at <u>that</u> sheep, Kes. Doesn't that remind you of Life?"

There was plainly something wrong with it. It didn't seem to be able to predict the lie of the land. Dips seemed unexpected and it stumbled against slight upward slopes. As we drew near we could see that its eyes were milky and stone-blue. It was completely blind. I put down my rucksack and spent twenty minutes running around, trying to herd the pathetic beast closer to its flock.

Kes sat on his rucksack & yelled guttural Yorkshire commands, like "Ay oop. Leeft. Run on!" and whistled a lot, as he watched.

We were now pretty thirsty and I was getting worried. Looking around at the landscape I saw that there was a sudden belt of trees below, so we descended to find the water *they* must be finding. Sure enough, just above the vegetation, water seeped out of the mountain in a clear puddle. It was ice cold and delicious. We were on our second pint before I thought of hygiene.

"Be sure to spit out the sheep turds, Kes," I advised.

He looked satisfyingly aghast.

An hour or so further down the way, Claudio sat patiently on a rock, waiting for us, looking like a lanky, brown Buddha. He seemed concerned. I'd had some trouble getting up some of the slopes. It appeared that this total stranger was hanging back deliberately to make sure that we made it.

We walked on together, playing a game called 'Jazz'. We each were allotted, by Kes, an instrument, (I was assigned the tuba), which we imitated by suitable noises, and thus we improvised together. Sometimes a shepherd stopped in astonishment as three figures came over the horizon belting out a lurching version of Dixieland liberally decorated by explosions of helpless laughter.

****

Eventually, we seemed to be more often descending than ascending and far below us appeared the chunky monastery of Roncesvalles, low and rectangular with a zinc roof and rows of dormitory windows in a white block, it looked rather like Colditz.

It looked, far below, much as it must have always looked throughout the centuries that pilgrims had walked this route. The feeling was distinct that we had crossed some sort of invisible boundary, not just into another country but into another age. Somewhere in the mountains we had walked through some field of temporal translation. We were walking into history.

The descent continued steadily; at the steepest slope, cloud flowed off the mountains in a forty-five degree stream like a fluffy waterfall. We walked along a road beneath the fall as if beneath a ladder against a wall.

Down by a monument to a famous battle stood the T.V. crew, intermittently filming us, as we, footsore and weary, laboriously picked our zigzag way down the final descent. They had driven up by road. We had laboured twenty-four kilometres (about 14 miles) over the mountains, no villages. We were very tired.

As we eventually reached Angel, the director, he said, "Look how the light has changed just now, so beautiful. Just climb back up a little and descend again. So we can get you in this beautiful light!"

Carefully, in detail, we told him exactly what he could do with his telescopic lens.

Down the straight road we reached the monastery and were greeted by a monk in sunglasses, who told us we were just in time for Mass. Across stone quadrangles, through lofty halls, down dark medieval passages and wide stairways, we hurried down to the church and sat in its cool, wood-ash grey, simple interior while the monks, in lime-green and snow-white robes, went through the service. Another world, and a venerable one. The cool monk in the shades stood among them looking like a spy from the Mafia. At one point most of the congregation stood up and queued in the centre of the nave. I joined the queue and eventually the monk who had greeted us, still wearing his sunglasses, draped a scallop-shell on a string around my neck, while the T.V. crew dollied up and down the aisles filming.

Well, for better or for worse, I was an endorsed pilgrim now.

Chapter 5.

A change of pace

There followed a spot of form filling and we were issued with our pilgrims' 'passports'. Then we were shown to our dormitory; a large hall of a room carpeted with many inch-thick mattresses of foam, like soft graves. I took a swift, tepid shower, which Kes declined, and we turned in, very tired, for the night. Soon there was a body on each foam rectangle and we tried to sleep. It wasn't easy. It was quite hot with so many people in one room, and besides most were young and excited. For many Spanish, Roncesvalles was the obvious place to begin the pilgrimage, many here had not come over the mountains like us. For a long time there was a tedious litany of rude noises, much giggling, sudden mysterious announcements in Spanish, more giggling, and so on. Eventually someone fell asleep and began to snore. An indignant youth then made a loud, insistent clicking noise with the tongue which finally woke the snorer, and everyone else, and so the snoring stopped. This cycle continued until dawn, when suddenly, as the monastery clock struck six, the place erupted into action and excited noise. Clearly many had been lying awake, awaiting the bell. After a short hubbub, by 6.30 a.m. we were alone in the room and could get some sleep.

Much later we explored the place and found an old but serviceable pair of plimsolls that exactly fitted Kes. They were quite dusty and had obviously been there for some time. It seemed a fortuitous gift.

Outside was a grim, pyramidal building surrounded by a single-storey arcade, which houses the bones, stacked to the roof, collected over many centuries, of those for whom the haul over the Pyrenees had proved too much. Here the hope that Santiago might cure had turned to dust.

Standing by the chapel were, what appeared to be, three medieval pilgrims. They were three Germans who had walked from Le Puy, in France, in medieval costume. One wore a natty pair of black and white striped tights and the sort of soft black, wide-brimmed hat with the front folded up to sport the white scallop shell of St.James, which we had already seen on several statues, and which I now wore around my neck. He also carried a medieval rucksack: a huge wicker basket strapped to his back. Covered to keep out rain, it looked as if he had a monstrous, humped deformity. They told us it contained their changes of costume. Silver juggling clubs were strapped to one of the other, normal, rucksacks. They had no money but would pause in towns and villages to perform a show to gain enough cash to move on.

The scallop shell of St.James, used for centuries as a pilgrim badge, is an interesting symbol. There is an ancient story of a horse rider who strays into the sea West of Santiago, on the Coast of Death, (La Costa del Morte, it's really called that) and is considered dead but rises up from the waves, alive after all, and covered with scallop shells. To be dead and yet to emerge from the water, the womb of life, is an obvious indication of rebirth, which is the purpose of the Way. It is fitting that he rises out of the marine element, the blue matrix of Mary, for the scallop shell is also a female symbol, resembling, as it does, the mound of Venus, the female, convex curve towards the vagina, the entrance into life. There has long been a connection between the scallop and Venus (the Greek Aphrodite), and Botticelli's painting 'The Birth of Venus', which shows her emerging from a scallop on the sea, is only one of many such images.

But it is still more complicated than this, for turn the shell around & look into its concave interior & see that the ribbed scallop is also an image of the rayed sun, whose path Westwards the pilgrim follows as it rises at his back, curves over him each day, a cosmic shell, and sets before him at night. The sun is a male energy. So the scallop depicts the amalgamation of male and female in one, from which all proceeds. Where male & female unite expect rebirth.

****

We walked cheerfully on, down a muddy path amid tall pines, in sporadic sight of a long, straight road to our left, to reach Burguette, our first Spanish village.

Burguette is a dapper little place of two-storied, chunky white houses, mostly with cabbage-green doors and shutters. The road through it has a lethally deep trough for a gutter either side which must have broken many an overburdened ankle. We stopped to get provisions in the first shop and found it well stocked with boots. Pilgrims having trouble with footwear on their first day was obviously not unusual. So Kes acquired another pair of boots. A man stopped us here to ask if Kes was walking all the way. The first of very many. I kept forgetting that Kes was only nine and that it must look strange to see one so young, with rucksack and all, on a 500 mile walk. Learning the truth, the man ruffled Kes' hair (which he hates) and told him enthusiastically that he was very brave.

"Valiente! Valiente!" he shouted, ruffling his hair once more, and beaming at a disgruntled Kes.

On through the village, then briefly down a gravel path flanked with shrubs of every shade of green, to the next village: Espinal. Ahead of us in the main street, we saw an old couple with rucksacks turn into a bar called Toki Ona ('Good Place' in Basque), and so when we reached the bar we went in to find out who they were. The bar was refreshingly cool with a white marble floor and dark wooden panelling. A relief, as the heat was already mounting outside.

We sat and I tried to order a beer. Realising the centrality of it, I'd previously looked up the word for beer in my Spanish phrase-book: "cerveza", not an easy word as the 'c' was a soft 's' and the 'z' was pronounced 'th' . Still, I confidently asked for a beer and awaited the refreshing result. The bar-owners looked at each other in momentary confusion and then directed me to the toilets (servicios). The lean, old chap we had followed in, laughed and ordered my beer for me. He was called Otto and had suffered from angina and had had a heart attack but had prayed to St.James in his sickness, promising to walk to Santiago if he recovered. He looked sprightly and bright-eyed and was here paying his religious debt. They had paused, however, because his wife had found it too hard over the mountains yesterday and was ready to give up. She would walk the rest of today, she said, but no farther. She wore light blue denim shorts, a red vest and a straw hat. Her quiet, sagging mood of failure contrasted with her husband's undaunted eagerness and enthusiasm for life. Otto was sharp as a bird as he looked around the bar, his senses alive and alert, interested in everything. He shone anew and his wife wilted in his shade. They were Norwegian and he was a retired director of a ferry company.

Meanwhile I became aware that the owners of the bar, a burly man and his plump wife, were gazing at Kes in open admiration. Kes had seen it too.

"Oh no," he sighed mournfully, "I think I'm in for a touch of the Valientes."

The man barrelled around to us and smiled down on Kes.

"How old is he?"

"Nine."

"And he walks all the way?"

"Yes."

"Oh Valiente! Valiente!" he exclaimed, ruffling Kes' hair.

"I'll hit him in a minute," said Kes, through clamped teeth.

Eventually I freed him from his admirers and the four of us hefted our packs and moved on.

The path turned off the main street between two houses and undulated over pleasant fields. Here lush jet-black butterflies flitted among the green; their wings plush-black with an edging of cream. It wasn't far to the village of Viscarret, but the heat was intense and we already needed water. At the entrance to the village, just before the dazzling white houses with their rows of brilliant red geraniums, was a low cattle trough with two constantly flowing taps and the Australian girl, Ariane, already quenching her thirst.

"Come and try this water," she said, with relish, "it's delicious."

We did and it was.

"Isn't it good?"

"Excellent. Oh, and by the way, you're standing in a particularly fine cow pat."

"Oh Jeez!"

The water was indeed superb; an apparent infinity of water, forcefully flowing, ice-cold and pure, having slowly percolated through the mountain for God knows how long. In the heat it was better than wine.

"So this is how you turn water into wine," I said, "live simply in a hot climate and need it."

We subsequently became connoisseurs of water and at fountains would remark on the quality, the temperature, the taste. Standing in this baking village, quaffing from the unlimited supply, we knew what it was to be rich. There was no greater criticism of a village than that it had bad water.

Our experience with water was only the first of many which brought focus to the ordinary and released its richness. Most people's lives are packed, jumbled with stuff. As a life gets filled, and over filled, it clogs up with the sheer quantity of what there is to see, hear, respond to; people defend themselves from the excess by skimming over their lives instead of living them. They move on all the time and do not linger; so that, paradoxically, their lives get impoverished by plenty. The Camino, by imposing the obligation of going slowly and providing comparatively little to respond to, allows the redemption of the simple experience. And, like a true miracle, the ordinary gives out its wealth.

****

At Viscarret we caught up with the German medievals. Having been on the road for weeks, they had acquired a slow, thoughtful pace not just in walking but in talking too. They invited us to share their lunch. We found this generous attitude of sharing all the way along. It was reassuringly contagious. But it took us a couple more weeks to acquire the calm, patient attitude to time that they already had. The pace of the city was still in our blood like a pollution.

We ate swiftly even though we tried to take our time. We were too insecure in our faith in events, unsure that we could get through the day's walking, find somewhere to stay. Our itchy feet were an infection of the psyche and urged us onwards. So we left the Medievals still leisurely progressing through their meal and moved on.

The Camino had other ideas, however. We set off eagerly, determined to do some miles, only to be arrested one kilometre down the way by the sight of Claudio's lanky form in the doorway of a bar, at his ease, relaxed, and devouring a massive tortilla (an omelette in a hunk of French bread). The sight of him embodied another attitude to time, leisurely, framed like a picture in the doorway. So, of course, we had to stop; I walked in and called for a beer - and was directed to the toilets. Claudio laughed, ordered the beer for me, and we sat down to chat. The Camino had taken our haste, punctured it and tried to give us back our time.

On the Way friends are another elemental wealth. There is a fund of them. They flow down the Way like a stream of refreshing water, and are equally vital. People meet and part, walk on at different rates and meet, or not, once more. Friends fall out and go their separate ways, groups form and split and maybe reform. You never know whether the companion who walks at your side and chats, and strides ahead, will ever be seen again. Any meeting, any exchange could be the last. This gives a piquancy to the apparently coincidental reunions.   This is true of the Way of ordinary life just as much as the Camino, but it is harder to appreciate there. Here it was a node of experienced fact.

Despite the extraordinary variety of pilgrims; all shapes and sizes, all walks of life (as it were), a motley of nationalities, ages, there is the unifying sharing of a common goal - Santiago, which calls from such a distance and draws this diversity together. The random groups which form and dissolve become concerned for each other's progress, for each other. A problem for one becomes a problem for many and it became difficult to imagine abandoning a comrade in difficulties. I can't tell you how refreshing this was in this time of cynicism and the primacy of personal ambition. It sounds idealistic and we so distrust idealism, but on the Camino mutual help was a fact, one of the great gifts of the Way, and cynicism withered under its influence.

So, we stopped and talked with Claudio and he told us of a lone Spaniard from Murcia who had just left, and we told him of the Medievals. In this manner news would travel up and down the path, so that often when we caught strangers up, or they caught us up, we would already know something of them and they had already heard about us. Thus this long, long trail formed a chain of mutual interest, a human telegraph, transmitting messages forward and back by means of casual exchanges.

Soon, more relaxed, we shouldered our loads and prepared to wander onwards. As we were heaving our rucksacks on, Claudio remarked that there was a common belief that a pilgrim's rucksack represented the weight of their personal burden of sin.

On the path, after Linzoain, were dull, rather grey grasshoppers at our feet, but as we stepped close they leaped to the air and spread their wings to reveal vivid flashes of powder blue.

Snippets of revelation hidden in the ordinary.

Soon we entered a refreshingly shady and cool section of dense woodland, mostly pine. The loud buzz of flies reminded us of the nearby heat. The path was wide and obvious and we didn't need to concentrate on the route so much. I found an owl's feather and put it in my hat. Tentatively, I asked Claudio about astrology and explained my sceptical attitude. He scorned the horoscopes to be found in daily newspapers and sketched the complex mathematical process of ascertaining the moment of birth in consideration of geographical position, calendar variations, things like hours added or subtracted in summer or winter, and then calculating the relative position of the planets. And that was the easy bit, he said, nodding thoughtfully, then came the interpretation of all the mutually influential planetary bodies in three-dimensional dynamic, the meaning of these ever-changing relationships.

"Yes, but how can that happen?" I responded, "that's the problem with astrology, isn't it? There's the planets in various geometrical relationships to each other & the Earth. There's the mind & life of the individual, but what connects the two? There's no mechanism, or rather no explanatory theory."

"I don't know," said Claudio thoughtfully as we made our way over a ditch and through a cloud of gnats, "but it is enough for me that it works; and it *does* work. I know that. You're a philosopher, you want to know the explanation for everything."

"Actually, it's worse than not having a theory," I went on, "if you try to envisage what an explanatory theory for astrology might look like, it's clear that it's unlikely to look like anything in respectable science. That's the real problem; we'd have to ditch great chunks of physics and psychology, and refashion them otherwise. Not much motivation in doing that, so astrology can't be allowed to work. Of course, physics could be radically incomplete."

Claudio looked puzzled; he frowned.

"How, I do not understand?"

"If physics finds it needs concepts of mentality. I mean, if it discovers that in order to describe what physically happens it is obliged to use concepts applicable to consciousness, like intention, metaphor, meaning. If it needs those then astrology, and most religions, are possible; otherwise not."

"Does it need those things?"

"Maybe. I think there are at least two areas which might necessitate concepts of mentality."

"What are they?"

We paused to watch an electric blue dragonfly coming towards us. It paused to hover before us & check us out, then went on its way.

"Well, the placebo effect, for example. With the placebo effect, a person thinks they have had an effective physical treatment and they haven't, but they get better anyway. The effect is well documented; it's real. But the physical ailment is cured when the physical cause for the cure is not present. It follows that how the person thinks, their beliefs, effect the cure. Concepts, and their pattern in propositions and beliefs, have a physical effect. I don't think physics or biology have an explanation for this. It rocks the boat."

"And the other rock of the boat?"

A woodpecker drummed in the far forest like some lost tribe passing a message.

"Synchronicity, meaningful coincidence. This is more tricky, it's not a documented phenomenon, yet. But if it happens then physics is somehow radically misconceived. If things can happen which are not just effects of physical causes, but have meaning for those who experience them, and happen because of the meaning, then the world works in a way which includes meaning and metaphor. The world is a poetic place. I don't mean that you might see a sunset and write a poem about it, but that the world would work as a poem works, in structures of related meaning. Actually operate like that."

"Synchronicity is very common on the Camino."

"Maybe."

Claudio smiled, "You will see."

He paused & leant on his staff. Midges flurried around his head.

"I think it the other way round," he continued, "astrology works. And because it works, the world must be the sort of place where it works."

"I'm not convinced it works."

"You will see," repeated Claudio.

In the quiet pause that followed we heard a distant, despairing cry. Looking back down the path we could just make out the diminutive figure of Kes hurrying through the trees.

"I'd forgotten all about him, poor kid."

Absorbed by the conversation, we had slipped into a natural pace which was plainly much too fast for Kes. He must have been desperately rushing along for ages trying to keep up and calling, while we plunged onward ever further ahead.

We had reached the edge of a small clearing, so we took off our rucksacks, propped them up against some trees, and sat and rested back on them, awaiting Kes. We sat in silence in the cool shade at the edge of the dappled clearing. It took some time for Kes to come along. He looked hot and flustered.

"Don't go racing on like that. You forget about me!"

"Sorry Kes."

"I've been shouting for ages. Have you seen any yellows? I don't think we're on the path."

Yellows?

The way was sporadically marked on the ground, or rather on anything that presented itself. Yellow was a colour we were already habituated to noticing. As we walked we were constantly scanning for a flash of yellow; an arrow painted on a road or a wall or a tree. Sometimes there was only the faint vestige of an old, faded patch, sometimes nothing. But Kes was right. Come to think of it I couldn't recall a yellow for a long time.

"OK. sit and take a break, Kes. We'll scout around."

Claudio and I went off in opposite directions, yellow hunting. Ten minutes later we were both back - nothing.

"Well, the only thing to do in this situation," said Claudio, slowly and calmly, "is to retrace our steps and find where we went wrong."

"But I can't remember the last yellow. It could be a long way."

"It could be."

"And this could be the right path anyway."

"That could be so."

"We're lost aren't we?

"Being lost is part of the Way," said Claudio, smiling.

"So, lost in a dark wood already."

"It's not so dark. You will rest here, I will walk back and find the way. It does not need us all to carry our packs searching."

"OK."

"What about a cup of tea?" asked Kes.

So Claudio ambled off back down the path while I brewed up a spot of tea. Take a break, have a cup of tea. Kes took his tea, swirled it round with the spoon, hooked out the tea bag and sent it arcing out into the forest. I watched it.

"That's a really sweet curve," I remarked casually.

"Try not to think of women so much," said Kes.

"No, I mean the trajectory of the tea bag. A beautiful low arch; just right."

"Yes, Dad."

I fell to musing; my back against a substantial sapping, sipping hot tea.

We stop and find the thought of tea. The stopping cues the thought and, sure enough, we have a cup. I began to think of just how many such cues there are in ordinary life, each spawning its habitual behaviour. Up in the morning to go to work, bath-room there, wash, dress, breakfast, an established sequence. But more than that: whatever is on the walls, the objects, pictures on the wall, the furniture; all embodies a life, patterns of behaviour, of values, of preferences. It all speaks me, tells me who I think I am, reassures.

Kes, I noticed, had started peacefully carving a stick. We were both at ease & untroubled.

Home is not just a place, I thought. Things have been chosen & put there to reflect back who & what we think we are. It confirms our self, our identity. And, in the process it becomes a sort of soft & congenial prison. No wonder we need holidays. There's a need to get away from our self.

There's two sorts of homesickness: a hankering for the security of what we have been, and an intuitive ache for what we could be.

Pilgrimage is about the journey from the one to the other.

I glanced up to see Kes. Carving away.

The forest buzzed with insects. A blackbird's alarm call briefly sheered across the peace.

No sign of Claudio.

Now I think I see why some people take such huge packs, solid with stuff. Some with so much that they can hardly get along. It's not their *sins* they carry, it's themselves. All the bits and pieces that will reconstitute themselves in this strange, challenging other place. There is a sense in which they do not carry their rucksack, but are carried by it. They take their home with them, or as much of it as they can; the burden of their old selves on their back. They carry their fears.

Kes, I notice, is not purposelessly whittling, he is fashioning a staff, decorating it, carving patterns in the wood.

And at long last I saw Claudio patiently picking his way down the path towards us in his slow, unhurried, meditative manner.

He arrived and smiled in what seemed to me to be a knowing way.

"You have had a good rest, I see," he said very quietly. And I realised how peaceful and patient we had become in this enforced clearing of waiting. The urgency to get on, make progress, had become subdued.

I smiled back.

"Yes, it's been a good break."

"You must have needed it. The Way has a habit of giving people what they need. Which isn't always what they want, or what they think they want."

"Have we come far off the main track?"

"Yes, I've found a yellow but it is a long way back."

"Do you need a break, Claudio?"

"No, it is a rest to be without the rucksack. And it is late, the sun has begun to set."

"OK. Kes, let's be off. Saddle up."

It was indeed a long walk back down the path to the point where Claudio silently pointed out a faded yellow arrow on a weathered post, mostly hidden by leaves.

We proceeded in the new direction, encountering great, flat slabs of rock underfoot at angles to each other all set in the flank of a large hill, so that the feet could never touch ground evenly. This was hard on the ankles, and tiring. We seemed to labour through this shattered landscape for hours, got glimpses of the burning, copper-coloured sun hastening to the horizon on our right. A Spaniard caught us up and chatted to Claudio.

"Can we have a tea-break, Dad?" said Kes, a little breathlessly.

"No, Kes you've had a long break and it's getting late."

I glanced at him and he looked bushed. It had been a long day. His eyes had a pleading in them. Soon we got beyond the awkward, angled rocks. I changed my mind, & took off my rucksack.

"OK. this will do. Break time."

When Claudio and the Spaniard caught up I explained that Kes needed a rest and we all settled on the narrow path. Claudio made coffee, I brewed tea. We weren't at all sure where we were, nor how far it was to the next village, Zubiri. Yet there was an easy atmosphere of trust in circumstances about our little group.

Now that we had stopped, I became aware of how hungry I was. It was a long time since we had last eaten. But I'd run out of food much earlier. Then I remembered an orange at the bottom of the pack. I dug it out and began to peel it. As I was peeling it I noticed my intention to eat it alone, and it became impossible to do so. I split the peeled orange into four and silently passed a section to the others. Such a simple event, but there was much going on. My unthinking action would have been to sit and eat my orange. It was my last and only food, yet the rightness of this simple act of sharing was transparently natural and the memory of my initial unthinking inclination felt shameful. I am usually a rather selfish person. Sometimes I'm aware of this and strive against it. But here there was no sense of effort. A quarter of an orange is not much to allay hunger, but it was very, very sweet, not just in taste, of course, but in feeling. Something in me was being unpeeled and given away.

Soon we were up and moving cheerfully, relaxedly, onwards. The ground began to slope down and the forest cleared. A bridge appeared below us and it was plain that we had rested only a few hundred yards from Zubiri.

Chapter 6.
Allowing Feelings

As we crossed the old, stone bridge over the Rio Arga, Claudio said that he would go and search for the refuge. We had no money for hotels, and besides it felt as if the relative luxury, and the privacy, of a hotel would elevate us out of the experience. On the Camino are periodic refuges that vary all the way from a floor in a derelict house to a hostel with bunk beds. They are usually free, or very cheap, and maintained by local people.

Hearing voices to our left down by the river, Kes and I strolled down a dirt road to find a large, four-square, stone house on the river bank. Three-stories of white and grey austerity, it felt grim, but there were rucksacks near the granite doorway and three teenage girls sat stretching their long, tanned legs.

"Refuge for pilgrims?" I asked in Spanish.

"Yes, but no room here," answered one in a surly voice. As we scarcely knew the language, a person's gestures, tone, manner became more important. We were like children, attentive to the context of speech rather than the content. This greeting felt like a slap.

Actions, and feelings, are contagious. We live in an atmosphere, a fluid of mutual feeling, and how we act, respond, gets into the mix and has consequences. Acting badly is like pissing into the water supply; it contaminates the medium in which we live. Growl at someone and they are liable to snarl back, or worse, snarl at someone else later. A smile is liable to be returned. A generous act, or the opposite, can ripple through people who happen to meet, like a breeze through a wheat field. We are all responsible for the temper of our communities. There is no shrugging the responsibility.

So we didn't snarl back, but we went in anyway. The house was empty, and filthy. Thick dust everywhere and stuff stacked up, mostly piles of old tables and old doors. A hoop rested forlornly against a wall, by its side a block of wood with an axe embedded in it. On the back wall a sign announced "Sex Pistols" in shaky silver letters. One of the girls had followed us in.

"No room, no room!" she repeated urgently.

"I don't think we're welcome here," said Kes ironically.

Well, not everyone seemed to feel the camaraderie of the Way.

"Let's go and see how Claudio is getting on."

As we left I glanced back, to see the young woman slipping off her shorts, and hanging them on the axe.

Homeless, we wandered back up the dirt road. Every day would end with this search for somewhere to stay. The pilgrim is a vagrant.

Back at the bridge Claudio told us he'd found a schoolhouse, on the main road, where we could sleep.

Old Zubiri is down by the river; higher up, along the main road, parallel to the river valley, were blocks of workers' flats. The school was up among these. The two-storied, bland, white and cream schoolhouse was empty; it was the school holidays. We unpacked our sleeping bags and laid them on the floor.

Then we went and sat on the steps outside our temporary home.

"This is a good place," said Claudio, joining us, "we have electric light and water." The implication being that there were refuges further on with neither. Claudio had done the walk before and knew.

Down the road came a singing troupe of pilgrims led by a priest holding aloft a large, wooden cross. All smiles and friendly laughter. We waved and they came over for an exuberant exchange before we directed them to the old house by the river which they were seeking. Minutes later there followed a small truck carrying their rucksacks.

"That's cheating," responded Kes indignantly.

I found a visitors' book for pilgrims inside and scanned it for something in English amid all the Spanish and French. A seeking for kin. I found some sensible remarks by one Phinella Henderson and a cry of pain from Guy Keloso lamenting a love for Madame Debril.

We found a shop, completely indistinguishable as such, in a street of white houses with rows of delicate pink geraniums beneath the first floor windows.

Back at the school we sat on the floor to eat: fresh bread, blackrinded sheep's cheese, a livid red sausage that tasted like curried rubber and a 50p litre-carton of rough, ruby red wine. It was all delicious.

Meanwhile, Claudio made his Rice. This was a semi-religious ritual having a kinship with the Japanese tea ceremony. Things had to be placed just so. Different ingredients added at exactly the right time. Cooking was an alchemical adding of this and that in casual, intuitively exact quantities, at casual, intuitively exact moments. Then the stove was turned off and the whole apparatus left and ignored for some, doubtlessly astrologically significant, period of time whose conclusion was determined by bowing down on all fours to the cooling dish and reverently listening to it.

Eventually we lay down in our thin, ultra-lightweight, and very cheap, sleeping bags to rest, much contented, on the hard, wooden floor, for the night.

Pilgrimage teaches what you can do without. And what is indispensable.

****

I was woken by a factory siren. It was still quite dark. To my right looming above me, was an amorphous lump of a dark triangle, mountainous, with a yellow light, like a hole through it, near its summit. Gradually I made sense of this weird shape. It was the black silhouette of a priest in his robes, sitting hunched on a child's chair, his head bowed, reading his Bible by means of a torch.

To my left people were stirring. A young woman dressing, her arms raised, delicate new light respectfully touching the gentle curves of her naked body. A dark jumper fell like a curtain over her breasts.

It was surprisingly cold.

Obviously more pilgrims had arrived after we had turned in. I turned over and returned to sleep.

When I awoke once more it was fully light and the school-room was empty save for the inert shapes of Kes and Claudio, plus three middle-aged women and a girl of about twelve. The women must have slept on the floor like us, but already it was impossible to know that. They looked so dapper and spruce. They were packing up, everything was carefully folded and put in its place. Neatness incarnate, domestic order in triplicate. They fussed about in calm and intricate regularity. Various creams and lotions emerged from packs and were applied suitably.

All was not well with the young girl, however. She was distressingly skinny, sickly pale and had a racking cough. One of the women brushed the girl's long, cinnamon brown hair, pausing when she coughed. Another prepared her breakfast. The third packed her tiny rucksack. They were like a retinue, a conspiracy of domestic service.

I watched as I made, and drank, my coffee, then dressed and went to try to find Kes' Mars bar.

Let me explain. Kes was not good at getting up. Left entirely to his own devices, he would awake and fuzzily and reluctantly begin the long and arduous process of reconnecting with his body, sometime in mid afternoon. However, by an expensive sequence of trial and error, I had eventually discovered, on our earlier walks, a partial remedy: a Mars bar. I would wave the Mars bar beneath his nostrils while subliminally whispering, "Mars bar, Kes, Mars bar." Eventually, one arm would move almost imperceptibly and the hand start to grasp and ungrasp. Quickly I'd remove half the paper and place the bar in the groping hand. In to the mouth went the bar and jaws moved slowly as, eyes still firmly closed, he began to eat. This would eventually induce partial consciousness.

All this went well, and Claudio woke and we prepared, slowly, to move off.

Through the village and across the old bridge, we then followed a footpath paralleling the river along the left side of the valley.

Crossing a field, Kes complained of pains in his calf. Claudio carried a compact, rectangular, heavy pack. We were to find that it contained an astonishing range of gear, much of which was not particularly for his own benefit but to aid those in need. He rummaged in this cornucopia and produced an engraved pot of thick, black paste called something like 'Mrs.Garcia's Magic Herbal Muscle Stuff' This was applied and seemed to do the trick.

Beautifully undulating, darkly forested, low hills both sides of the valley here.

Onward, a low hum and a clanking, knocking sound throbbed; and there appeared below us a sprawling Magnesium factory (Claudio told us what it was). There seemed no plan to it. It spread along the valley with variously shaped buildings irregularly dumped between gashes in the ground and piles of light grey material like bleached slag-heaps. Much large industrial equipment lay about like rusting mechanical abortions. It felt eerie and alien. The land had been opened up for brutal surgery and the innards left obscenely visible. It was like coming across a crudely raped woman, left for dead, which, in a sense, was exactly what it was. We walked silently through the devastation as if we were skirting an accident.

With some relief we found the path rising slightly up the valley side to reach the villages of Ilarroz and Esquiroz. Quiet and empty places with dignified stone houses like massive dog kennels; white with dark grey quoins, few windows and plain Romanesque doorways; five foot agaves and shrubs of hostas clipped and shaped to look like variegated eggs here and there, and vines meandering up the walls spreading their leaves against the white. 1747 it said on one house. A motley of dogs, seven or eight of them, came out to greet us and were friendly for a change. Claudio walked on ahead and was soon lost to view.

The way bent back down to the river where we could see a road-sign outside the infernal factory announcing that it was 666 kilometres by road to Santiago, the Biblical number of the Beast.

Larrasoana looked ugly ahead so we turned off left, up the valley side once more, towards Aquerreta. We strolled through farmland and fallow fields edged with teasels and sprinkled with vivid blue cornflowers. Swifts swooped overhead and a fine male bullfinch fled before us. A bird of prey, a black kite, posed nobly on a post, and what I think was a Scarce Swallowtail butterfly skittered past in the thick heat. Such simple riches. Then, ahead on the narrow path of rather orange soil, sat one of the women from Zubiri, reading. As we drew near we could see a padded sleeping bag laid out on the path by her and in it lay the girl with the cough, asleep. Pale and corpse-like she lay like an emaciated sleeping beauty, scarcely breathing, peaceful and vulnerable; the shadow side of all the vibrant life around us. We tiptoed past, nodding greeting.

Descending towards the river, the fields closed in till we were hemmed in by humid vegetation. A pipe issued from a bank flanking the path and we took some welcome, cool water. A weir and some rapids appeared and we took a break beneath the trees by the river bank.

"Just look at those sinewy swirls of water, Kes," I observed, "like tree roots."

"Looks more like the top of a Mars bar," he replied poetically. "You making some tea?"

I did, and we rested content by the flowing stream. I threw my tea-bag into the river and mused on the beautiful curve it made.

"Feeble," said Kes, and threw his somewhat further.

Despite all the peace around me I felt restless, agitated, as if we were trespassing and might be discovered at any moment. I found myself nervously returning to the path, and walking up and down. Kes ignored me and started making little boats of dried leaves which he launched on the water. I returned to the river bank further down, and something on the ground caught my eye. I knelt on the thick grass. Deep in among the green blades I could see a tiny flash of red and white, and, exploring, found a narrow box about two inches long like a minuscule coffin. Through its transparent plastic top I could see something glinting. I opened the box to reveal an exquisitely made fish, a fisherman's lure, in perfect condition, realistically iridescent in shiny white and watery green. A beautiful thing. The print on the box was in English. It had been made in Ireland.

There is a tradition on the Camino that things that you just find are deeply significant for the finder. You have to see them as symbols. To do so is part of the training that the Way encourages. This I knew.

So I watched my reaction to the find carefully, my feeling was a mixture of astonishment and that startling sensation when a new idea first dawns. I knew something about fish and their meaning. There is scarcely anything more sacred. Fish are the creatures of the water of life, the element of intuition, of creativity. They are at home in that world and partake of it. Their shape is a pair of arcs gently touching like a pair of praying hands, slightly curved and open. A human sign of homage and humility, and the shape that my cupped hands were making now, with the fish in one palm like an embryo. The double curve, like two crescent moons, that come together to make the Vesica - the shape of the lens which focuses light, the shape of the ark, the shape of the open vagina, the shape of freshly parted lips about to speak. The fish is the sign of female creativity, of things coming into birth, a gateway to another world. It is the sign of immanence. It is the original Christian symbol, pre-dating the cross.

As I looked at this fish in my hand each association spawned another, many others, fast, like fire spreading, multiplying; my mind teemed with thought, of other meanings, further connections. It was like splitting a pomegranate, and all the seeds spilling out, and each seed splitting, and so on. In myself the ordinary world parted and out of the clearing tumbled more fruits of the imagination. I felt flooded, dizzy, my mind dropped in a whirlpool, and I wasn't sure I could cope.

This was silly, but happening. The pace of accelerating thoughts scared me, so I plunged my hands through the wet grass to feel the reassuring solidity of the earth. I calmed and settled, stood, and walked slowly back to where Kes had climbed out into the river, on a series of irregular stepping stones, and was happily launching his boats. I sat down and watched the intricate flow of the river. As the water swirled, eddied and tumbled down among the rocks it made a haze of spray, and in the spray were evanescent, miniature rainbows.

Kes returned from his boat building and sat by me.

"Pretty place," he said.

"Sure is."

We quietly began to pack up our gear and prepared to move off.

Chapter 7.

Finding Place

The path bent closer to the Rio Arga and crossed an old bridge and up to a road. Two kilometres or so of noisy, smelly traffic. Hotter still here, as we had lost the cool presence of the river and the road itself reflected the heat back up at us. We laboured, stunned by the heat, through Zuriain, until a welcome yellow directed us back to the river towards Iroz. By the bridge here was Claudio, in a swimming costume. He waved.

"Hot today, why don't you take a dip in the river?"

"Now that is an excellent idea."

We walked along the bank a little to find a shady spot and shed our clothes. I laid my shirt, drenched with sweat, in the sun to dry. The water was deliciously cold, a touch of the high mountains. I lay in the healing, rippling, cool flow and let the current gently massage and the chill penetrate. In contrast to the icy water, I slowly became aware of my own body heat, deep and warm like the memory, or a promise, of sweet, secret love. A brushing slither announced a passing fish over my chest and down my side like a tender greeting, so sensuous. With my eyes just above the surface I could see iridescent damsel flies skimming the water, rainbows in their prismatic wings. Life, so sweet and subtle, I felt literally immersed in it and deeply content.

On the bank I could see Claudio getting dressed. I stood and waded out.

"I have to meet the film crew in Pamplona," he said, "we must spend to-morrow filming. I'll probably see you there."

"Fine," I replied. It never occurred to me at the time that there might be any problem finding him in a city.

"Tell me," I asked, "are there any dangerous creatures in the rivers here in Spain?"

"Not usually, although I once put my hand down in the water and something moved under my hand. It was a water snake. I got out very quickly."

"Are they dangerous?"

"Some of them."

So off he went. I watched him, slowly, patiently walking off, his long, thin, brown legs, and his gait, like a camel's. The sweat on our clothes had dried already, leaving fringes of white salt. Kes was still cheerfully splashing about so I took the opportunity to wash our clothes in the river. (We carried two sets of clothes each, one on, one off, so there was always washing). I laid them out on the grass to dry and sat in the dappled shade and wrote some letters, updated the perennial notebook, then fixed some food: hot dogs and onions and sweet tea.

Some time later, and much refreshed, we moved off back up to the road at Zabaldica then into the landscape, as the river valley, and the road, swept off to our left. The path widened to nine or ten feet of white, crumbly dust, as if the pulverising sun had beaten out all colour. The scene opened out to a wide, fertile plain of wheat-fields and dark poplars, and above, an even wider, intense blue sky. Turning a corner to see the plain, that huge space, was like the first sight of the sea on childhood holidays: the spirit expands to fill the space it's in. Wide open space beckons the soul, as the sky does.

The path looped around hillocks of dark pine forest gashed with fire-breaks.

We sweltered on, the path baked hard and shade scarce. In the heat, we were already well used to scanning the landscape for shade. It was stupid & unthinkable to take a break in the open sun. Falling asleep could bring sunstroke.

We classified shade according to its effectiveness. There was simply 'shade': technically shady but minimal, better than nothing, thin and maybe dappled. Then there was 'good shade': thicker and involving several trees, or one large one. But best of all was 'deep shade': cool and refreshing; a female, moony place of recuperation; Blake's Beulah, a healing, mending envelopment we descended into with gratitude. We became connoisseurs of shade as we were of water, for they are akin. So just as we stopped for the blessing of cool water whenever we happened upon it, so we often took the hint, and the gift, of deep shade and took a break to allow its softness to work its magic, and temper the fierceness of the brutal sun.

"Unless we climb up to the forest it looks like we're out of shade for a while," I commented.

"Something may turn up," replied Kes.

We ploughed on through the turgid heat until, much later, we found some moderately good shade and sank down for a rest amid a flurry of Clouded Yellow butterflies; their wings deep orange with dark brown tips as if burnished by the sun. Out in the bright light, the ground was smitten with heat, the sparse grass was yellow and brown although there was some scabious, cornflowers and thistles. Kes quickly fell asleep and I sat alone amid the hum of flies.

Eventually a young man in his mid twenties appeared on the path. He wore only a white vest, shorts and trainers, and was browner than my tea. He carried an alpine ski-pole as a walking stick. I hailed him and asked him if it was useful when walking. It was, he said, but he kept dropping it. Patrick, he told me, Belgian.

"Are you going to Pamplona tonight?" he asked.

"I don't know," I replied, "we just walk and look for somewhere to stay when it gets late. Are you going to Pamplona?"

"Maybe, although I think I might stay with the nuns."

"With the nuns?"

"Yes, there's a refuge not far, run by nuns."

He left. I let Kes sleep until the sun got low in the sky.

Eventually, we moved off and each settled into their own pace until I reached a yellow arrow on a fence. It was a bit worn & unclear. Kes arrived.

"What's up, Dad?"

"Look at this yellow, Kes."

"What's wrong with it?"

"Well, it looks as if we are supposed to go over the fence. All this time so far we have never had to climb over anything. What do you think? It's a bit faded."

" Looks like it's over the fence to me."

" OK. Let's go."

I started to heave myself up & climb the bars of the wooden fence. When I got down, backwards, on the other side & stood back a little, I could see that Kes hadn't begun.

"Come on, Kes, it's a bit awkward with the rucksacks, but it's not difficult."

He didn't move, just stared into space.

" I tell you what, take off your rucksack & hand it over the fence to me, then you can climb freely."

He remained staring.

"Come on, Kes, you can do it. It's not that high."

"It's not that," said Kes, thoughtfully.

I was getting a little impatient.

"Well, what is it then?"

"It's the bull," he said, firmly.

I glanced over my shoulder. There in the middle of the field, & advancing rapidly towards me, was what appeared to be a diesel locomotive with legs.

"Bull! Bull!" I shouted, rushing towards the fence & then climbing as fast as I could. Unfortunately, I caught my foot as I climbed, tipped over the top, performed a sort of bent handstand on the uppermost bar, did a vertical forward roll & landed flat on my back on the other side, my head towards the fence, looking up.

"Oooof, " I said, winded.

"That was brilliant, Dad," said Kes, " most people need a swimming pool to do that sort of thing."

I gave him one of my Looks.

Meanwhile the bull had arrived & was looking down at me over the fence as I lay on the ground. Its eyes protruded wildly & its mouth was flecked with foam & blood. It clearly wanted very much to be on my side. It snorted a lot, & stamped, & pawed the ground.

"He's not a happy bunny," I said.

"No, Dad," Kes stated, "it's a bull."

I got up & checked myself out. Right shoulder a bit bruised, otherwise alright, the rucksack had broken my fall.

"Ok," I sighed, "onward."

We took a long diversion around the field & soon reached another river, the Rio Ulzama, and a low, stone bridge that ended in a stone, round-headed arch over the path. This led straight into the ground floor of a plain, rectangular building, so that the bridge and the building were all of a piece. Here, in the shade under the arch, was a double brown door with florid, black, cast-iron hinges which included decorative dragons.

Dragons are complicated, but they are essentially akin to snakes and fish in iconography. Another symbol of female power; scaly animals, fire-breathing flying snakes that knights love to skewer with their phallic lances; and guardians of treasure. Some Greek temples were built over snakepits. The oracular priestess at Delphi was called the Pythia, from which we get 'python.' Delphi itself is named after a female dragon (or serpent) called Delphyne derived from a word meaning 'womb.' There are Cretan sculptures, among others, showing priestesses holding snakes. Then there's Medusa, not to mention Eve.

This must surely be the place.

I knocked. A middle-aged nun opened the door.

"Peregrinos" (pilgrims) I said, "do you speak English?"

"No," she replied, "do you speak Spanish?"

"No," I answered, smiling.

She beamed at me and sort of twinkled; it was an emotional iridescence, a flickering in the affective ultra-violet; so I beamed back and tried to twinkle too. She laughed heartily and gave us an enormous key and directed us around to the side door.

The refuge was one long, shady room that reeked of tranquillity. Heavy beams crossed the ceiling. Partitions were made with cork sheets producing several rooms. There was a lounge, male and female bathrooms, a kitchen and several bedrooms of various sizes and capacities.

"Wow, this is luxury," I said, "more like a pilgrims' suite than a refuge."

The place felt so restful I decided to take a nap and I lay me down in this haven of peace; this womb-like space of warm, soft air. I dreamt. I like the Greek (and earlier Egyptian) idea that a dream provides an intuition into the place where you sleep. It was a simple dream in which I was welcomed by a group of women. They stood as a small, excited, friendly little crowd of about seven people. Their ages ranged from about eighteen to around fifty. They greeted me simply, as an old and well-loved friend. There was much smiling and touching, embracing and kissing. The oldest, a matronly, big-bosomed woman dressed in warm shades of purple, orange and violet, her arms folded beneath her breasts, looked on and smiled in recognition, twinkling.

"Well," she said, "you certainly took your time."

****

When I awoke, we went off to find a supermarket to get some food. I let Kes choose. Then we stopped off for a quick drink in a bar. The walls were entirely decorated by Asterix cartoons. In the wood above Zubiri, Claudio and I had discovered a mutual admiration for Asterix adventures. I especially liked Obelix; the bumbling innocent, the open-hearted fool; whereas Claudio went for Getafix, the Druidic sage, the Celtic magus. Claudio even looked a bit like Getafix and resembled him in his love of things Celtic and his esoteric knowledge. He was steeped in the Celtic and had travelled to Ireland several times. He even knew some Gaelic. He had spoken appreciatively, in the cool wood, of Galicia, the last province on the walk, and how it was lush and green and wet and magical, and quite unlike anywhere else in Spain. It reminded him of Ireland.

Back at the convent, I took a shower and then went to the kitchen to cook. Patrick, the Belgian, was already there cooking.

"Would you like to eat with me," he said, "I've bought too much wine for one."

"I'm always willing to help out a fellow pilgrim in difficulties," I replied.

So we convivially chatted as we ate our lentils and Ravioli and bread and cheese, plus red Rioja wine (full of sun).

Patrick, it turned out, was a driving instructor from Brussels, addicted to long-distance walking; a laid-back character who loved to be alone in wide spaces and walking fast.

Afterwards I went out in the cool evening and sat by the river for a last smoke. Reflections beneath the bridge lazily shimmered like a spell seeping through the air. The grey-stoned, medieval bridge was festooned with greenery, while below it the olive river, highlighted with white flowers, imperceptibly flowed to a weir, so that the scene was imbued with the soft sounds of falling water. The light had become creamy so that the orange sandstone and rich, deep green vegetation and pastel blue sky, mirrored in the river, became a Cézanne composition.

Frogs croaked, like sheep with a death rattle.

Chapter 8.

Synchronicities

I was up at 8.30 and popped out to find Kes' Mars bar. Sounds of a loom, or some other machinery, came from the upper floors of the convent. The nuns were already at work. The sun had started burning a hole through the blue sky.

Back at the refuge, everyone had gone and Kes was still deeply asleep. I found a forgotten staff and a length of scarlet cord and fashioned a hand grip and a loop for my wrist, so I couldn't drop it. I was to become very attached to this stick. People do. I've seen tears in the eyes at the realisation that some tatty bit of wood has been left behind in a bar. Things that we rely on get invested with our appreciation, I suppose; even inanimate things. I came to feel I could understand somewhat the naming of swords. We bestow humanity, like a knighthood, on the instrument which earns it. So, we name our ships, our houses, and some their computers.

Around eleven we were ready to go. We were already on the outskirts of Pamplona, so it was all road and urban traffic. I posted my letters. As we strolled through the busy streets I told Kes about a second dream I'd had in the convent. It was a much more intellectual dream, as if my logical side was trying to compensate.

I'd dreamt that I was lecturing, and my subject was Fate. Fate, I had explained, was a mathematical discipline, like physics. What happens to a person is a consequence of two things: their desires and their needs. The desires are rational. People plan, and try to achieve what they want. Needs are usually not known or very poorly known. They are not known because people don't really want to be aware of what they need. What actually happens is whatever is the stronger: the desires or the needs. People try to organise their lives so their desires are satisfied, but when a need is stronger the desires are over-ruled and something else happens more conducive to the needs. Very often, because the needs are resisted, the pressure of the needs become very strong and they forcefully overcome the desires. The resulting events are disruptive and maybe even traumatic.

However, this is complicated by the sheer number of people. Each person's desires and needs go into one common system, like different objects in a mutually created gravitational field. So what actually happens depends on the relative strengths of desires and needs of everyone within a complex, inter-active psychological system.

I had regularly glanced at Kes while relating all this. He looked puzzled, as well he might. I kept forgetting he was only nine. Maybe this was all too difficult, or too weird.

"It was just a dream, Kes," I said, softly.

"Sounds about right," he said thoughtfully, "it must be something like that."

He paused. We crossed a side street amid the busy crowd.

"I had a dream last night too," said Kes, warily.

"Did you? That place seems good for dreams. What did you dream?"

"I dreamt I'd given birth to a black baby."

"Now that's a deep one."

I launched, as teachers are prone to do, into the significance of black and white, and day and night, and one emerging from the other and cited the Taoist symbol.

"What's the Taoist symbol?"

"You know, the Yin/Yang sign: circle with a double curve down the middle, black one side, white the other, and so on."

"You mean like that over there?"

On a white wall that we were passing at that moment was an enormous, elaborate, painted mural, some thirty feet long, with a large Taoist symbol in its centre.

"Bloody Hell!" I cried in astonishment.

To the right of the Taoist circle, as we looked at it, on the black side, was a dark, volcanic landscape in the shape of a face with a single, sinister green eye and a cone of fire as the other socket. On the left, on the white side, was a flying white dove framed by a sun over a beautiful, blue waterfall. It summed up what I'd been trying to say. We looked at each other, a bit stunned. I took a photograph of it in some confusion. We walked on in serious silence, only to be faced with a large graffiti, on a wall, in English.

"Keep Laughing." It announced, inexplicably. So we did.

"This is getting a bit heavy," I said.

"Perhaps we needed it," said Kes, grinning.

Soon we crossed over the Rio Arga once more, walked along a park by the massive, mossy city walls and entered Pamplona by an ancient gate.

The cobbled streets with their five and six-storied houses, with many iron verandas, were strung with Basque flags. A busy, picturesque city. Slim, pretty young girls seemed everywhere, like a flush of jasmine, with that stylish, pert, elfin look I associate with Paris. Here were shops for artists' materials, potter's studios, a restoration workshop, craft shops. This place had style.

In the centre was a wide, airy square with plane trees, a bandstand, and pigeons bathing in a fountain; around the edge of the square were tables outside many bars with neat waiters in aprons. It was all rather bustling and we felt lost. We had got used to wider spaces and there was too much going on here.

"What shall we do?" asked Kes.

I consulted the map.

"Well, there's a refuge just a couple of kilometres beyond Pamplona. I vote we take an easy day. Walk to this refuge. Dump our rucksacks and then come back into Pamplona for a look around, and try to find Claudio."

"Fine, let's go."

On the way through the town we shopped in a supermarket for some food, pausing just beyond the checkout to dump all unnecessary packaging to save weight. The cardboard box over a tin of sardines, for example. I poured the coffee from its jar into a plastic bag and dumped the jar. Half the bag of sugar got thrown away.

Sugar is very heavy.

It was a short, easy walk to Cizur Menor. Here a passer-by directed us to a large private house as the refuge. We knocked gingerly on the huge door and were very politely greeted, in English, by a petite woman, Maribel Roncal, who maintained this refuge out of the goodness of her heart. Many good women on this route, it seemed. She showed us into a room with sturdy wooden bunk beds and urged us to make ourselves comfortable and to use the large garden just outside. The garden was well cared for and rather English, save for the palm trees.

Collapsed in the shade was an enormous dog. A great lump of doggy flesh, it looked more like a small bear. I'm not up on dogs, but it looked like a St.Bernard to me. The poor thing, slumped on the ground and immobile, panted heavily and its immense sad eyes seemed to say: 'Do something about this heat.' It was not a suitable dog for Spain.

"Sort out your pilgrims' passport, Kes, we'll get them stamped in Pamplona."

Our passports had to be rubber stamped each day to prove that we had traversed the entire route.

Back in town, we tried the cathedral for the stamps. Not a pretty building, a classical design, twin towers and a portico, looking more like a public library, or a London college, than a cathedral. It looked as if it had been cut out of cardboard. Severe, gloomy and unfriendly inside; except for the cloisters with delicate tracery of cusped circles and stars of David. Gravestones in the floor here with numbers, and holes like tiny letter boxes. A really snazzy last address: 228, The Cloisters, Pamplona Cathedral, Spain.

Back in the nave, we knocked on the sacristy door where a crusty old man reluctantly let us in. Here we were left in a tall, tawdry room in faded plush that looked like a failed, posh tea-room. No sense of the creativity of rebirth here, just the decay of slow dying. The excessive height of the room, trying to impress, only diminished. It was an attempt to belittle, as the posh usually is, rather than elevate its occupants. The old man, so often in this space, defended himself by means of a tetchy self-importance.

Half a dozen priests arrived in full regalia. Clearly the disrobing room. At first they were stern until one told the others that he'd seen us the day before walking down the main road in the heat of the day. Suddenly they were all smiles and questions, and there was much "Valiente!" and scuffing Kes' hair.

"What do you get for thumping a bishop?" said Kes, grimacing.

Then one, still in full ecclesiastical dress, processed to a huge cupboard and returned with stamp and pad aloft and ceremonially stamped our documents.

"Are we married now, Dad?" said Kes sarcastically.

There was much hand-shaking all round.

Outside, we were strolling around aimlessly when we bumped into Claudio.

"Hello. Do you want to see some filming?"

"Yes!" said Kes.

"No, not me. You go with Claudio, Kes. I'll go for a wander. I'll see you here in an hour."

"OK."

I wandered around until I found a terrace with a wonderful view of the plain we had crossed, with the mountains in the far distance. It was at the elevated corner of the city walls. An official notice announced, in English: "Don't remain on the wall bord. FALL DANGER." There were fine old trees and plenty of good shade. A breeze sighed through the translucent, mint-green leaves. Dotted around were stone benches, tables like miniature dolmens and a small fountain, like a font, in the shade. People sat around, or lay stretched out on the sparse grass, talking and laughing like a scene in Renoir. Suddenly it felt a long way from home. I didn't belong here. I was a transient, passing through. Then, amid the Spanish chatter, I heard some English. A stocky man sat talking to a small group nearby. I went up to him.

"It's good to hear English," I said, grateful.

He introduced himself: Rudy, a Mexican American and we started to chat. Meanwhile the group faded away. He had been reading his poems to them.

"Let's go and have a drink," he suggested.

In the corner of the terrace was an attractive bar, the Meson del Caballo Blanco (House of the White Horse); an exotic place, light grey stone with sandstone lancets and a rectangular tower. Inside it was dark like a chapel; a stone ceiling and the only light, apart from the door, from a glowing wall studded with thick, brown and green bottle glass. He ordered red wine, swigged his down and immediately ordered another. He had a dark complexion that looked as if it had suffered thousands of insect bites. He began to tell of his wife, who was Danish; she had left him. He lit an American cigarette and put out the match with his fingers, without licking them first. Then he stuck the spent match in his brawny forearm. Seeing me stare at this, he did it again. He had big hands, heavy and awkward, like hand-shaped boxing gloves. One thumb constantly twitched, the knuckles of both fists were, I noticed, heavily callused. This guy liked to fight.

"We will go to another bar," he said, "you're my friend."

Then he announced loudly to the entire bar, "We go now and we do not pay."

Everyone ignored him.

"Er, well, actually I've got to meet a friend."

"We go to another bar," he shouted.

We went to another bar. He ordered red wine, sank it swiftly, ordered another.

"You a soldier?" he asked.

I was dressed from head to foot in khaki, with walking boots.

"No."

"I thought you were a soldier. All my friends are soldiers. Were soldiers. They're all dead now."

"Why are they all dead?"

"I was in Vietnam, and Angola, and Katanga."

Was that possible?

"The Americans weren't in Angola, were they? You must have been a mercenary."

"Yere, a professional soldier. All I know how to do is to kill. Now what do I do?"

"Katanga? That's the Congo isn't it? Have you read Conrad?"

"Conrad who?"

"Never mind."

"We go now and we do not pay," he shouted.

The next bar was full of Basque men. He was obviously well known to them. They were plainly sizing the two of us up, judging whether there was enough of them and whether it was worth it. I stood as tall as I could and tried to look military.

Suddenly he said, impetuously, "Life is a tangle. And death is only a double step. It's as simple as that."

"A double step?"

He froze, and feigned a collapse.

"It's as simple as that."

In the next bar he announced to everyone as we arrived that I was his friend. It was intended as a warning. I tried to look casually mean. Doing my Clint Eastwood impression, rolling an invisible cheroot from one side of my mouth to the other.

"This is a good bar. You can get anything here. Any drug you like you get here," he said proudly.

I found myself, appropriately enough, torn by Rudy. He was clearly dangerous, and I wanted to get the Hell away. On the other hand, he was such a desperately lonely man, and full of anger. If the only possible human contact for him was with his callused knuckles, that would do. His knuckles spoke of him; there was something raw and vulnerable but scabbed over. I didn't want just to dump him like useless packaging. But I didn't know how to get away from him without making things even worse.

After the next bar, he hesitated, considering where to go next, and I began to walk in the direction where I knew Kes must be waiting and getting worried. So, via another two or three bars (I lost count), we got to the point where I could see Kes in the distance and I waved and shouted. He came hurrying up.

"Where have you been? You're well late."

"I'll tell you later."

"Is this your friend?" said Rudy, in an odd voice. "It is your son. I can see. Father and son, walking together."

His hard-bitten face softened. Kes embodied all he hadn't got. He struggled with his feelings and lost. He began to weep. He embraced me, his heavy body shaking in my arms. He turned to Kes.

"You look after your old man, he's my friend."

I shook his hand and we walked away. Rudy shouted after us.

"Anytime you're in Pamplona you look me up. Ask anywhere. Everybody knows me."

I waved.

Chapter 9

Being in the Right Place

The walk back to the refuge sobered me up a bit. About a dozen more pilgrims had arrived. We sat in the garden and ate a simple meal of boiled eggs, fresh bread, olives and cheese. I let Kes have the red wine and I drank lots of tea. We shared the eggs with three, bold, black and white kittens, still wobbly on their little legs. I found a magpie's feather and put it in my hat.

"We've just missed a fiesta here," said Kes eagerly.

"I know, San Fermin."

"They let bulls loose in the streets and people run in front of them."

"I know."

"One man got killed."

"Really?"

"Yere, and they jump from the top of the fountains."

"The bulls?"

"Don't be silly."

The fountains were typically ten or twelve feet high with a wide basin beneath.

A friend back in Ingatestone went to San Fermin every year and had told me much about it. He regarded it as a period of temporary insanity that enabled him to stay relatively sane for the rest of the year.

Then the Red Cross arrived. They had come to treat an injured pilgrim. We went to have a look. A big American had one foot up on a stool. Most of the nail on his big toe had come off, somehow turned over on edge in his boot and cut into the flesh. The nail had moved around as he had walked and cut deep. It was an ugly wound. He wouldn't be walking any more.

"Surely you could feel it as you were walking?"

"Yere, but you get used to the pain after a while and I didn't think it was this bad."

He was very despondent. All the way from the States.

Kes turned to me.

"Why don't you go and let the nurse look at your ankles?" he said.

I glanced at the attractive young woman.

"OK."

Some years ago I'd damaged both Achilles' tendons walking in the French Pyrenees. They had never really healed and I'd been getting by since St.Jean Pied de Port on daily pain killers. Kes called them 'Ankle Pills.'

She gently examined my ankles and tried some massage. Each had a lump on the back like a little Adam's apple. They were very tender. After, I went back to Kes who was playing with the kittens.

"What did she say?"

"She said it could be serious and I should pack it in and go and get them x-rayed."

"Are you going to?"

"No. I'll see how it goes. I'm not giving up unless I have to."

I gazed around the garden, somewhat despondent. One woman sat alone & quiet, in the dappled shade of a large sapling, eating fruit. She was not dressed for walking in heat. She wore a long dress of soft brown, the skirt in folds like Greek drapery. The hem, wrists & neckline were a band of ornate mid-green symbols. Around her neck, resting on her ample bosom, was a necklace of chunky orange beads. Her movements were confident with a calm grace as if her eating was some kind of ceremony. I felt drawn to her & in the easy habit of the camaraderie of pilgrims, I left Kes to the kittens & went & sat at her table, opposite her. Her hair was jet black & hung, straight & heavy, to her shoulders. Long, opalescent orange ear-rings drooped like elegant fruit. Her deep brown eyes seemed elsewhere. We both stayed silent.

There was a sense of warm serenity as if she was meditating on some ultimate home & the experience had changed the very air around her. She turned her head very slowly towards me & nodded once.

"You are walking the Way," she stated & looked directly into my eyes. The mood of restful contentment deepened.

She picked up a pocket knife with a brown, wooden handle, pulled out the blade, twisted the ferrule on the handle & began to cut up an apple.

Everything seemed in slow motion.

"There are special places on the Way," she said, paring out the core.

"So I understand."

"No, you don't," she asserted, holding a slice of apple between thumb & knife & taking it with her very white teeth.

She waved the knife in a dismissive gesture.

"These places are not in the guidebooks," she said, firmly, dipping her head towards me showing a flash of ear-ring.

"Then how do you know where they are?"

She pointed the very sharp point of the knife towards me & jabbed three times.

"Use your feelings. Trust your intuition. You can do it."

Then she seemed to mellow out. The slight tension that had built melted in a gentle smile. Her eyes softened.

"Think of it as a sort of test. There are five places. Find them."

She jerked the knife in the air several times as if fending off a wasp which indicated plainly that the interview was at an end. I rose in a bit of a daze & went back to Kes.

What on earth was that all about? It felt a bit silly.

Later, we went for a stroll down the village and popped in to the Bar Tremendo. The T.V. was on and the 'A' team was fighting some people with a machine that fired cabbages. After that, football. I didn't pay much attention until I heard a few English names. England versus Spain! I looked up in time to see England gain possession in mid-field. There was a good run on the left wing and a neat cross and ...

"Gooooaaaaal !" I shouted.

There was a heavy silence. I turned to see a dozen pairs of hostile, Spanish eyes.

"You're not very diplomatic," said Kes quietly.

"I forgot where we are."

We went and sat in a corner.

A small man with a droopy moustache, wearing a pink shell-suit came over to talk with us. The 'talk' was hard work, with much gesturing and mime and drawing of pictures. He repeated something that sounded like "artista de ceramica." Some sort of potter? He took us out to his car and showed us the models he had made; neat little replicas of churches, chapels, hermitages, then he proudly displayed his kiln in the back of the van.

Pamplona was turning out such a mixture of the violent and the creative. Yin & Yang.

It is said that 'Pamplona' comes from 'Pampas de la Luna': fields of the moon. There is much creativity in Pamplona because there is such need for it. Somehow in the character of this place male bravado flourishes; a need for a test, a hankering for a fight, facing the bulls. The city has emerged from history with thick, defensive walls. In this wide and fertile plain something is challenged. And as each thing creates its compensatory opposite, there is a sensitive empathy also. Or rather, to take the hint from the Taoist mural, these opposites exist in mutual presence. However it comes about, I can't recall a more naked confrontation of the traditionally male and female forces as in this place.

During the day the sun had pounded down, now the garden shone with a delicate, silvery light.

That night I dreamt of a mature woman with an owl on her shoulder carrying a chalice, behind her in the rich , blue sky, a full moon. She beckoned, smiling.

I woke up the next morning with the mother of a hangover. Maribel was shouting at me. We were very late and must go now. She wanted to go and get some shopping. Maribel jerked curtains open angrily and the hot sun flooded in. I looked around. Everyone had left except Kes and I.

"Come on Kes, we've got to go."

"Wha ....?"

"Go. Come on. She wants us out."

"Wha .....?"

I busied about, packing my bag. I'd wash some other time. Then I started packing Kes' rucksack. Maribel flitted about banging things, very irritable, tidying up. She really was most insistent.

"Come on, man, on the road. We must shift."

"Wha ...?"

Slowly, painfully slowly, Kes, zombie-like, began to show lethargic signs of what passes for life with him when he wakes up.

It took me ages to get him up and out, and then only into the Bar Tremendo for a Mars bar and his usual three cups of coffee.

After a short bit of road we turned off into the huge plain, a vast sea of gently rolling golden wheat and stubble, beneath a delicate, cloudless, wedgewood sky. The path was bleached, white dust and sparse grass, hammered by the sun. A plague of cyclists passed us in ones and twos. A nuisance because we could never hear them until they suddenly appeared at our side and belted past.

We climbed a hill with difficulty, both below par, and descended through the village of Guendulain, scarcely noticing it. We trudged on, through the unpronounceable Zariquiegui, feeling bludgeoned by the heat into silence. Up and down the undulating path we laboured, the white and grey earth beneath our feet like cracked and rutted cement. Up again to a ridge, and a road, at Alto del Perdon, and a view of another sea; a patchwork of amber and sea-kale-green, and stubbled fields of wavering stripes of gold and chocolate. The baked stubble smelt like fresh bread. Butterflies flitted continually around us in this fiesta of colour, mostly with wings of sorbet lemon with hot orange tips, others plush black with cream splashes, light blues less commonly, and a flurry of black and white Magpie moths alighting and aloft around pale violet scabious.

Nothing moved, except us, in Uterga; life seemed wiped out by the heat. Permanent siesta stunned the place. At a horse trough we guzzled welcome, cold water. You could have fried an chicken on the stone.

"Hey, look at this," said Kes, leaning over the trough.

All along the waterline was a row of wasps, clinging to the stone, heads down, drinking. We bent over, like the wasps, plunged our arms in the cool water, splashed it over our faces and shirts. And a dozen steps down the road, it had all evaporated.

More fields beyond, where we found tall fennel which we snapped and sucked for the refreshing aniseed taste, and lavender which we collected to put among our clean clothes. Neat vines and huge exuberant sunflowers, taller than Kes, by the path to Muruzabal where we decamped into a bar. A line of local young men sat on bar-stools along by the counter, heads down, drinking. We had two quick beers and left.

Obanos, just down the way, was preparing for a fiesta. A gravelly area had been sectioned off and tiers of red seating were being erected. The heat intensified. We found some trees and took a nap.

Road most of the rest of the way to Puente la Reina (Queensbridge). Only mid-afternoon, but this was an important place, a place where three roads meet, we would try and stay here. A small square with a fountain appeared to our left. Here we paused to take stock. The sky had reached a depth of living blue that flowed into the self and joined with its kin within.

"Just look at the colour of that sky, Kes," I sighed in admiration, a mug of good, cool water in my hand.

Such a vivid, vital blue. Blue, the sacred colour of the Mother of God, the colour of death in Tibet. I recall once walking into a shop in London which sold material; cloth for dresses and curtains and suchlike. It was having a special indigo sale and the entire shop was enrobed with sheets of deepest indigo like slabs of oceanic marble. This beautiful colour was draped everywhere; the bass note of feeling, a serene fire, the shade of wisdom. It was like going home.

As I stared at the sky I seemed to dissolve into it. It had a pull that matched my yearning. It seemed to be drawing me out of myself into the wide, blue yonder. It offered relief from the burden of the trite and stupid narrowness of myself; the petty desire to impress and read off my value on the faces of others, all the effort required to move those faces till they registered my worth. Wasn't this, at heart, why I was a teacher in the first place? Why I would eventually try to write a book? I was being offered a vibrant death, a drowning in life, submersion in sky, and I could feel its sweet, seductive, pure enticement.

"Come, my love," she whispered, "Come and die."

Chapter 10

A Special Place

"Is there a refuge here?" asked Kes.

"I hope so."

I took out the day's sketch-map from my back pocket.

"Well, according to this, the refuge is just over there - a monastery: Los Padres Reparadores - the Repairing Fathers; the Healing Fathers maybe. Sounds about right apart from the gender."

We went and knocked on the door of the good Fathers. A very neat monk answered the door. Everyone has their own emotional flavour, the feel of their presence. This chap felt freshly scrubbed; he felt clean, uncontaminated, newly emerged from a mountain stream. He smiled and it felt real. He took us in, and then along to a small office where he meticulously filled in our details in a large ledger, each pilgrim listed and numbered. He stamped our passports. Order prevailed here.

Having literally booked us in, he showed us to our cells. We were each given a tiny room on the first floor, next to each other. Long and narrow, each had a bed and a small desk and not much else. Simple and adequate.

The window looked down on to a quadrangle. A simple, stone arcade at ground level, all the way round. Then two plain brick stories with anonymous rectangular windows, cell windows I suppose. Everything spoke the same note: calm, plain, unfussy, dignified order. Sufficient and unpretentious. It was indeed refreshing.

Down within the quadrangle was a formal garden; small, regular lawns, roses and cacti in the beds. In the centre four very tall, thin trees forming a square of pillars framing a brick plinth with a modest statue of Jesus (or perhaps the founder of the order).

How right that a discipline, a community of monks, should be called an 'order.' At least it felt exactly right here. I was amid an order. Uncluttered clarity. I've little doubt that were you to go there tomorrow it would be little changed. Not much room for Dionysus here.

Meanwhile, Kes had arrived from next door. He didn't look happy.

"What's wrong, Kes?"

"I don't like it here."

"Seems OK."

"I don't like being on my own."

"Next door?"

"Yes. Can I come in here with you?"

"Well, there isn't much room in here. Still, I don't see why not."

So we carried his mattress into my room and laid it on the floor. A bit cramped but more chummy.

Downstairs we found Claudio.

"Michael and Kes! Good, just in time. You must come with me, now, quickly."

He paused, and went through some sort of inner rewrite. It was like watching someone run, full-tilt, into a sand-pit.

"If you want to, that is, and, of course, not being in a hurry. But we all should go quickly now, while not being in a hurry."

"Go where?"

"Eunate. The film crew is waiting for me at Eunate."

"What's that?"

"It's a church."

"There are so many churches, Claudio," I sighed, wearily.

"Eunate is different. It is a special place. The bones of pilgrims have been found buried there."

"Is it far?"

"No, it is not far."

But it was a fair way out of town, in the landscape. It stood isolate, surrounded by the stubble of wheat-fields, or rather, it seemed to focus and concentrate the fields, as a nut might concentrate a tree. Where the late afternoon sun hit it with light, it glowingly reflected back its brilliance, as did the golden stubble fields and the hard earth around it; on the church's shady side the stone became sombre and sorrowful, introspective, like an echo of the stone of the church at St. Jean. Roughly circular, it was as if a three-dimensional Taoist symbol had grown up out of the ground.

While Claudio went off, with Kes, to film, I walked a circle around the church, at a respectful distance, through the stubble. The building had concentric layers. The outermost was an encircling stone wall five or six feet high. Inside that was a ring of arches, an ambulatory, maybe twice as high. Rising within that were the outer walls of the octagonal church itself. And within that was, of course, the interior. The architecture imposed respect. I began to understand why I had instinctively encircled the building. Here was some power. We are cagey about power. All powerful things - a pylon, a turbine, a medieval relic, a python in a zoo - acquire a respectful space around them. In many parts of the world where there are pilgrimages to holy mountains, the mountain has to be circled by the pilgrim before it can be climbed. Presumably, visitors to ancient Athens would circle the Parthenon, viewing its processional frieze, before processing into the temple. The concentric design of Eunate signalled its power. A female power, for the curve in all its forms signifies female power as the straight line signifies the male. So the crescent moon, the tumescent womb, the sinuous snake become, in architectural terms, the arch, the dome, the arcade. As I walked around it I could see that to walk in was to have an experience of curving around the building and penetrating through walls of increasing height. The male visitor, in effect, spiralled in, and fertilised the building.

Around the dark side the building bulged into a lower, semi-circular apse. Looks pregnant, I thought. Mother and child, yes, this is Madonna and Child in architectural form, but the child isn't born yet. Or to be more accurate; the daughter. It could not be a son in this female, counter-cultural site. This place of death is a homage to birth. If 'Eunate' is derived from Greek and Latin, it means 'well-born.'

The floor of the inner ambulatory has thousands of long, thin stones arranged in a wave pattern, like the sea. I absent-mindedly brushed my hands along a wall as I reached the door and something fell into my palm. In my hand was a small yellow snail, its shell mimicking the spiral around the church I had just walked.

Inside it was gaunt, bare rock, undecorated arches. It felt like being within stone, elemental and forbiddingly cold, not warm and womb-like at all but alien, primal as a mountain is. It was like being buried.

An altar is the hearth of a church, special and auspicious, a focusing core that draws and invites, sacred to Hestia. The niche and apse at the climax of the chancel are holy wombs in which the mystery of creation takes place. Approaching an altar, I often feel a sense of heightened expectation, a small thrill of potential. Not so here. Standing before this altar was unsettling. There was something bleak, even cruel.

When the Greeks built temples they did so to mark a place, a special place. You couldn't build one just anywhere. The temple surrounded the spot, the grove or spring, or site of a remarkable event, and made it more visible to those of poor emotional sight. Reverence partly, so that the inept did not blunder into the sacred like Oedipus at Colonus, but also to protect the insensitive and the foolish. The poor things should not be subjected to an unsolicited brush with cosmic powers. A temple is the ancient equivalent of a hazard notice: level crossing ahead, beware low-flying aircraft. I'm sure that the notion of building a church just anywhere would have been not only barbarous, but stupid in the Ancient world.

Meanwhile outside, round the sunny side, Angel the director, wearing the darkest, most impenetrable sunglasses, was seriously into film directing. I watched it for a while, not understanding what was going on too clearly, when one of the crew appeared, dressed as an Arab. This obviously wasn't part of the script and there was some arsing about and general laughter.

When the filming had finished, Claudio took me aside and asked if I would be interested in participating in the creation of an 'energy field.'

"What's that?"

"You will see?"

"What does it involve?"

"We will meditate, and I will speak a prayer."

"In Spanish?"

"Yes."

"I won't understand much."

"It will not matter. The sounds will do their work."

So we went into the church, and sat peacefully, and quietly meditated. After a while Claudio began, softly, to speak a prayer, although it was more like a low, vibrant chant. I understood not a word. Then a zinging sensation began in the base of my spine and started to rise up my back. When it reached my head, it filled it with an effervescent tingling, like Perrier water; a light, aerated spring; millions of tiny silver bubbles welling up, gravitating upwards, and bursting like an offering of themselves. Claudio said nothing afterwards, but smiled shyly. Not a word.

I knew I had found the first Special Place that the woman at Cizur Menor had spoken of.

I told Claudio about her.

"Oh, you have met Margaritta."

He looked impressed.

"You know her?" I asked.

"No, but I have heard of her. She is from Venezuela. She is well known on the Way."

"Does she walk the Way?"

"Yes, but not as others do. She goes very slowly & when she feels that there is someone she must talk to, then she stops & waits until they catch up. When she has spoken to them, she moves on. It is a great gift that she has spoken to you. You must think very carefully about what she said."

"Yes, I must," I said thoughtfully.

Back in the town the mood was utterly different; there was much preparation for a fiesta. There were tiers of seating around the edge of the small main square where a stage was being fitted up with microphones, huge loudspeakers and much other gear.

However, along the tall, narrow, cavernous streets the mood was not at all festive. The atmosphere was serious. In innumerable bars, and down in dark subterranean private dives, men stood in the stone-chilled shade drinking red wine, looking grim. Outside, eddies of people were beginning to collect at points of vantage. So we stood amid an excited group of young women all wearing loose, cotton, low-cut, summer dresses; their soft, creamy brown arms palpably radiating the day's heat. Above us, and down along the vista of the street, there had been draped white sheets over the balconies. Soon a parade approached, led by men and boys dressed in immaculate white shirts and trousers, each with a startling scarlet sash around their waist and a matching bandanna around the neck. On the shoulders of four men, a gilt litter carrying a life-size, standing figure of St.James garbed as pilgrim with staff, and a gourd for water. He wore a pea-green robe and a deep blue cape with scallop shells as decoration. Then more impeccable, white-clad men without the sash but with scarlet berets instead. They carried small, blue and gold horns which they blew to warn of the approach of the Gigantes - the giants: twelve-foot high effigies of a king and queen. Each had a wooden cage beneath its robes which a man wore on his shoulders along with the whole towering figure above. The effigies eerily trundled towards us, and then as a band struck up, began to dance. As they moved forward, they twirled around over the uneven, sloping road. A feat that took strength and balance.

Smaller figures, with huge, grotesque heads wandered around the crowd, terrifying the children. Finally a column of pairs of men and women danced an unending, swirling dance. The music had a cyclic quality; round and round, changing slightly like the folk music of Brittany. It was music for whirling, for twirling, like dervishes.

We had seen the German trio pretending to be medieval. This was the real thing. Plainly the king and queen represented male and female principles, but so did the colours. Traditionally, white is male because of sperm, and red is the female colour of creative energy, because of menstrual blood. This is why we have the mistletoe & holly at Christmas, because of the white & red berries. I took the dancers to mean the harmonious interplay of male & female, on and on, world without end.

We stopped off at a shop on the way back to the square with the fountain, here we had our picnic. Kes chose the food. Kes is to the sandwich what Archie Shepp is to jazz: innovative, but on the whole he produces a gruesome mess. On this occasion a creative mixture of chopped ham, cockles and Tabasco sauce, washed down with rosado wine.

Back at the refuge we discovered that Claudio had met a couple of women he knew and, as the monastery was full, had retired to somewhere in the basement to practise techniques of spiritual harmonisation.

It had been a long day, so I was glad to get back to our cell and get my boots off.

"Hey Kes, come and have a look at this."

"Now, that's clever, man, how did you manage that?"

Both my feet were bright blue.

"This, Kes, is a profound religious event of deep significance. Blue is a sacred colour. Feet feature prominently in the world's scriptures and so are meaningful entities, cosmically speaking."

"Naaah," responded Kes, "yer sweaty feet have made the dye in yer socks run."

We went peacefully to bed.

Chapter 11

The Ethos of Place

I woke early, and so, amazingly, did Kes. A dodgy moment. Things looked bad.

"Wha .....? Wha ....?"

Eyes rolling upwards.

Swiftly, I rummaged in my rucksack for the emergency Mars bar and administered it directly to the mouth. Slowly, slowly he began to re-engage with his body. A close call.

We were out before the heat had a chance to build and Kes got his coffee-fix at a pavement table by the main road. We sat beneath the leafy branches of a long grove of plane trees, a natural nave vaulted with green. They met in the middle and were lush with leaves incessantly, delicately mobile in the light breeze.

I recalled a moment somewhere in the books of Sacheveral Sitwell. Aestheticism was his religion; he lived for the experience of beauty. After he had seen Europe (no less), he travelled to South America in search of the Baroque. After one particularly arduous day, hunting out remote churches in the depths of the jungle, he ruefully observes that the most beautiful thing he had seen that day was the single rose in his hotel room.

Soon we crossed the ancient bridge. As the bridge at St.Jean marks an intention, so the bridge here marks a confirmation. A bridge is a path over a boundary, a sign of acceptance, of moving further out, away from the old self, into the unknown. The elemental space of the Meseta was ahead.

We followed the path near the Rio Arga once more. To our right appeared a flock of flying harlequins, astonishingly colourful birds, gliding effortlessly on stiff, pointed wings. They had a bright lemon throat and back, a turquoise breast and wing-tips, and a chestnut head. Bee-eaters, looping and lilting like a carousel.

Immense herons flapped leisurely, elegantly over the course of the river above mists of midges. A Red Kite soared, threatening, high in the sky and even the herons squawked. The sun rose higher and prepared to smelt the earth. Across the dusty path columns of ants trailed, on some mysterious pilgrimage of their own.

The path curved away from the river and climbed a cleft between two red hills. We took a water break here amid turtle-doves purring in the few trees. A posse of French cyclists panted through, eager to make tracks.

"Claudio is up ahead of us," observed Kes.

"How do you know?"

"Look here in the dust. These are his footprints, see. Completely flat sandals with no heel and no pattern."

"Oh, yere. That's sharp."

These breaks were so sweet. Mostly we just chatted about simple things, banal, not worth reporting - what we thought and felt about this or that place or person, the state of our feet, the shape of a cloud, the colour of the soil, how far to water or food - but we had so much time to chat. All day, every day together, for weeks. Few parents experience such a gift. We began, naturally and unforced, to form a bond. The shared activity drew us together, the trials and pleasures. We grew to know, and like, each other.

Only our sixth day walking but I felt accommodated to the landscape. It was where we lived. Checking for shade ahead was now automatic. We carried little water. Never ran out. Filled up when we found it. Judged the time by the sun.

There is something in the dynamic of walking that the mind likes. It is a regular, rhythmic activity; a sort of physical chanting, the same actions repeated over and over. Breathing inevitably matches the pace, regular and easy most of the time, deep on hills. I found that all the stress of work, and not just stress, but all the snarls and hang-ups that get swirled into knots of emotional energy and leave nothing to live on; all the petty angers, the trivial humiliations, the casual put-downs, the implied insults, had got pounded out by the very action of walking, step by step, down the legs, through the feet, into the good earth. The huge, deep earth could take it all, silent and uncomplaining.

We moved on over easy undulating paths flanked by stubble and vines and one beautiful field of cultivated fennel; feathery plants like delicate Christmas trees with tiny, yellow fruit like fairy lights, their roots earthed up like potatoes. Then, on a path of bare, parched ground, a pigeon-sized bird: soft, light orange on head, breast and back; the rest black and white stripes. With a silent touch, I drew Kes' attention to it, whereupon it unfurled a crest of orange feathers with black tips in a fluid movement like opening a fan.

" This world is so weird, " said Kes, firmly.

A Hoopoe - bizarre and exotic.

Cirauqui appeared ahead, a low mole-hill of roofs with a church at its summit. Swifts weaving over it like a cloud of gnats. Just beyond the town, a stretch of cobbled and rutted Roman road sloping down to a ruinous stone bridge. Then the path became pulverised white dust flanked by hard-baked chunks of cracked earth with huge, spiky thistles, brown and withered. The sun had bludgeoned the blue from the sky till it had become a fierce, bluish-white. When we stopped to take some water from our bottles, it was too hot to drink.

Lorca, the next place, is the archetypal Camino village. Permanently sleepy in the baking sun. Little more than one street, leading to a main square like an oven, enclosed by glaring white houses frilled with scarlet geraniums. To the right, shaded by a single plane tree, a horse trough and delicious, cool water. We shed our packs and sat in the shade and munched carrots.

Two German women arrived of mythological proportions. Huge Amazons fit to wield a broad sword and mate with Gods. One had a knife at her belt the size of a machete. Kes, somewhat unkindly, seeing them approaching, asked me if they were going to plunge their heads in the horse-trough to drink. But no, they merely asked directions for the bar and strode off for a hogshead of ale or two.

"That was close," said Kes, "we could have been sexually abruised."

"Might have been worth it," I said grumpily.

I know people who have done the walk, and say they grew more and more ethereal, more spiritually pure and disembodied. It did not affect me that way. As I came to be more present to the place I was in, more aware of my perceptions and feelings, more in touch with my body, I became increasingly randy. It became a problem, the access of new energy took that form. It was awkward, I'm not a philanderer, twenty-three years happily married and counting; I didn't know what to do with this strong, insistent pressure.

We ate some very juicy pears and some sunflower seeds. (It was my turn to choose the food.) A van stopped before us and we bought some bread.

A Spanish couple went through, not noticing us in the shade. They didn't stop for water. On such a day, this was sinful. He was a tall, athletic young man in shorts and vest, behind him a slim young woman in a black dress limped painfully along, ("a limpette," suggested Kes). He waited for her to catch up and then began to march swiftly, calling out what sounded like the Spanish equivalent of 'left, right, left, right.' She did her best to match his stride and pace, grimacing.

"Bastard," said Kes succinctly.

"They're not going to get very far like that," I commented.

Up to the road from Lorca, and it got hotter. The sun blazed at us, the road glared up at us. Soon my shirt was soaked, back and front. I thought the sun was affecting my eyes. I kept having to squint and blink, until I realised that it was sweat coursing down. My arms were glistening silver with sweat, my eyebrows filling with sweat and pouring constantly.

There is something humbling about the Spanish sun. It is a blatant manifestation of natural power. It brands the individual with a bodily knowledge of the appropriateness of humility. Feel this, it says, this is unconquerable.

A hard, long walk to Estella. Stella for star.

We couldn't find the refuge. So we popped in to the police

station where a couple of dapper, and very bored coppers, gave us a map and marked the route.

Estella is a biggish town. The refuge was quite a long way, cross town. It was a technical college, empty for the summer. A small, residential campus with poorly designed blocks of stained white buildings like a fifties housing estate. The caretaker's dog, panting in the heat, chained up by the gate in the sun, no water nearby, was a sack of bones. You could see all its ribs. The fat caretaker sat nearby in the shade.

A resting fellow pilgrim directed us up to the third floor of one of the blocks. Here were two of the women from Zubiri who had been tending the sick girl: one emerging from a shower room, a towel around her head, the other sweeping a dormitory. I nodded and smiled but they didn't seem to recognise me. Kes rested on a bed while I took a shower. The water was very cold. Perhaps this would make me more ethereal.

I let Kes sleep in the feathery, tactile warmth while I went shopping. When I returned, we stretched out on a lawn beneath gathering storm clouds and ate a leisurely meal of crusty bread, English ham, cheese, spring onions and strong red wine. Then chocolate doughnuts and luscious Spanish plums.

Back in the dormitory every one of the tiered bunk beds was taken. One of the Zubiri women was putting everyone's boots outside on the window-sills and shutting the windows. Then she stood in the doorway surveying her good work. No nasty, smelly boots anywhere inside. After she left, I retrieved *our* boots and opened the window nearest my bunk. Despite the breeze, it was still a night in a sauna amid crashing thunder storms. Strong winds lashing the building.

In the morning there was much philosophical debate concerning the fate of boots and the rights of the individual. The discussion was vigorous. Spanish is a wonderful language for a row. It crackles, and the whole body is used.

A few sorry-looking boots were to be seen on the window sills outside. Many people couldn't find their boots at all.

Some people, it seems, had wet boots, inside and out, while others were bootless, reduced to wandering the wet campus in their socks seeking their footwear outside. And everyone was a bit ratty from disturbed sleep. It was all rather chaotic.

As this human storm raged around me, I lay safe in my elevated upper bunk, smug in the belief of warm boots somewhere down below.

When things settled down a bit, I got up and brewed some coffee. Couldn't find my boots anywhere, till I discovered that somehow, in the scramble, they had wandered down the corridor.

For some unknown reason, forty scouts from Seville, only a little older than Kes, arrived on a truck. Kes woke in the hubbub, was up with astonishing speed, and began rushing around, clumping in his boots, playing various games. No problem whatsoever with the lack of a common language. A child once more, with the relief of someone to play with. How could he be so articulate and mature and still play tag? It made me realise how much I'd been treating him as an adult, and obliging him to act like one.

I took the opportunity to wash some clothes and pegged them out on the back of my rucksack to dry as we walked.

"Why are you flashing your knickers on the back of your pack, Dad." asked Kes, "Are you advertising?"

We left rather late and followed the Rio Ega through a park to the main road out of town. A British car passed, GB plates, and I waved and they looked puzzled. As we strolled along the road I wondered how it might be possible to convey nationality solely by gesture. What could I do to say to motorists: 'Look, I'm English.'? The only thing I could think of was Winston Churchill's 'V for Victory' sign.

We soon turned off the road and followed a rising path to the monastery of Irache. A tourist attraction; there were coaches and a picnic area and Claudio reclining on the grass, taking a break. Finding a face you recognise on the way is like a miniature homecoming;

something familiar in the constant change. After water, companionship is the greatest human need. We sat down and he made us camomile tea.

"What's that other building, Dad?"

There was a large shed with 'Bodegas' written on the wall.

"It's a winery. They make and store wine."

He stared at the sign.

"How do they make wine out of body gas?"

The path took us past neat managers' bungalows and back to the road. Down the long straight road, another British car approached us, and as they came within hailing distance I greeted them with a cheery wave and Churchill's V sign. This was not entirely successful. The driver just looked confused while the passenger made a vigorous upward thrusting motion with his right forearm.

The car's horn blared discordantly.

"Must be from Thurrock," said Kes.

Along a dusty path parallel to the main road we came upon a tethered donkey. We fed it carrots and it brayed pathetically as we left. No water within its tethered range.

By the road, just before Azqueta, we rested by a horse trough with excellent water and a wide view back across a patchwork of fields to the foothills of the Pyrenees, looking chalky from here in the harsh sun. A dead viper nearby like a huge Bombay Duck in the desiccating heat. We crossed the road to sit on a green bank and drink in the immense expanse. Claudio began to pay close attention to the vegetation.

"Yes," he said, in triumph, "I thought so. This is rosemary. I will take some for my Rice."

He cut some bunches and tied them onto his rucksack to dry in the sun. For days afterwards we knew when Claudio was not far ahead as his passage was marked by the aromatic fragrance of rosemary.

A pilgrim came along the road apparently wearing a mask with some red lines. As she came closer we could see they were the marks of recent wounds. She told us a harrowing tale of walking along with her hands in her pockets, and tripping, and falling, but not being able to get her hands out of her pockets fast enough to save herself. So her face crashed down into the stony dust, then her rucksack, a fraction of a second later, hit the back of her head, pounding her face into the stones again. She was fresh from the hospital and numerous stitches, but very resolute to continue. Her will was adamant and she was plainly more interested in plunging onward than in stopping to chat with us. She pounded away and we remained sitting among the rosemary letting the fragrance, and the view, slowly seep into us.

Onward, eventually, through the quiet village of Azqueta passing a farmer, wearing a black beret, astride a donkey flanked with two huge panniers of deep baskets like bass drums. He nodded respectfully towards us, slowly and with immense dignity, as we passed. His action had a natural, easy grace. It felt exactly tempered to the moment with just that right degree of recognition, that sensitive accuracy of pace that constitutes grace of motion. How delightful it would be to always act so. To live a life of elegant rapport in the simplest of actions as well as in the thick of troubles. A life of Chinese brush-strokes, exact and exquisite. Imagine what trust, what faith that would require. Would that not be grace?

We turned off on a wide track of dull orange dust with the baroque church tower of Urbiola rising like a rocket in the middle distance. At a curve in the track was a dilapidated sandstone building like a lone garage. It covered a medieval well. Inside, steps sloped down to a chill pool like a Roman bath. The place felt creepy, there was a sense of mould and corruption, and no-one was tempted to try the water despite the mounting heat. Littered around its doorway were broken stones that were green inside. The shade behind the building congealed the acrid stench of urine.

We moved off and into a long, lonesome valley flanked by low hills like shoals of flat-bellied, grouper-fish clothed with vegetation like some marine fungus. The valley floor was fields of chunky, cocoa-coloured soil with stubble sticking through it like new feathers on chicks. Linnets skimmed in flocks past us, seemingly quitting the place, twittering. Puffs of dust, the colour of dried blood, marked the landing of the occasional wheatear, which then stood up proudly with a military bearing, watching us pass and ensuring we did.

Other than that, not a soul. On and on we walked as dark clouds massed and the light grew dull. As the rest of the world receded, the valley felt increasingly alien. We felt unwelcome here. Bales of hay, like giant Weetabix, were piled up to make the play-houses of the children of giants. Nearby, a dead magpie, iridescent feathers sticking up at odd angles like an exotic wreck. We strode on in silence in a bubble of shared loneliness.

Then the storm broke. Gusty rain slashed at us. Hailstones, the size of marbles, pelted us. Heads down, we plugged on, splashing through rivulets of stale blood. Eventually, the path turned off left between the hills and we emerged, dripping, into the small town of Los Arcos.

None of the sparse inhabitants seemed to know where the refuge was, and we were preparing to walk straight through and go on to the next village when a dubious-looking chap, like a seller of dirty postcards, beckoned us over to his house and suggested we could stay there. We walked in to his large garage suspiciously, to find it full of damp pilgrims, including all the scouts from Estella. They were opening huge tins of soup and meatballs with Swiss knives. Kes was greeted like an old friend. But the place was too crowded for us to lay our sleeping bags anywhere, so the owner beckoned mysteriously once more and showed us through a tiny garden and into a large shed.

"Your room, gentlemen," he said lugubriously, "this is a good room, it has all necessaries. This hole through which we have entered is the door. This other hole in the wall, here, is a window. At your feet is the floor and above your head is the roof. Everything a room needs."

What he omitted to mention was the thirty thousand other things the room contained. It looked like a long-lost Noah's Ark for endangered objects. There were vintage agricultural implements of all descriptions: spades and rakes and scythes and shears and hoes and wheelbarrows; a motley of tools propped up and laying about: saws and chisels and axes and hammers; there were saddles and bridles, brooms and bags of fertiliser; drying herbs and onions hung up; screws and nails and nuts and hooks were scattered about everywhere like acorns in autumn. There was a spinning top and piles of newspapers, ladders and mattresses, drums of tar, nose-rings for bulls, a lavatory seat, a sheep castrator, buckets and ropes, planks and paintbrushes, bits of bicycle, feathers, a car's engine and a battered teddy-bear. The whole ensemble was sepia-toned with a layer of ancient, brown dust and the floor was littered with broken nut-shells.

Our host grinned shyly at us.

"Now this is the business," said Kes approvingly.

We shifted in our gear and swept the floor just enough to fit in a couple of sleeping bags.

Back in the garage the scouts were comparing feet. Claudio was doing his rounds, looking for blisters, which he relished.

"Ooh, now that's a lovely one," he cooed, reaching for his medical kit, "and just ready."

Alone, in the corner I found a bemused Italian, contemplating the scene before him.

"Let me show you something," he said softly.

He removed his trainers and socks. I've done a lot of walking in my time, but never, before or since, have I seen anything like this young Italian's feet. They were scarred with concentric rings everywhere as if branches had been growing out of the flesh and had been broken off, and the raw remainder had healed. This man had had blisters all right. Huge ones. And they had burst and the exposed skin had half healed and fresh blisters had formed on the tender site of the old. And these too had burst, and so on. All his toe-nails were black. You see a lot of injured feet on a long walk, but these took the prize.

"I have walked from Italy," he said wistfully.

He didn't need to tell me. You could see the evidence of the miles engraved in these appalling feet.

I glanced up at his face. He was gazing at the scars, his eyes unfocused, in loving admiration. He was proud of them. They were marks of devotion, a sign of his endurance, unquestionable evidence of his worthiness, branded medals of sincerity of purpose. I thought he was quite mad.

Kes seemed happy with his friends and Claudio with his medicinal good deeds, so I went off to get some food. I had trouble finding a shop that was open and could get neither fresh bread nor wine, but returned with freeze-dried shepherd's pie, doughnuts, plums, some cut bread called Bimbo, and biscuits, whose name I could not resist, called Mildred. I inquired about getting sellos (the rubber stamps for our pilgrims' passports) and was told the priest would do the job after mass.

So, after eating, we went down to the church. I thought that the best way of ensuring meeting the priest was to attend the service.

The church was dark and grim inside: late Baroque carving everywhere in profusion, all knobby and curly in frantic excess. It had once been pristine and gilden but hadn't been cleaned in an aeon or two and had become tawdry with grime. It was all too much. In the effort to express exuberance, to impress the worshipper with the sense of God's overwhelming bounty and its golden worth, the builders had produced an insistent, warty monster. The spirit of our host's shed had been taken up and made pretentious and vulgar. It was like being submerged in the forgotten remains of Santa's grotto.

The congregation was a few substantial old women, buried in black. We sat and rose, and sat and rose, as the service dragged lifelessly on like a dreary lament for a rumoured joy that nobody really believed in anymore.

When the service finally died the priest smartly disappeared. One short, but bulky old woman, remained and tidied up. We appealed to her for the sellos. For some reason that I couldn't fathom she insisted on showing us the cloisters.

The walls were of a gentle honey-cream stone pierced with ground-level windows with beautiful curvilinear tracery. The square beneath had been made into a flower garden; dark green foliage with many blooms in sepulchral white and maiden's blush pink, but there was just too much of it. The small space was crowded out and cluttered with plants. It was the same spirit of rampant disorder expressed in the church and the shed.

Here, in Los Arcos, people had gone about their business for centuries and yet had regularly produced a similar ramshackle jumble. What is it about a location that can result in such repeating expression?

Back in the church, I asked about the Black Virgin which I knew was supposed to be here somewhere. With a tired gesture, the woman indicated the top of the huge mess of an altar-piece. Atop this over-elaborate stack, like a diminutive Guy Fawkes on his pyre, was a doll that looked as if it had been steeped in dilute peat. She was a grubby brown. It was impossible to tell whether the material was actually that colour or whether she had suffered the same degradation by neglect that was all around her.

I had read about Black Virgins back home. The subject is complex and controversial, but one theory has it that there was, and is, a cult dedicated to the female side of the cosmic force represented by these dark statues, some of which are a rich jet-black.

Demeter, dark Mother goddess of the earth, who converts dead and buried seed into golden wheat, was worshipped at a cave in Phigaleia in the form of a wooden idol known as 'The Black'. She is supposed to incarnate an alternative, subversive, compensating power of the dark earth, hidden truths of the unconscious. Here, however, she was an impotent irrelevance hidden near the shadowy roof. A disappointment.

Her representative on earth reluctantly stamped our cards as if we were criminals seeking an alibi.

****

The floor in the shed was cold. We slept on the filthy ground under sheep skins, with raw, red tattered edges, that we had found amid the debris.

I was up at seven in the morning and tried to wash some clothes. The discoloured sink in the garden had no plug, so I used a single pink household glove I found nearby. The fingers bloated up from the plug-hole, beneath the water, like some drowning virgin. Behind me white rabbits pottered about the garden, nibbling on the spinach. Four mirrors and a picture of the virgin protected the outside toilet.

Then I went and bought some envelopes in a cluttered shop. The deserted streets were being cleaned by some men with wheelbarrows, shovels and witches' brooms.

Back at the garage, the scouts had gone and Kes was up. We sat on our ram's fleece and drank mint tea. Claudio snored quietly. We left him to sleep and Kes and I were off about ten, we walked through Los Arcos and its warm, cosy smell of freshly baking bread.

At the edge of the town was a litter of old roadside markers collected and dumped. Plump white tombstones with a red cap, they lay amid weeds and haphazard grasses in random disorder like the outdated residue of many forgotten Christmases; a last echo of the ethos of Los Arcos.

Chapter 12.

Seeing otherwise

A long, straight dirt track of stony white powder, already reflecting a powerful glare, led through bleached wheat stubble. We crossed an equally straight road that swept relentlessly to the horizon.

Reaching Sansol, we passed along the Calle Real, Real Street, 'so, here we see reality' I thought. In the road, half way along was a dead kitten.

We sat to have breakfast on a hill overlooking Torres del Rio and watched the scouts filing down the road below. Not a cloud in the vibrant blue sky; the dull orange earth beneath us already softly warmed, like fresh bread; the low, plain houses of Torres clustered in the landscape like a crowd of friends; we sat and aimlessly chatted, in no hurry at last.

The pilgrim is a nomad. He moves on constantly, sets down no roots, not even temporary ones. Each place to stay is a one off, new and fresh. The horizon continually beckons. Who can tell what is around the next bend in the path? There isn't time for a dulling by familiarity. There is nothing to hurry on to see. No appointments to keep. Everything can be taken at a pace suitable to what's happening. He joins no society, except that of other nomads. The result is a freshness of experience, an attending on the moment. Time and the quality of life is retrieved. Ripeness is all. We sat and savoured the calm originality of the new day.

Kes got out his knife & started to cut his staff.

"Spain's weird," he said, casually.

"How?"

"It's just weird."

"How do you mean?"

He glanced up at me to see if I was in a serious enough mood. He clearly had something he needed to sort out.

"Well, you go along and you see a rock or something. And you look at the rock and you think: 'Oh yere, that's interesting.' And you forget all about it. Then, a week later you see something else and it connects up with the rock and you know what it means. And it goes on and on like that all the time. How does it do that?"

"I don't know."

"Well, it's weird."

"Certainly is."

"It's such a shock, you know. You think: 'Now wait a minute. What's going on here?' I can't handle it."

The scouts reached where we were sitting & filed past, they must have stopped for breakfast somewhere: each wished us good morning, politely.

Kes collected his thoughts and went on hesitantly. He looked me straight in the eye & then held out both hands as if holding a small child.

"It's a bit scary. But sort of exciting. Like I feel: 'Wow, this is really it.' It seems really important somehow."

"I think so. I suspect it's like that in England too."

"Do you?"

"Yere, but we don't notice. Too busy doing other things. We don't stop to look at the rock in the first place."

He looked down bashfully & rolled his head.

"Yere, you're right, we don't give it a chance."

He whittled his stick, nervously. Down below us in the village a greengrocer had parked his van & a line of housewives were chatting, waiting to be served.

"It's like that with people too," Kes continued, watching the housewives.

"Is it? How?"

I stretched my legs out more comfortably.

"Well, you talk and talk and you listen to talk but don't realise what's going on. Then suddenly you realise what's really happening, what people are trying to say, underneath what they're actually saying."

"That doesn't sound like the same thing."

"The feeling's similar. Like you're connecting up and it's really important and the rest of the time isn't."

"I see."

He paused & twisted up his face trying to find what he needed to say. He slashed a bit at the stick he was carving.

"It's good it doesn't happen all the time," he said.

"Why?"

"It would get ordinary and stop feeling important."

"I'm not so sure of that. Maybe everything would feel important all the time."

"Maybe."

There was a long, pregnant pause. He dug at the earth at his feet with the tip of his stick. He really needed to uncover something with this chat.

"Yeah, your *own* talking's weird like the rock," he concluded, looking up at the women at the van , now arguing loudly.

"How?"

"Same way. All that talk, and it goes in and you forget about it. Then it goes round and round and does what it does inside. Then a month later something happens that makes you realise what you were talking about. If you're lucky."

"I don't think it's luck."

Another long pause.

"It's like cats," he went on, smiling.

"Cats?"

We had four cats at home.

"Yere, cats. You know, one is on a chair and another jumps up and they're both all spiky towards each other for a while, until they sort out the territory bit."

This wasn't vastly clear.

"What's that got to do with it?"

"Well, you realise, watching them, that they're locked into this funny catty world with its own catty rules. And each cat is locked into its own world with its own personal rules and they don't know they're a cat and they don't know they're <u>that</u> cat. They don't know what's going on. Everything gets processed into their catty world and their own individual world. There is something else going on but they don't know what it is and they can't know until something happens that won't process. If they see a rock and later something else and there's this feeling of weirdness, that means there's another way of putting things together."

"Just the same with people."

"Yere, but you don't realise till you get here. That's why Spain is so weird. All the rest, at home, is looking into a mirror and talking to yourself. There's someone else here. Someone really else."

We grew silent and I stretched back and took a nap.

Afterwards, we packed up slowly and walked down towards Torres.

The path was pure white, like talcum powder, with small, brown lizards, like ancient embryos, scurrying at its edges. In the fields on the edge of the village someone had used half an old car as a shed. Nearby, an old woman swept up the dust with a besom broom that had a bent branch as a handle. Her house had large cacti in pots at the base of its rough, white wall; black plastic sheets, held down by rocks, covered the holes in the roof, and white plastic bags hung on her washing line to dry.

We passed a stream that had been diverted into a trough with concrete tables nearby where the three Zubiri women (the smelly-boot-haters at Estella) and their young charge were having a picnic. They were reverently wrapping the remains of sandwiches with foil, while on a table was a cornucopia of lotions, salves and cosmetics. I nodded greeting but they ignored me.

Beyond Torres the path continued as a very light brown talc flanked by fields of what looked like chunks of chalk. The vegetation was sparse and poor, desert-like, withered in the cruel sun. A long, brown snake slithered desperately off the path out of the heat. We sweltered on like legionnaires. Kes sang Buddy Holly songs, lustily.

A pair of pilgrims caught and passed us. He was a big, strapping chap and carried both rucksacks. She was petite, in a one-piece black dress like a long vest, and had a dainty and mesmerising wiggle.

"I bet she whims to his every desire," said Kes.

"I see her as Play-pilgrim of the year," I replied, "posing naked with staff and, suitably located, scallop shell."

"You would."

We passed a startling field of sunflowers like thousands of sweet, young Victorian girls wearing vivid yellow Salvation Army bonnets, then silently through a small conifer plantation which smelled, strangely, of warm after shave.

"Why is it just the same at home?" asked Kes, as we emerged.

"Pardon?"

"You said it was just the same at home, and it isn't."

"What isn't just the same at home?"

"Connecting up. You know seeing one thing and later seeing another and it making sense. Rocks and stuff."

"And cats."

"All that."

"Well, it happens back home but less often because we're too busy, too programmed."

Kes scuffed his feet & kicked up a flurry of dust.

"What do you mean 'programmed'?"

"Things to do, places to go, people to see, deadlines to meet, timetables to obey. There isn't the leeway to allow for the linking, so it doesn't happen so often and people think it doesn't happen at all. Or if it does they're too busy to pay much attention."

"I'd pay attention."

"Maybe, but would you be loose enough to let it happen in the first place?"

"What do you mean?"

"Well, what if you saw a rock twenty metres away from the path and had a feeling that you should go and have a look?"

"I'd go and have a look."

"You sure?"

"Yere."

"What about on the way to school?"

"I'd still go and have a look."

"No, you wouldn't. You get up at 9.15, on a good day, to be in school by 9.00. You wouldn't have the time."

The conversation faded like sunset.

Towards the road there appeared a bleak, square hermitage; locked. Nearby, on a glaring concrete slab was an amateur altar; a cairn of small rocks held a makeshift cross of twigs, while before it had been placed a few cigarettes, some biscuits, the dregs of a bottle of wine, and some sheets of paper with pious words of mutual encouragement from passing pilgrims.

We climbed to a broad plain of low, patchy scrub with a few distant plantations of vines and dark conifers. No shade here, even the lizards were hiding. In the roasting heat, it looked like a scene in Arizona. By the path was a beehive shepherd's hut like a primitive oven built of grim, grey stones; here we ducked through the low door and took refuge inside from the furnace of the landscape, sitting like lobsters in a pot. What was left of our water was too hot to drink, so we made tea with it.

Viana appeared deserted until we toiled up the steep stone steps into the old, walled town. A fortified town on a low hill. Sometime in the past this place had needed to defend itself against something. Inside the walls, men in shirt sleeves were industriously fixing wooden and metal barriers all the way down the main street at every side junction. At first we were puzzled until I suddenly realised what it was all about.

"They're getting ready for a running of the bulls. It's a mini-Pamplona."

"Oh, wow, can we stay here, Dad?"

"I suppose so."

Crowds were gathering excitedly behind each barrier as it was completed. We mingled, and eventually, with a whoosh, a bang and a cheer, a rocket went up and a wave of excited chatter flamed through the crowd, but as the bulls appeared, the talk turned to cries of consternation. Somehow a pilgrim was trapped the wrong side of the walls. Still shouldering his rucksack and with a scallop round his thin neck, he anxiously watched the bulls at the top of the long street baring swiftly down upon him. Tall and emaciated, with a short grey beard, he belatedly strode sedately, with long gangly strides, towards us, calm and dignified, and was let through a small door just as the bulls thundered past with young men leaping onto windowsills and clinging to iron wall bars. They leaned down and swotted the bulls with rolled newspapers.

Except, I could now see, a lot of them were actually cows; mean cows no doubt.

A square had been converted to an arena, and here had been dumped a wrecked car. A confused bull wandered around unsure of what was going on. In and on the car were a motley of young people, their faces painted in black and blue patterns, shouting and gesticulating, waving flags. They were stocked up with an armoury of small, but heavy, objects which they periodically threw at the bull with theatrical gestures and a fair bit of sneering. Occasionally one would leave the protection of the car to race around towards the bull to taunt it at closer range and maybe throw a spanner at its eyes.

No-one seemed to object to any of this, or to find it in any way unusual. We saw a fair bit of habituated, casual violence towards animals in Spain. It made me wince with shame; as did this goading of the bull. There was something adolescent in it, something bullying and ugly like misplaced vengeance, as if the inaccessible and unconquerable strength of the sun had become bull-shaped and could be poked at and wounded with sharp sticks. It was mean-minded. As I watched, it made a sort of tumour of soft regret somewhere inside to be hung up deep in the soul with all the others.

A brave young boy scampered out into the arena, his jacket in his hands, which he flounced at the bull, till it turned towards him, then he high-tailed it back to the barriers. The crowd laughed and cheered. Then a young man sped out from the car and threw a flat iron at the bull which bounced off its shoulder. I rather lost interest after that.

We left to find the refuge, and, buying some food on the way, I discovered I was short of cash. I decided to economise on cigarettes.

The refuge was in a peaceful square, the ground floor of a four-storey stone building with cages over the windows and a carved coat of arms; a single room through old, heavy, wooden double doors. The walls inside were smeared whitewash. There were two tubular beds and five very dirty mattresses on the floor. At the back, a tatty, dark red settee, and littered about, a small round table and a couple of plastic chairs. Two naked light bulbs. Everything was beyond the second-hand, and dirty, the floor was sticky and the place smelled of pee. I found a mop in the toilet and some ammonia cleaning fluid and set to clean the place up while Kes had a nap.

Afterwards I was desperate for a fag, but fortunately found some large dog-ends among lots of oval shapes, small rubber bands, at the murky bottom of a waste-paper bin.

I sat, content after my labour, in the stuffy little room and smoked. There was no traffic noise, no voices; all of Viana seemed at Siesta. Kes, stretched out on a mattress, looked so small and vulnerable as he slept: spindly little legs like a chicken; green shirt with tide-marks of salt from the sweat; his blond hair, bleached fairer in the sun, unwashed and getting long. In the close heat, he was like a cell-mate in some dishevelled South American jail. It didn't seem right that something so small and fragile should have to grow up and face life. I couldn't bear to imagine him standing alone as malevolent troubles charged at him; it was too painful to consider.

I drew luxuriously on my salvaged cigarette.

I wasn't sure how far we'd walked, a hundred miles or so maybe, four hundred to go. It wasn't worth thinking about. Far to go. Un poco y un poco - little by little. Weeks of walking still. He hadn't complained much, except when he was bored. A good lad.

One of the more tender revelations of parenthood is the ache of the knowledge of the vulnerability of your child. No matter what joy attends as you hold your child you also embrace fragility and helplessness. That tugs the heart-strings. At the core of all happiness lies the awareness of its ephemerality. This child will suffer the trivial, excruciating wounds of everyday life, will be smitten with heartache and disease, and will eventually die. It is quite intolerable. It would be easier if we didn't care, but love opens the heart to life's arrows. This is the paradox of love; that the more a person loves, and the wider the range of that love, the more they take on the burden of the pains of others. Compassion hurts. This is why we defend ourselves against love; it is self-protection. As Chogyam Trungpa says: he who pursues the path of love and compassion has a fuller and fuller broken heart. Spirituality doesn't include strolling around in permanent bliss, grinning like a Californian Buddhist. It is a matter of how much you can take. Love, like Truth, needs courage & strength.

Kes awoke and sat up. staring fuzzily into the waste bin where I had found my cigarette ends.

"What are all those round things in the bin, Dad?"

"Rubber bands."

"Rubber bands? Why are they moving then?"

"Moving?"

I looked more carefully. No, not rubber bands, moving indeed and with little twitchy bits at one end.

Oh no, oh no!

Cockroaches! Huge disgusting cockroaches! In the waste bin where I had found my dog-ends.

"Aaargh!"

I ran to the sink and washed out my mouth in a panic.

"What's the matter, Dad."

"Oh no, no, cockroaches."

Horrible. Horrible. The thought of cockroaches crawled about in my mouth.

"I've got to get a beer," I shouted, fumbling with the massive door. In my mind the cockroaches were shitting on my tongue; minute, rancid, alien shit.

I ran out and across the square desperately searching for a bar.

Everything seemed normal in the Bar Las Vegas. I swirled the cold beer around in my mouth, trying not to think of cockroaches. I looked around seeking distraction. The T.V. throbbed out 'The Heat is On'. The accompanying video was a nasty piece of work. Not having seen much T.V. for such a while, I was especially vulnerable to its violence. Isolation from the habitual crudities of our culture had made me fragile. My feelings had a gold-leaf sensitivity. The crass and cruel distressed me. On the T.V. a grinning driver smashed through cars. Lots of guns and aggression; very ugly.

"The heat is on. It's in the street."

Around me, paunchy old men wearing black berets, slammed down their dominoes on the table as if angrily smashing insects. My beer swilled the thought of roaches away somewhat. Only somewhat. All of a sweat, I turned again to the TV for distraction. Another rock song, a hairy group of blokes were trying to pick up an attractive young girl, slim and blonde, but she wasn't interested. Then, suddenly, they were on stage, pounding out a powerful heavy-metal beat; a band of leather-clad gargoyles grimacing and sneering. How dare any mere girl ignore their desires? The girl was also on stage. The group ignored her completely. She was in a long, rectangular glass tube. It was filled with water. She was plainly drowning. Her hair spread about her like fragile sea-weed in a slow current. She mouthed her distress silently, palms flat against the glass. The fate of Aphrodite in the modern world. This place was full of nightmares!

I fled.

In the next bar, I checked out the T.V. first just in case, it showed comforting, rolling hills, green and lush. Beautiful; such long, gentle curves and the plush grass like a refreshing drink after the sun-shrivelled landscape we had been living in for days. I realised how starved of green I was; the clarinet colour of nature. The flying camera swept back to show a cathedral, then a line of familiar white cliffs. As I recognised them, I wept.

By the time I was ready to go back, I had become more calm. I strolled down the canyons of narrow streets with their tall houses either side. Canaries, in tiny cages the size of shoe-boxes, sang sweetly. Out of the corner of my eye I caught the image of a white bird lilting down towards me. As it brushed my head I caught it; a pair of white cotton knickers, warm and soft.

I looked up whence this promise had fallen, like manna from the goddess. A torso thrust out above me from the side of the building like a tongue from a giant. Charcoal black hair, swept back tight to the head, she gobbled a spate of Spanish and disappeared.

Oh my prophetic beer!

I awaited consequences with rising expectations.

Soon a girl of about ten or eleven was spat out of a doorway nearby, plainly a splinter off the Carmen above.

She snatched her mum's knickers from my hands, lasered me a silent look spiked with etherised hemlock, which could have withered the testes of a fighting bull at forty paces, and retracted into the building accompanied by more crackling Spanish.

Back at the refuge, Kes had filled the waste bin with water, but the cockroaches were swimming about unconcerned. He seemed demented. He poured the water out carefully, leaving the damp cockroaches at the bottom. Then he stabbed at them, pounded at them, with the handle of the mop. They cracked and crunched like snails under foot. He was enjoying it. Kes, who would daintily step over an ant if he saw it in time, was pummelling them to death.

I took a nap on a dirty mattress.

****

We carried the table and chairs outside and I cooked there. Octopus with white beans plus sausage and mushrooms (and Tabasco sauce), fresh bread and rough red wine. A long, slow meal while we chatted amiably.

Later we took a stroll and found that the narrow streets had been filled with trestle tables, and plump women and their daughters were covering them with a feast: plates of very red meats; golden rings of fried squid; fiery tomatoes glistening with oil; tender lettuces of fragile green; huge creamy cheeses; livid red and cool green chillies; some pungent, steaming black stuff that looked like the insides of many black puddings; and much, much else. Members of the families would arrive in big cars, and were embraced and kissed amid much excited noise of reunion.

Soon the streets were full, as people chatted loudly, paused to take some wine or sample a dish offered insistently, or wandered in and out of the bars. The place hummed with cheerful good humour. Huge jumping crackers were let off amid screams, as they were thrown into crowds. Men set off rockets by holding them in one hand and lighting them with the other, until it caught and the force was strong enough to let it go swishing aloft. A tin bull appeared covered in fireworks, it rushed about chasing people as they fled, the fireworks cracking and banging. It must have been dreadfully hot and noisy inside.

It was late by the time the large band began on the stage in the main square. Mostly brass and percussion, there was an energetic vitality to their music, punchy and strong. They belted out up tempo numbers into the clear night air that must have been heard for many miles. I stood amid the paired dancers feeling a little lonely, when I became aware of a tug on my trouser leg that had been going on for some time. Looking down I was transported into one of those sentimental scenes in Chaplin. A Spanish waif in a party dress stood staring up at me. Her big brown eyes looked anxious and questioning. She had a runny nose and a pathos like Satie's music; a melancholy child.

"Papa Noel?" she asked plaintively. Are you Father Christmas?

Well, the beard must be getting long.

I could see plainly in her face what she wanted me to say. Her fathomless eyes harboured an ache, like a ghostly mist in a deep well. I knew the right thing to do.

"Si," I told her gently, smiling.

She gulped, breathless for a moment, then ignited with pleasure and rushed off in high glee to tell the amazing news.

"Daddy, Daddy, Father Christmas is here, Father Christmas is here!"

I sloped off quietly back to the refuge.

Flies buzzed around the whitewash, while mosquitoes waited, hanging from the wall in silent malevolence like scattered musical notation. I killed them all with a discarded woollen sock which I found in a corner; lurid purple flapping down from otherwhere dispatching them to oblivion.

Chapter 13

Tenderness

I awoke in the morning feeling vaguely anxious. There was something threatening here in Viana. Something that required a response; a cool courage, a panic, a manic killing, a strong sense of family unity. I couldn't see what the threat was, but I could feel it. There was a need for a mythical figure of bonhomie, a Father Christmas.

Kes didn't appear to be in his sleeping bag, or in the room. I eventually found him, dead to the world, curled up like a wood-louse, in the bottom of his bag.

Outside the morning had dawned cool. Men in blue boiler suits with black wellies and straw hats flushed the streets clean with hoses; the water sparkling in the crisp, early sun. A donkey was being shod and bridled in a corner of the main square.

I popped in to the main church, lit a candle to my unknown grief. Nearby was an extraordinary statue of a woman, Mary Magdalene, coquettish and sexy, naked to the waist with long, seaweed-like hair and a sensuous tilt to the hips. The skirt was a penitent sack tied with the pagan symbol of the female. Here was the potent, and dangerous, Aphrodite who could make men violently ill; destructive Helen who could innocently start a war; energetic Lillith demanding satisfaction and insisting on her pristine independence; Artemis attracting suitors like crazed moths ready with her arrows to shoot them in the back. I have never seen the like in any Catholic church; a celebration of temptation, an honest whore knowing an alternative truth, cutting through pretence with an arch look; the youthful version of the force at Eunate before it had matured into an ancient shrivelled fruition. I shivered, Eunate still stuck in my heart like a granitic arrowhead.

And here too. I found, out by the porch, was a large ancient tombstone set into the pavement; a single name recorded its restless contents. It was the tomb of Cesare Borgia; the model for

Machiavelli's Prince.
****

We set out, late, for Logroño, the next town; a big city.

In the quiet, as we walked, conversation emerged naturally, like an unfurling frond. For some reason, Kes wanted to talk about the silver car. Back in Ingatestone, in the early stages of preparation, we had taken a few short walks around the village. One sunny day, we were walking down Stock Lane, a narrow country road, when the roar of a powerful open-topped sports car ripped through the peace. We stood well back on the verge as it reached us and thundered past. At the wheel, a young man, almost too young to drive. He was gunning the car hard, showing off. I can see his face now, the grin of the pushy adolescent, as he turned to his girl as they bombed along, terrifyingly fast. She squealed by his side in excited fear; head thrown back, mouth wide in wild abandon, like a climax. Her scream echoed around as the car rocketed over the hill ahead.

"Much too fast, much too fast," I cried in consternation.

We could only hear, from far ahead & out of sight, the desperate shriek of brakes and a series of ominous crunches. We hurried along. Soon an ambulance passed us howling urgently. By the time we had topped the hill and reached the scene the quiet of the countryside had returned once more. A farmer told us how he had seen the car shoot over the brow, take to the air, plunge down nose first, and cartwheel over and over. In the stunned silence there was now only the wrecked car, metal twisted like toffee, broken glass, the farmer's urgent need to talk, and blood everywhere.

Here in Spain, we talked it through. Both of us still needing to exorcise the shock.

We took a break en route at a church like a hacienda, made of sandstone blocks, with concrete picnic tables like raised tombstones mushrooming in the shade. Whitethroat sang in the trees. A strong, blond cyclist wandered around taking photographs; fine professional camera; sturdy, fit chap, like a Dane. We chatted a little and he turned out to be an American taking photos for a book. He wanted to do the walk one day. We shared an apple and a cigarette then he pedalled off strongly down the rutted, lion-hued path. Above him a flock of storks spiralled lazily in a languid carousel moving steadily East as they rotated, maybe fifty or sixty birds; dark beneath, each flashing white in the sun as they turned.

Fairly dull, the rest of the way to Logroño. As we steadily trudged, I found my mind taking stock. After a while you don't consciously think, just let the thoughts rise, like a spring, and note what they are as they pass. The question that I couldn't ignore, which formed in the dullness, was: what was I doing here at all? What was I looking for exactly? The Santiago of the soul, I had told myself; but what, precisely, was that?

Here I had been given the gift of time. Time at home was so packed, and so empty. So much work, so many deadlines, so much to do. Even entertainment filling time, yet somehow irrelevant and beside the point.   Distractions everywhere and a growing ache that had become urgent to find out what lay hidden beneath; what I was covering by the work and the frenetic play.

I had read Kierkegaard and had been moved by his account of the hedonist's increasingly neurotic determination to dispel the bogie of boredom. Entertainment was a defence mechanism against the fear of boredom. But what was it in boredom, in effect in time and consciousness itself, such that the mind was scared of it? The irony was that in order to produce an effective defence mechanism at all, the mind had to know somehow what it was defending itself against, otherwise how could it construct something that would work? So I already knew, somewhere in there, what I was so scared of. Bateson wrote that entertainment was the food of depression.

What distinguishes a pilgrimage from spiritual tourism is the journey, not the destination. The struggle is all. It's what you're there for. The walk, like the writing, is full of dull stretches, and in those dull stretches up come the thoughts you need to deal with. In the monotonous passages, the dreary road to the horizon, there was much to be found, much to speak of. When a plain, long path presented, there was nothing to do but walk it. No distractions, no entertainment, nothing to interest and divert; and I found something there awaiting my attention. I found me. I lurked beneath the demand for amusement, waiting, like a bandit, to pounce. All the things I didn't want to encounter, the things the entertainment was used to hide, waited patiently; and slowly, as I walked, I ran out of stratagems to conceal, and what I needed to face, repeatedly, and more plainly, emerged. The bandit, grinning like a clown, whispered to me the things I feared to hear. The dull stretches were among the most testing and productive times. There was gold in the boredom. Consciousness itself, the bare Cogito, contains its own remedies. If we allow it.

Just above Logroño, an old woman suddenly appeared on the path out of a nearby hovel. She fluttered about waving pamphlets at us. Her bright, porcelain eyes, sunk in her creased, reptilian, brown face were full of enthusiasm. The pamphlets showed the whereabouts of the refuge in the big city ahead. It was apparently some sort of social charity called JOC. We thanked her and she glowed with the pleasure of giving, then skittered into the shade like a lizard, waving good-bye, to await the next pilgrims.

Logroño was an emotional mess; a big city with a big city's confusion of feelings. So many people going about their business; clutter and noise and fumes and bustling disorder. I could detect no overall quality of feeling. Though cooler today, a tower in the centre had a display which read 33 degrees Centigrade.

We found the refuge easily; a tatty street with lots of police hanging about and men sitting on the kerb with vacant eyes. We dumped our gear. Kes took a nap while I went to get some new socks, white cotton ones, some cash, and to hunt for a cobbler.

My old boots had acquired a startling slope on the heels so that I walked with a bandy gait like Popeye. I was beginning to get pains in the calves and hips from the unnatural stresses. The cobbler was not hopeful that my boots could be repaired, but he would try. He wanted me to come back in the evening. We had intended to go through Logroño but it looked like we were staying. Nothing to do but wait around.

When I went back in the evening he had done a good job. I struggled to express my satisfaction.

"You are not a cobbler," I said, in faltering Spanish.
I thought he was going to hit me with his hammer.

I went on swiftly, "You are an artist in shoes."

He beamed and whipped out a bottle of red wine from nowhere and we toasted the health of pilgrims everywhere and the noble art of cobbling. He showed me how strong the boots were now, bending the sole back with powerful fingers, and I admired his work once more.

That night I lay restlessly awake on the floor of the refuge. The room had a city's humidity in the close heat. Orange street lights shone into the room, a touch of Raymond Chandler. Then a voice outside called in the night.

"Hola. Hola."

Only Billie Holiday could have got so much carressive innuendo into the two syllables of this 'hello', and for the same reason: it was a condensed message of availability, laced with the hard-cased vulnerability of the fallen. It had street cred, the offer of temporary tenderness, love for sale, and a self-defensive cynicism ready to curse and spit - a whore at work. I could hear the fawning and the claws:

"Hola"

She went on and on like a cuckoo till I fell asleep. I dreamed, luridly, of a harem.

As we turned to leave in the morning down the seedy street, a woman came out of a nearby doorway and greeted a friend. At once I knew her. The tones were unmistakable. She was tall and scrawny, like a chicken that had been starved, plucked, and stretched on some relentless rack. She glanced into my eyes and I saw a lifetime of bleak struggle, honed to melancholy hardness. The little hope there was only a lingering question; still looking for business.

Further down the sordid street, a barefoot child played alone in a pot-hole in the road. She wore a poor, frayed dress and dirty knickers. She chatted to her imaginary companions. My heart, tender as a wound, melted within me. Her impoverished, disabled future seemed to float around her. I looked on her with acute distress, a sharp-edged splinter in the soul. Such wounds do not heal, only recede. What can be done with such things except to move on? I walked on through the bustling streets, the honking cars.

Chapter 14

Losing the Mask

Logroño stretched forever with shops and factories (41 degrees, it said on the tower) till we turned off left into a parched landscape. Dust devils swirled like wraiths. A figure appeared ahead, shimmering in the heat, running towards us across the uneven ground. A jogger, in this heat! As he passed us he yelled out, "I am completely mad," and pounded on.

We took a break in the shade of some sweet smelling pines. I made tea with the last of our water.

I was getting to enjoy making tea, the ritual of it; unpacking the nested equipment, pouring just enough meths into the reservoir, having a stick nearby to adjust the damper if necessary, lighting the vapour. The process itself was pleasurable, a pocket of order. I began to understand a little more about Claudio's Rice.

As we sipped our tea, a hoopoe flew by like a crippled jay, quickly and desperately flapping its black and white wings with its fingered edges. It struggled to keep airborne, as if the ground's pull was too strong for it. It landed heavily and squatted low like a dachshund; dappled apricot breast and neck, and a crest like a cockatoo; a clown of a bird. A show off, a bird with a burden like a self-obsession. It attempted magnificence and only managed the ridiculous.

At least I was beginning to understand what was going on here. I've said that as I walked I found myself feeling increasingly wicked, not that I was filled with evil intent, quite the contrary. I was also realising what really matters and what is merely peripheral, and how the trivial can come to seem important if there isn't the time to allow the recognition of real worth. These important things were simple like water and companionship. Well, one of the really important things that becomes pressingly clear is the need for love. It just rises up and confronts the psyche. I found this embarrassing. It seems so wet and inadequate. But there it is, the need for love is basic and vital.

And this is much more a need to care rather than a need to be cared for. It takes us out of ourselves, the narrow boundaries of self-interest, so it isn't even good enough to care for those who care for us. That is too selfish to satisfy, that reinforces self. It has to be disinterested, a concern for those who, should we do something about our caring, would not be in a position to reward us for our effort. The love which nourishes is a free gift: giving without the desire, or even the expectation, of return. This is why I felt tender towards waifs and wastrels, and even actresses in pop videos. I was feeling for the unfortunates whom I could not help. What made it infinitely worse was the knowledge of my systematic incapacity to deliver such selfless care. I knew I wasn't good enough, couldn't be good enough. So I felt faulty, defective; I felt wicked.

I shook off these depressions and packed up our gear.

We walked on through an immense leisure park with a lake; mobile homes, an ice-cream van, people in swimming costumes. People relaxing, people enjoying themselves. I could find no sense of empathy for them. It all seemed trivial and irrelevant. Petty people about their petty business. With a sudden shock I realised that shaking off depression, I was sinking deeper.

I climbed up towards a big road; the lake, far below now, a sheen of blue silk. On the top of a stalk by the path was a magnificent swallowtail butterfly: cool lemon wings with black markings on the leading edge like piano keys. It fluttered in a semi-hover, struggling with its bulk, over sun-dried flower heads. I turned to share the sight with Kes but he was nowhere to be seen. I hurried on up to the main road, where he was waiting for me.

We trudged in silence down the ferocious road. It was full of huge lorries which slammed past us, nearly knocking Kes over with their slipstream. The brutal heat pounded down and was doubled in the reflection back up from the melting road. We walked against the hot air as if combating a force, it had a pressure, an immovable soft wall like an enveloping liquid, which we waded through streaming with sweat.

On the horizon, a huge silhouette of a black bull, some sort of advertisement, loomed above and ahead of us like an obstinate negation of the sun.

We took a break at a petrol station, swigging water from the freezer to replace the sweat, while lorry drivers sluiced the cabs of their trucks with hoses.

It was a relief to turn off down a lesser road. A van pulled up driven by a priest and youngsters piled out, others drew up in a posse of mopeds. They were marking yellows on the road. They were very lively and there was much backslapping and 'Valiente.' I smiled and smiled but was relieved when they went, I wanted to get on, not walking so much as to try deal with the feelings that the Camino was throwing up and obliging me to deal with.

The mind doesn't like defects, they are where it doesn't run smoothly. A defect is an inconsistency. Established thoughts may be mutually incompatible, or some emotional habits not square with others, or actions not fit with what we think or feel we ought to do. There's plenty of scope. Even if we achieve the massive task of getting consistent thought, harmonious feeling, and compatible actions, and squaring all three, there's the higher level task of getting all of them to marry with the prime directive of selfless giving.

Cards are stacked against us by the fact that the apparatus to perform effective changes is acquired late. In early life we just live. We are having our character formed while we are incapable of conscious character building or effective character change. By the time we are self-conscious enough to be aware of what our personality is like, it has already been established. The defects have got built in.

Worse, our personality is our identity, so a challenge to our personality is a threat to our identity. We are not disposed for self change.

Worse still, we will have unconsciously devised various stratagems for concealing these defects so they are not recognised as such. There are many mechanisms for this. Here is one of them. From time to time a defect will have a consequence in action. The results of this action reflect back at us. This is an opportunity to recognise the defect and decide to address it. It is also a chance to construct a bit of self-defence to conceal the defect from ourselves. Let us say that we have acted unkindly, contrary to our own stated principles of fairness. We could tell ourselves that this action was necessary in terms of independence and personal freedom. We convert it into something admirable. We have not acted unkindly at all, we have preserved our freedom against someone who tried to take liberties. Our principles, or our vocabulary, get altered to fit. The defect gets more firmly embedded and more difficult to even admit, let alone remedy.

Individuals incorporate these deceptions into the mask of their identity; at the personal level, at the level of private relationships, at the wider social level. The skills of maintaining the mask become refined, habitual, sometimes added to. These skills are legion and, with unconscious practice, become sophisticated and harmonised among themselves. The coverings for our faults are carried around like a psychological face, markings on the shell, part of what we are, scarcely noticed.

Eventually, most of the individual's psychological energy is being used to sustain the mask, a complex mask with structure and substructure. It has a neuronal reality which is sustained, and fed and nurtured, with our life's blood. It's in our brain like a spidery parasite.

So the malfunctions in our being remain, and spread, and our social context feeds them. The need to throw off the trap of our relationships becomes urgent. Then the Camino calls, however we may express it.

Carrying all this churning, I had reached another main road, crossed a footbridge, climbed a steep path, and arrived at the edge of Navarette. I stopped by a trough and fountain for a welcome drink to wait for Kes. I had been walking fast, self absorbed. He was nowhere in sight. I waited a long time, sluiced and filled my water bottles. Had a fag. Two. Still no Kes. I began to get worried. I reluctantly hoisted my rucksack on again and started back down the trail; down the ascent, over the bridge, into the fields. No sign. Panic kindled, but I kept it tight and small. I retraced my steps slowly, forward again, scanning the dust at every branching path for his footprints, following side paths up and back, checking out shady places where he might rest.

Nothing.

I waited once more at the fountain. Where was he? His Spanish was minimal. He could never explain his situation. I imagined him setting off in the wrong direction. He must be miles off course by now; alone, scared, lost in the immense countryside without a map or even a clear idea where he was going, lacking even the name of the next place on the Way. I fretted and accused. He must be desperate by now, stumbling tearful through the fields in the fading light, all of Spain around him.

I went on into the village and into the first shop.

"Mi hijo. My son," I said, hysterically, and held my flat palm at roughly his height.

"Peregrino. Pilgrim," I said, and made gestures to indicate that he was lost and that I was desperate. The shopkeeper and his customers discussed the situation but obviously could not help. I ran out and down the main street, going in bars and shops repeating the scene, to no avail. Dusk was settling, and it was growing misty.

I tried to keep calm and think what Kes might do. Well, surely, he must have realised by now that he'd taken the wrong path. The sensible thing for him to do was to retrace his steps to find the last yellow. We'd done this together many times. So I went back to the fountain hoping to meet him returning to the right path. He wasn't there. Getting quite dark now. I went back down to the road, and there he was, tramping down the road towards the village.

Thank God!

I shouted, "Kes! Kes!" and ran towards him, ignoring the pain in my ankles, my rucksack bumping heavily on my back. I'd got quite

114

close before I realised it was a very short, and totally mystified, young man with a humped back. I was desolate.

Well, I could do no more tonight, except perhaps alert the police at the refuge. So back to the village once again. At the refuge, a monastery, I tried, incoherently, to explain that my son was lost, to a young monk with a crew cut. He was callously unconcerned and took me out of the main building, past an open-air swimming pool, and into a large garage. There, resting comfortably on a foam mattress, was Kes.

"Aw, yer wee bugger," I said, lapsing inexplicably into vernacular Scottish in relief.

"What kept you, Dad?" he said.

"Just in time for some Rice," said Claudio, who was squatting on the next mattress, smiling, attending to his camping stove.

I didn't calm down till the third glass of wine.

"This is good wine," I said, in a bit of a daze.

"It is the wine of the region," said Claudio, " the wine of La Rioja. Some say it is the best in Spain."

"It's excellent."

"Rioja is named after the Rio Oca which we will reach in two days."

I think he was basically shy and hid it with instruction, like many a teacher.

"The Oca is important for the Way. We meet it many times. It means 'goose.' It is connected with a game for children."

He described the game.

"That's Snakes and Ladders!" said Kes.

"Not quite, but related. It is the pattern of the Way," Claudio went on, "you think you travel far, and then you fall back, perhaps to the beginning and you must go on again."

"I see, and the last square is Santiago."

"No, the end of the Camino is Finisterre," said Claudio firmly. "The Way is very old, older than the Christianism, and it does not go East, towards the rising sun, the direction of the Christianism. No, it goes West, towards the setting sun, the Celtic direction. To finish the game you must go to Finisterre, the end of the earth, and watch the sun set into the sea. It is important."

His eyes were unfocused. His attention was turned inward; he was talking primarily to himself. Though who could tell for certain, things get said for all sorts of reasons; it must have got said in my presence for some purpose. I glanced up at him, he looked grimly serious.

I was reminded of a day in two of the big art galleries of London. I had toured the Impressionists and was full of light and the intoxication of things, then I encountered the Spanish room in the National Gallery with all its brooding shadow. Claudio had a morose streak.

"Santiago is quite far enough," I said quietly, "Is Finisterre much farther?"

"No, three, maybe four days."

"Why is it important?"

"It is necessary to die; to contemplate your own death. It is part of the Way. The most important part."

"We're going to sleep outside, under the stars," said Kes, brightly.

"It is a warm night, and the garage floor is hard," explained Claudio.

It also stank of oil, gurgled with plumbing, and was alive with flies.

So after Claudio's excellent Rice, mixed with tomatoes and tinned sardines, we took the mattresses, and our sleeping bags, outside and laid them on a slight slope above the swimming pool. The sky was stunning. The mist had cleared and the velvet sky was smothered with stars, the milky way a scintillating swathe.

"The milk of the goddess," said Claudio, "it marks the direction of the Camino."

I settled down, content, reunited with son and friend, in the warm and astonishing knowledge that I loved them both.

We slept late. I was woken by shrieks and cries. Crowds of handicapped and retarded teenagers were excitedly teeming out of the main building, some of them in wheelchairs, some on crutches; so this was why we had been banished to the garage. They chimed, "Buenos Dias", as they filed past. A late morning dip.

Soon some were splashing and yelping in the water, while others, patiently waiting their turn, sat on the grass playing games and laughing frequently. Toothy grins with wide-spaced teeth. I lay propped up on one elbow, on my foam mattress on the grass, enjoying their liberated enthusiasm for life. They appeared transparent, feeling into action, instantly.

Feeling refreshed by life's unfortunates, I strolled into the village to locate Kes' Mars bar. The people in the shops were anxious to discover all was now well. I wandered round the place. So often, on a long walk, there is nothing to do but wait, stand and stare. A useful skill, to wait with ease.

On the way back, a bizarre and poignant object by the roadside: a dumped teddy-bear. It's throat had been slashed. It had been mutilated, a slaughtered toy, ravaged and abused by some maniac child. I found it unsettling.

It was some time before I returned to the pool. Only one young woman remained, stretched awkwardly on the grass. She looked broken. She spoke to me as I passed, but I couldn't work out what she had said. I smiled back stupidly. Swallows skimmed for insects over the empty pool. Kes and Claudio were stirring. I delivered the Mars bar and sat to write a poem.

<u>Road-kill</u>

Face down by the roadside
a discarded teddy bear.
I turn it with my foot
and see its throat slit,
its eyes wrenched and absent;
just a strange shaped bag;
a wreck of love.

Over by the pool, I became aware that the young woman was calling. I went over to her and tried to decipher her Spanish. She lay with her head face-down on the ground, her mouth close to the earth. She patiently repeated herself several times until I had worked it out.

"Please," she had said quietly, out of the side of her mouth, "can you turn me over, I am burning on this side."

I did as she asked, of course. It was like manipulating a rigid, limp doll. It felt like an insult to be healthy.

While Kes and Claudio were getting ready, the rest of the disabled emerged in theatrical costume. They were having a Roman day and all were got up in home-made gear; decked out in paper and cardboard armour and togas. Most were in wheelchairs, some made their own, painful way. One young man lurched past me, stiff and contorted, his arms hung lifeless on his torso carrying his shield & his short sword, his head drooped to one side. Each step was a turning swivel as he dragged a leg around to flop it down ahead. He fell frequently.

An organiser began a mock slave auction. He went up to a mass of warped flesh which had been unloaded into a wheelchair and cried out, "How much for this one?"

He felt a withered arm, bent back at an impossible angle.

"Excellent muscles!" he shouted.

The guy in the chair grinned lopsidedly and dribbled with glee.

"Here, see, good teeth! How much, what am I bid?"

A young woman bid extravagantly. The organiser did an exaggerated wink and they all laughed uproariously.

Chapter 15

Time & Time Again

The walk to Najera was dull; much road, no fountains, and long, dusty paths made of face-powder; while, swaggering across the clear sky, the coarse sun mugged the earth. An ugly factory by a river fitted the mood of crude oppression. Only a canal with deep, swift-flowing, dark green water spoke of relief. The fierce Spanish drivers careered past us as if infected by the loutish sun. The big problem was when they were overtaking, which they did in the most unsuitable places. This wasn't so bad with oncoming traffic, we could see what was coming & take evasive action, but sometimes a pair of overtaking cars would come up unseen from behind and scream past inches away. This lethal stream had slaughtered a variety of dead animals whose corpses accosted the nose. Dogs and cats, small mammals, birds, snakes had been mashed into a lurid mess. Knocking down an animal was no cause to stop.

There is a class structure among pilgrims. The aristocrats are the rare horse riders, elevated and stately, above the rest. Then come the nobles, the thoughtful walkers. After that, the yeoman cyclists. Everyone looks askance at the peasants, the motorists.

Claudio spoke of the Rosicrucian movement, alchemy, theosophy, medieval mystics and the Catholic Mass, of which he seemed to disapprove. He said that he often wakes himself up with his own laughter.

The first building on the edge of Najera was the Bar Sancho where I downed three beers in swift succession. The discovery of the slang for a glass of draught beer, una caña, had solved the premature toilet problem. (Remember: 'Servicios' –toilet, 'cerveza' – beer).

The bar was tiled throughout in cool white with a huge black Spanish fan, too big for any woman to use, on the wall. The only other customer was a grizzled old man who looked as if he'd been left in the sun for a month and it had turned his brains. His skin was burnt dark, like an Arab, and shrivelled like a prune. An unlit cigar hung limp from his mouth, a battered straw hat adorned his head. He stared blankly through burnt out eyes, and said nothing.

We plodded across the bridge over the Rio Najerilla, though there wasn't much of a river beneath. Frogs croaked below, like sick Brent geese. Through the back streets, I glanced through a grill in a wall to see a coven of skinny feral cats; a scrawny mother feeding her scrawny young. A host of suspicious lemon eyes with chocolate slits accosted me wildly.

A stork's nest, like a compost heap, topped a church tower.

Claudio took us straight to the monastery of Santa Maria La Real, where the surly custodian was most reluctant to let us in.

We were eventually shown into a long, narrow room with a very hard, and cold, marble floor. Sleeping bags were arranged around its walls. We found some spaces and staked out our claim.

People around had wet hair and enquiry revealed the place had showers. I couldn't remember the last time I had a shower. It was delicious and worth the queue.

Kes had hobbled the last few miles into Najera. I couldn't find anything obviously wrong with his feet, so I massaged them with lavender oil and gave him an Ankle Pill.

I could find no English entry in the Pilgrim's book, although one Spanish girl had signed with an imprint of her lips in lipstick, a soft, sensual pink, which troubled my dreams.

We ate out at the Hotel San Fernando which did a discount for pilgrims. Chicken and chips. The waitress said something about me which caused Claudio to laugh.

"What does she say, Claudio?"

"She says you have emotional hands."

The barman was tying fishing flies.

While we were eating, the light-fitting on the wall smoked for a while and then burst into flames. A waiter dealt with it calmly, unmoved, as if it happened every day.

Spanish wiring is a nightmare, they have half a dozen items piggy-backed off the same socket, worn leads taped over, or twisted together.

Risk is part of Spanish culture.

Back in the pilgrims' room, at a large table by the door, some Spaniards were talking excitedly. One had his very small rucksack on the table. You can take what you like on pilgrimage, your life's journey, as long as you can carry it. Vicente had the essentials with him: a spare T-shirt, shorts, socks; and three recorders of different sizes, plus a great wad of sheet music. He lovingly took up one of the recorders and played a Baroque piece to illustrate his point. Kes admired a Spanish pilgrim's leather hat and was presented with it as a gift. Soon a guitar appeared and a lively sing-song developed. Smiles and friendly feeling everywhere, till a middle-aged man came in and told us we were keeping the monks awake and would we please stop. I went off to my hard bed.

The man next to me snored loudly. He got the full treatment: hisses, tutts, clicks, a flashing torch and, eventually, coins thrown at him. He slept on unperturbed. I stuffed some toilet paper in my ears and went to sleep.

****

Although Kes had slept next to me, on the other side to the snorer, he was nowhere to be seen in the morning. I found him half way down the crowded room, having in his sleep somehow negotiated all the intervening bodies. He was flat on his back with his legs vertical up a wall, still sleeping.

Claudio, like Kes, was a late riser. Having to wait for them did me a lot of good, I was still too frequently restless to get on, and wandered about. At first I felt frustrated, yet I gradually realised that I already knew that being somewhere else wouldn't make any difference. I would be restless in the next place too. Thus the frustration. The restlessness was to get to a different psychological place, to be otherwise, not to reach somewhere.

I took a stroll around the monastery. The cloisters were exotic; a well, and tall palm trees in the centre; extraordinary tracery in the windows full of fat, curly animals arranged like an espalier tree; a woman, her legs widely splayed, at the foot of one; celebrations of fecundity. The tracery threw lacy shadows on the floor of the honey-sunned walkways.

The scale of cloisters encourages thought. Followers of Aristotle were called 'Peripatetics', wanderers, because of their habit of walking around the precursor of cloisters discussing philosophical problems. The architecture embodies the process; round and round, returning to the problem, getting back to where you were, seeing the problem differently each circuit. Here a problem could be walked through under the auspices of sun and fertility, male and female.

We climbed out of Najera, under a cloudy sky, along a path made of pale rust, flanked by faintly red rocks, through a conifer forest and then into open country. My spirit eased as I climbed, and opened somewhat as we reached the wide spaces.

Just before Azofra we caught up with a handsome Brazilian woman, maybe in her early forties. We talked in hamstrung French. She chatted in a manner which fended us off. Her troubled eyes troubled me, always flitting painfully elsewhere; deeply unhappy, and self-obsessed, she was at the edge of tears and ready to give up. I couldn't find anything I had the ability to say which might break through. It occurred to me that a simple hug might say much and would have gone a long way, but I was too English to dispense it. We had an awkward drink together in Azofra and reluctantly left her there when she stayed to eat. She was unreachable.

Azofra is a brick village with a dirt and concrete main street, it had tractors and farm wagons parked either side. Dogs slept on the shady side, an idiot sat on a kerb mumbling to himself. On the left, at the end of the village was a neat little park with a fountain where Claudio paddled in the basin to refresh his feet. The main crops in the nearby allotment were spinach and gladioli. Three deaf pilgrims arrived, but were wary; an insular group.

A little farther on, a thunderstorm broke suddenly just as we passed an abandoned van in a field. It stood alone as if the fields had worn away around it to reveal a monstrous, alien skull. It was yellowy white, the colour of old bones, with irregular spatters of rust, the empty sockets of its headlamps like gouged eyes. We took refuge in it, laughing at the automatic sprinklers continuing to spray the drenched fields in the heavy rain. I brewed up some chicken soup. When the rain had stopped, I decided to take the number plate as a souvenir. It was a Logroño number and so had the prefix 'LO', this was followed by 'VE.' So, it read LO-VE. I showed it to Claudio who thought the number itself, 21634, was also significant as it added up to 16, which made 7. Apparently this is a very fortuitous number. The letters and the number were red on a white background.

Back on the way, nothing but a bare stony path to the horizon between stubble fields. On the next road, we passed a sign to the right for a place called 'Curvas de la Degollada.' I asked Claudio what it meant.

"It is a very strange name," he replied. "It means 'Curves of the Woman with the Slit Throat.'"

I went cold, and told him about the slashed Teddy bear at Navarette.

"You are a see-er," he said, "When is your birthday?"

"September 11th."

"A Virgo. It must be somewhere else in your chart. At what time were you born?"

"I don't know."

"You must find out, and I will do your chart for you."

"OK. I hope this slit throat business doesn't point further into the future."

Claudio said nothing.

We took a long, long break in a field littered with straw, a proper rest with our boots off. Like a cat at a shut door, I could only rest and learn patience. Patience, clearly, was what I needed. Kes busied himself in the straw while Claudio and I talked. There was so much time.

We discovered that we had a similar conception of the word seer, or see-er as Claudio pronounced it. A seer experiences time differently from the norm. For most people time ticks away, the present slips into the past which becomes forever lost. The future has yet to be. Only the present truly exists. It's not like that for seers. Things happen that make meaningful bridges across time.

Brain researchers tend not to talk about the mind perceiving time any more. They speak of the brain representing time. It makes its own. Mostly it works hard to match its inner time with the way the world works. If you are a slip fielder, you have to correlate what you do with what the world is doing. Equally when crossing a busy road. But the neurologists have found the inner mechanisms for making our own time & this means we can change it. If something happens so that we need to slow time to give us more space to act, then we can do it. There are other instances of our capacity to manipulate time. The seer joins events from the past to what is happening now & what is yet to happen. Somehow.

I was worried about the bear with its throat cut. Maybe someone I knew had died, perhaps violently.

"Maybe, but perhaps not. These things are symbolic," said Claudio quietly.

I told Claudio that I found him a calming influence.

"I am not naturally calm. I am nervous and have to get things right, a Virgo like you, I check everything over and over. But I have a bad heart and it would not be good to get upset. Not long ago, when my typewriter jammed, I smashed it in anger."

"Typewriter!"

"I don't like modern things."

Claudio carried a portable sundial rather than a watch.

"Come and see what I've made, Dad."

I saw a huge pile of straw fashioned into a hollow doughnut, maybe nine feet across.

"Very good. What exactly is it, Kes?"

"It's a stork's nest."

"Ah, so it is. Well, make sure the stork doesn't bring you something you didn't expect."

"You do talk rubbish, Dad."

"Thanks, Kes."

"Can't understand you half the time."

He busied himself tidying up his nest.

When he joined us, his socks were spiky with straw.

"You cannot walk like that," said Claudio, "Give me your socks, and I'll take out the straw."

It took ages. He was painstaking. We had some more tea. At long last every shred was removed and the red socks returned to Kes. Twenty minutes latter, they were smothered with snippets of straw all over again. Claudio smiled and sat and removed each piece once more.

****

We lost the Camino and its harsh, arid, stone-riddled paths in the wide plain around Santo Domingo and just aimed for the baroque church tower.

On the edge of the town, in an alleyway between two factories which smelt of burning tyres, my rucksack fell off my back. Something had snapped. Your rucksack is your home. It felt like a disaster. I picked it up in my arms, like a huge child, and carried it through the alleyway to the edge of a field.

Meanwhile, Kes and Claudio, who had been ahead, had realised something was wrong and strolled back to me.

We stared at the casualty on the ground.

"What are you going to do, Dad?"

"I'm going to have a cup of tea."

The rucksack wasn't going anywhere. The problem wasn't going to get any worse. We left the bag where it lay, went into the field, and brewed up.

Kes had a fast-swelling insect bite which I treated with Lavender oil and an anti-histamine tablet.

Down the path came a short, bearded pilgrim wearing blue jeans, a white shirt and a badly tied turban. He had no rucksack, only a small shoulder bag obviously almost empty. We offered him some tea, and bread and cheese.

He replied in a strong French accent, "No food. I do not eat much, you know. I do not need it. I live," he gestured around at the landscape, smiling, "on the Spiritual Food."

"You don't carry much I see," I remarked.

"My first Master, he say, 'A man must carry little on his path.'"

"Er, right. Master? You follow some particular sect, some group?"

"My second Master, he say, you know, he say, 'A bee sucks at many flowers.'"

He nodded sagely.

"My first Master, he say, you know, 'There is more than one path up the mountain,'" he went on.

"Oh, well, where did you find these Masters?"

"India, you know. I go there many years. I nearly die there."

"And now you're walking to Santiago?"

"Some days I walk to Santiago, some days no."

He sat, arranged his legs in the Lotus position, looked around, nodding his head slightly, smiling, as if Spain belonged to him.

"I have, you know, no money," he told us smugly.

"None at all?"

"A little. I beg. The people give. It is good, you know, for them to give. If I got money I eat. It is good. If I not got money I not eat. It is good too."

He grinned spiritually.

I got up to take a closer look at my rucksack. A metal ring which held the bag to the frame had sheered through. I didn't have a replacement. We searched the dusty path for something to use as a temporary fix. I found a white feather for my hat, and, eventually Kes found a ring-pull from a can. Cut through and bent a bit, it did the job. We walked on, waving cheerily to the Light of India who was settling down for a nap.

The hostel at Santo Domingo was a gem. Through the ancient wooden door was a cobbled courtyard, the stones in a chevron pattern. A wooden farm-cart with studded wheels was parked in a corner, shafts up in the air. A cartwheel candelabra swung above. Upstairs the dormitory was homely; a rich, warm carmine, stone-tiled floor; walls and ceiling of wooden beams with a white plaster infill. Real beds with chequered blankets in red and blue. The room had a gingham feel to it without there actually being any. Someone cared about how it looked and felt, and had made it domestic and welcoming. People lounged about comfortably, writing diaries and postcards. They nodded greeting amiably. Through the window we could hear the clacking beaks of the storks fussing over their huge, untidy nest on the church tower. There was a kitchen with an oven that worked, and plenty of pots and pans and utensils. Showers even. After half an hour, it was our home.

On the wall was a poster advertising an exhibition in the town: 'Life on the Pilgrimage.' It showed four late medieval pilgrims in long, one piece gowns in brown, red and Mary's indigo; flying-saucer hats, thin gloves; their eyes resolutely ahead, large staves ready. At their feet, ignored, was an immense, winding snake, brown as dust.

The Mayor arrived showing someone around. He wanted to know if we were settling in all right. The town was proud of its hostel.

A blind French pilgrim arrived with his helper. I imagined them toiling over the rocky slopes of the Pyrenees, hand in hand.

We all took a late siesta.

In the early evening, Kes and I went for a stroll, the streets were full of young men promenading, pushing buggies, pushchairs, prams, heads high, proud of their podgy, overfed infants. We went into the bar Los Arcos for a drink. A thick set man, black hair and dark, furtive eyes, overhearing our English, came and introduced himself: Andreas, a Basque from Bilbao. A nervous man, and slightly drunk, he kept looking over his shoulder as if checking for spies. He sat hunched as if burdened with worry. Basques were persecuted, he explained, the Spanish did not like Basques, did not trust them. When he drank his red wine and coke, he threw the glass at his mouth, splashing the liquid over his jaw. He spoke fast, in fragments, his eyes darting about neurotically. He asked me if there were books on eschatology in England. (The study of death and judgment day and life after death). Sweating profusely, he explained that there were no Spanish books on the subject; the Catholics didn't allow it. He made it sound like a conspiracy. Theatrically glancing over his shoulder, he confided to us that the world was going to end in seven years. No doubt about it. Was Finland a good place to die, he asked anxiously, explaining that he did not want to die in a hot country. Perhaps Finland might escape the End altogether, he inquired. I told him that it seemed unlikely that anywhere could escape such a time.

He asked me if I knew any nice English women who wanted to get married. Men were no good, he said. Cared only for football. Trivial, superficial, materialists. Did I know of a woman who might go to Finland to die with him? I promised to keep my eye open for one. He insisted on swapping addresses. We shook his large, sweaty hands and left.

We went from there to the theatre which advertised a 'Spectacular', a one-night-only free show. The 'Teatro Avenido' was a shabby genteel place that had seen better days. Posters outside advertised 'La Vida de Brian', the Life of Brian; inside they had a variety show, allegedly from Madrid: lots of skimpily dressed chorus girls, some singers and a smattering of comic sketches. Kes got bored and went back to the refuge.

On stage, a monk in his habit conversed with a wisecracker. I understood little, but it was clear from the sharp intakes of breath from the audience, and the gestures from the cast, that the patter was full of dirty jokes, or worse, anti-Catholic jokes.

A substantial matriarch rose to her feet at the back of the auditorium and loudly, magisterially, issued peremptory commands. Nobody paid much attention to the sketch, the drama was elsewhere. A string of children at the front got up silently, and obediently trooped out like a line of goslings. The sketch proceeded in desperation, while other big-bosomed mums in the audience popped up here and there, and clucked at their brood, ordering their children out; and they went. The audience buzzed with indignant disapproval at the luckless actors.

Sitting at the refectory table in the hostel, Claudio was crafting an entry in the Pilgrims' book. He'd drawn an elaborate Celtic cross, while the surrounding calligraphic text was full of astrological symbols.

"You have many feathers now," he remarked, his eyes pointing to my hat, "Did you know that it is a tradition for pilgrims to collect feathers and put them in the hat?"

"No," I replied, pleased that I had found a tradition intuitively, "What does it signify?"

"I don't know."

"It must have something to do with birds, of course. They are symbols of liberation. A desire to join the angels, perhaps?"

He looked at me oddly.

"Maybe so."

"Plato says in the Phaedrus that of all bodily things, the wing is most divine; it takes what is heavy and raises it up to the place of the gods."

In the kitchen, Kes was having a mime-and-gesture conversation with José, an abrasive young man from Navarre with a rough laugh. I joined them just as José pushed back the shirt-sleeve of his left arm to reveal some ugly suppurating sores.

"Santiago!" he said, vigorously, "wwhoup." The noise was like a brisk whistle made through pursed lips. As he spoke his other hand skimmed above his bad arm as if reaping the disease, the hand opened to the window as if releasing doves.

"Santiago!" he repeated strongly. The saint would cure his festering arm. It was a fact. His eyes fiercely challenged me to deny it. I looked away.

We had had a whip round for a communal meal. Claudio had been shopping and filled the table with fruits and vegetables.

"What are these long thin things, Dad?"

"Asparagus."

"Just the right shape for dipping in the chilli sauce."

Kes was dunking them in the Tabasco.

It was all far more than we could eat, so Claudio distributed the considerable remainder among the other pilgrims.

In the dormitory many were already abed. The three deaf pilgrims had arrived; a young, gaunt man with a scrappy beard and two young women. As he prepared for bed, he hummed loudly to himself, rustled plastic bags, banged about with his pots and pans, calmly oblivious, in his silent world, to the ill-feeling this noise created around him. People would resent this, and treat him coolly in the morning. No wonder he was wary of others, and, being the dominant one in the trio, he would set the tone for the group.

Chapter 16

Liberating Feelings

Out to a greengrocers in the morning, for some fruit. I was getting into the habit of using the gap between the times we got up instead of fretting at the leash. The shop was full of women chatting, more of a social centre than a shop. The jovial, balding shopkeeper, plainly contented in his work, seeing the scallop shell around my neck, served me first. No one minded.

I popped into the cathedral on the way back. Here, high up on a wall, is the world's most ostentatious chicken coup, elaborately ornamented with gothic stone carving, pinnacles and a decorative iron grill. A cock and a hen flapped about within. There's an unlikely story, concerning resurrected roast chicken, to explain this bizarre sight. The interesting question is why the people of this town should have acquiesced to a prominent hutch in a church, and not only tolerated it thereafter, but grown proud of it. The answer is the local spirit of place; Santo Domingo is a friendly, family town where homely values prevail; what better living image of that could there be than a cock and a hen in a coup? If family life and a sensible concern for domestic well-being matters, why not display the fact in a church? I could think of worse foundations for a religion.

We left Santo Domingo by the main road over the Rio Oja, except there wasn't a river, only a parched channel of stones and grass. A long, straight road towards Grañon on a hill. The lorries kept sweeping my hat off with their slipstream. By the roadside, a dead dog, bloated, teeth bared in frozen pain, stinking.

The other side of Grañon, we were crossing a field, when a strap on my rucksack broke. Relatively unperturbed this time, I replaced it with a strap I used for compressing my sleeping bag. Problems tended to occur singly, practical problems that is. We stopped and took a break, assessed the problem, decided on the best possible action under the circumstances, did it, saw what difference it made, did the best possible thing under the new circumstances, and so on. What else can you do?

We paused to see the famous font at Redicilla: a fat bowl, maybe four feet across, swelling upwards like most of a pumpkin. Within, where its seeds would be, is a pool of energy. I could feel it prickling the skin when I put my arms into the void. The segments of this vast, stone fruit were carved, layered with storeys of windows and dormers like a crowded medieval town, a circular town; a foretaste of the celestial city. For among many other things, Santiago is emblematic of the Holy City; the harmonious community of the enlightened which appears in many cultures - Jerusalem, Rome, Shangri-La, Shambhala, Eldorado, the Land of Oz, the End of the Rainbow. Places far distant and semi-legendary which the questing seeker aspires to reach. Spiritual places of the soul which, like Plato's Republic, have no physical existence and can only be founded in the heart and mind. Those who separately found (not find) the Holy City within themselves, enter its gates and join the community: the secret college.

Just after Redicilla (which means 'a small net' or 'a hair-net') a young woman caught us up. She was called Bienvenida - which means 'Welcome'.

The arrival of Bienvenida was both refreshing and disconcerting. She had reached that point in life of the first full flowering of womanhood. She was what my Granny had called 'well-blessed.' She was all fulsome curves, but had yet to gain the skills of coping with them. Dressed all in virginal white from head to foot, she wore only trainers and socks, a skimpy pair of shorts with white knickers beneath, an inadequate vest, and a white peaked cap above a face like an Aztec. This clothing strained to keep her newly blossomed flesh in, and manifestly failed. There was always some portion of her hanging out. The motion of her walking encouraged the more recent portions of her anatomy to attempt escape, which they almost, but never quite, achieved. It was a disturbing experience to walk behind Bienvenida; as she strode ahead, vast expanses of freshly pink and beautifully rounded buttock would be rhythmically revealed. It was decidedly hypnotic. The eyes were drawn, and rocked gently from side to side, in empathy with her motion. After a while walking became quite uncomfortable. The only chaste solution was to make sure of walking ahead of her. But then a glance back revealed a positive sea of breasts, scarcely covered and striving for freedom. Even without a look backwards the presence of Bienvenida could be felt like an ache. Like a major planet, she changed the shape of space all around her.

Even trying to concentrate on the landscape was no relief. It was undulating and treeless here, like a huge, recumbent Bienvenida. She seemed everywhere. Earth and flesh echoed each other.

The fountain at Viloria de la Rioja couldn't contain itself, and instead of a steady flow, ejaculated water bombs. Unaware of this, I bent over the bowl, pressed a button, and it shot me in the face. Kes fell about, laughing. Nearby, homage was paid to her power in the shape of a statuette of an almost naked goddess. Certainly Bienvenida was a true deep-bosomed daughter of Demeter. She embosomed fecundity. I'm sure, as she passed, the hot, cracked earth felt her presence, yearned into life, and seeds deep in the hard ground sprouted spontaneously. The Primordial Maiden did my rampant randiness no good at all.

We sweltered down more dreary, straight road, the constant roar hovering in the heat, until, just over a bridge, appeared what looked like a transport café, laid back behind a huge car park full of trucks. The Restaurante Leon had higher pretensions, however; red brick, like a golf club-house, set in trees, rambling roses and trailing ivy, with white, metal garden furniture on the patio. An oasis.

They made much of Kes inside, regaled him with 'Valientes' and brought out an immense book for us to sign. It had wooden covers, parchment pages, and furniture hinges to hold it together. Claudio and I dabbled in the pseudo-profound, while Kes wrote simply: "Kes 9 years, a pilgrim."

We ate a delicious meal of roast quail.

Back down the unending road, we passed two dead barn owls and a mole by the roadside like milestones. "Molestones," suggested Kes.

Our different natural pace sorted us into a single line. As those ahead passed a tree it was amusing to see that we had each, independently, acquired the same habit. As each person reached the line of the tree's shade, the hat was whipped off, like a salute, to give the head a breather. It remained off through the shade, to be replaced as each crossed the margin of the shade into the broiling sun once more. It was like a line of troops doing homage to the tree.

With relief, we turned off the road into Belorado. The refuge was a parish room annexed to the church; a hall with a rickety stage at one end, and a red and white chequered floor with a huge refectory table, its edges carved with a cross-in-chalice motif, in its centre. The table was covered with apples, oranges, tomatoes, cheese, bread and red wine in unlabelled sea-green bottles. Here sat Vicente, the music man from Najera, quietly smoking. I sat by him and offered my scallop shell around my neck as an ashtray. The irreverence amused him. I asked him how he was. He made a clown's face of sadness, pointed to his feet, and limply flapped his wrist in the gesture which meant: 'like, too much, man.' Then he pointed to his heart, made a gesture of opening with both cupped hands, and said, slowly and softly, "Wow!", beaming. He indicated the food with an expansive sweep of his arm, inviting us to eat, which we did.

In the late evening Kes went to bed with a touch of asthma, Claudio took Bienvenida for a walk in the countryside, to show her the position of Venus.

I took a stroll alone.

Belorado is a large village. In an echo of Santo Domingo, families promenaded around the main square, showing off their infants proudly, swapping gossip. Older children skittered about on bicycles. Teenagers posed by sleek Japanese motor-bikes. Much attention was paid to the new, solitary traffic light. People had driven in from surrounding villages to see it. They drove up and down to admire it from all angles, ignoring it if it happened to turn red.

The heart of Belorado was a spacious main square bounded by shadowy arcades and open-air cafés with striped awnings. In the centre was a bandstand amid three circles of luxuriant, cool plane trees. Here the Municipal Band played; three saxophones and a trumpet, two drummers. They wailed and oompahed through tunes while the old swayed and the middle-aged danced. One dignified old lady danced with her grand-daughter, looking very smug. Even the dogs leaped about trying to join in. Old men sat on park benches smoking.

A buttery almost full-moon in an intense, gentian sky softened the night. A single stork glided silently by the mellow moon to roost on its immaculate nest on the church.

****

A warden arrived in the morning. He tried to hustle us out until he realised that Kes was ill, then he made us some coffee. We left late.

The four of us, Bienvenida had joined our group, were quiet and walked separately in a long line, sometimes out of sight of each other, each alone with their thoughts. We met up beneath the trees around village fountains, like the one at Espinosa with its fountain like a long grave, its tap set in a column like a headstone, its trough swarming with tadpoles, but even here we sat apart.

I got Kes some Ventolin for his asthma in a chemist in Villafranca, and some bread shaped like a huge cow-pat.

Immediately beyond the town we toiled up a stiff climb through scrub, and then oak, to the Fuente De Mojapán; a welcome fountain with good water at the edge of the forest of the Montes de Oca, the Mountains of the Goose. Sitting there already was a Frenchman called André with startled, tender eyes. He told us he was recovering from a nervous breakdown, as if he were warning us to treat him gently. He passed the time while walking, he explained, meditating on his shadow. We rested, admiring the extensive view. Insects hummed constantly like electric transmission lines.

The orange path snaked through the trees. I entered a sort of trance as the miles unwound. Thoughts came slowly and time sped. I climbed to a firebreak in the thick forest; a long, broad path which had large crosses as markers down its centre. The earth was very white and stony, like the dry bed of a stream, but with patches of magenta-flowered ling. Dense pine and fir trees, and an occasional patch of oak, stretched deep either side like a presence, like guards. Humans passed through here, it was not their world.

One foot was well on its way to the ground when I spotted a slight movement below it. Viper. I threw my weight desperately to one side, swivelled, started to fall, leaped and pirouetted to compensate for the lurching rucksack, all in a trice. The snake slithered away, fast. I had avoided treading on it by half a cat's whisker. I stood panting, my temples throbbing. Kes caught me up.

"That was good, Dad. I didn't know you could dance like that. Can you do it again?"

I suggested something he might do with his pilgrim's staff.

He went on, I sat by the path to settle myself. Bienvenida waved as she passed. I sat some more, recovering from the passing of Bienvenida. Claudio came along and sat by me. The firs had a beautiful tinge of fresh green at the tips of their branches. So the forest had a haze of light green from all the new growth. The silence of the forest seethed with life. I began to feel the potential, the green striving. The feeling itself grew swiftly, I became light headed.

"Claudio?"

"Yes, Michael?"

"Do you feel anything odd?"

"Odd? No, nothing special."

"I'm feeling very strange."

The sense of energy, of power increased alarmingly.

"Strange? How?"

"I know this sounds silly, but, tell me, can you feel the trees?"

I glanced at him. He wasn't laughing, he looked interested.

"I see them."

"No, not that, the growing, the sun," I faltered, "the trees are yearning upwards. I can feel it. The whole forest. It's enormous, all that force."

It swamped me as if an emotional dam had burst. My body felt charged, my mind swooned, I felt plugged in to the current which powered the trees, it flooded through me. I lost myself. I was part of the forest. I grinned foolishly at Claudio.

"Can't you feel it, Claudio? It's so strong."

"I cannot feel it," he said seriously.

A group of swallows appeared in the empty sky above, circling, swooping. More came. Time seemed to expand. Soon there were hundreds of birds, immediately above us, turning & turning, silently.

"What's going on?" I said, a bit panicky.

"Look!"

He pointed.

Down the path to our left a mist formed. It wasn't possible in the hot sun, under a cloudless sky.

"I think we should go and see," said Claudio.

We packed up quickly and walked towards the cloud. I tingled all over.

The cloud covered a cross-roads, and down the dirt track careered a car in a billow of dust.

We both laughed, nervously.

"Not a miracle after all," said Claudio.

"You know, I really thought something very weird was going to happen."

"Me too."

We walked on into San Juan.

Chapter 17

Living a Myth

San Juan is nothing but a isolated monastery and half a dozen houses. A dirt road stops here, the domestic part of the monastery flanking it like a station; a terminus buffered by its church, a sepulchre for its founder. The path came up by the church's side. It was apparently windowless; blind, introspective.

The Brazilian woman, we had last seen in Azofra, sat on a low wall outside, being earnestly engaged in conversation by a well-built, but greying man, roughly her age, one hand on her knee, his intent face jutting at her bowed head. He spoke vehemently, the word 'Cristo' much used, with a squeeze on the knee for emphasis. She wept a little, moved by his faith.

Claudio went off to find the priest in charge, Kes and I entered through the garage and wandered round the labyrinthine building, and blundered into a hall where a large, formally dressed party sat at trestle tables heavily laden with the remains of an elaborate meal, listening to a speech. We stood in the doorway, sweaty, dishevelled and dusty, still burdened with our rucksacks. The man giving the speech faltered as he saw us, and the crowd followed his eyes and, seeing the diminutive pilgrim, roared in approval and clapped and whistled enthusiastically. We were feted; there was much 'Valiente!' and we were led like celebrities to a table where we tucked in to the leftovers of cold trout. Claudio returned and said he had found the priest and, as there were no shops or bars here, he would cook us some eggs if we wished.

The Light of India was already here, sitting on the floor, one strand of his turban hanging, eating with his fingers.

Seated opposite me was the most beautiful, mature Spanish woman. She spoke vivaciously to a man to her right. An elegant woman with silkily black, almost blue, hair tied in a short pony-tail with a scarlet scarf. She wore teardrop, pearl earrings and a plain black dress. She had classically strong features with thin, arched eyebrows. Her exquisitely courtly fingers gracefully toyed with a single yellow rose.

A crowd of children clustered noisily in the doorway, girls in white lace dresses and boys in cricket pumps and long-legged white shorts, excited both with the occasion and the one of their number elevated to the company of the adults. Kes soon found the attraction of some friends stronger than the attraction of food and was greeted like a hero as he shyly joined them.

I was sitting quietly on the low wall outside, by the sandy road, when I next saw him about an hour later. He came careering around the side of the building, his boots incongruously huge, pursued by at least twenty kids baying like hounds. He seemed exceptionally red cheeked, like a 'Fiesta' apple. He slid to a halt by me just long enough to shout, with manifest delight, "I'm completely pissed!" before roaring off.

****

In the morning I took a wander around. San Juan has a most distinctive atmosphere of its own. Atmosphere, felt quality, is as hard to describe as a flavour. It was like the touch of bare metal, or the taste of ice-cold milk. Here there is something smooth, unalloyed, basic; a simplicity, a purity, an honesty. And all this with a depth and a placidity that is quite exceptional. Everything here expresses a quality of elemental sufficiency, a limpid peace which has thrown off all elaboration as unnecessary distraction. It constantly and calmly whispers what we already know at heart: that we really need but little, and if we had access to our own fecund depths, it would be enough and more than enough. The place speaks of the death of effort.

The monastic rooms are spacious and simple. The church itself elegant and plain. San Juan has his tomb in the crypt, a potent spot. Silent and immaculately simple, yet it reeks with quiet power, like a pregnant pause in a symphony. Upstairs, in the main church, it is said that twice a year, at the equinoxes, a single shaft of light pierces the thin alabaster in a slit window above, to shine first on the carved form of Gabriel and thence, as it moves on, to the awaiting womb of

Mary nearby. Death below in the crypt, glorious life above; a place of Annunciation and joyful birth.

The heart of the other buildings is a sort of well; a small, dark courtyard with a primitive, roseate sandstone balcony, like an elevated cloister running around at first floor level. Completely enclosed, cool and shadowy, secretive and uterine, it has an ancient aura of profundity as if it were a fragment of a Tibetan monastery transplanted here.

Forget the history, and the architectural guidebook, San Juan is a mythic place. Not in terms of any particular myth, a specific story; but rather a place where things happen for symbolic reasons.

A myth is a story which maps a spiritual process. A hero is someone who lives a myth: someone who leaves their trivial self and takes on an immemorial role. A mythic place is somewhere that is embedded in the mythic consciousness. Someone approaching a mythic place in suitable conditions (driving up in a car for a look would not do) will enter the myth. San Juan is one such place. They are very rare.

I will try to explain. But first forget that myths are stories, fictional. Tolkien was once asked why an intelligent man, like himself, bothered to write fiction. He replied that he didn't write fiction, he wrote the truth.

Next, take on board the idea that there are places which incarnate a myth. Everything about them, their setting, the landscape, plants, buildings, even their names, but above all their atmosphere, and the events which accrue from it, are dynamically mythic. Any primed person approaching the place enters the myth.
The entire Camino incarnates the Grand Myth of the questing soul, striving to transcend itself, till it dies with the setting sun and is reborn transformed. But there are special sites on the Way which embody significant episodes or concentrate the whole like a seed. San Juan is one such.

I carried binoculars on the walk. Just another bird-watcher I had thought, but Claudio had insisted that it must be in my chart somewhere, that it was a significant fact about me, it meant something. My interest in watching birds is the exhilaration of observing flight. It is an empathetic experience. The spirit partakes of what it observes, be careful what you look at. When I watch a soaring bird, my heart goes with it and shares its motion. I escape my earth-bound self and feel a liberation. The bird-watching is not just a twitcher's hobby, it expresses my yearning to be free.

This is ancient knowledge. In the iconographies of the world and their mythic developments, birds are associated with release, knowledge, prophecy. They are not bound to the restrictions of the earth and its mundane gravitational limitations. They are up and away. They travel elsewhere and return with secret knowledge of far away and exotic places. So, to use the vocabulary of the past, birds depict the soul which flies free of the entrapping and limiting body when that body expires. And their transitional function between life and death gives them access to another knowledge, a knowledge of the future from which prophecies may be extracted by the intuitively gifted and trained. This is why angels, beings of a greater freedom, of another dimension of being, are winged. Winged beings; birds, angels, Hermes, Eros link heaven and earth. Shamans of all kinds wear feathers, Irish bards too, they say. Inspired poetry is the language of the birds.

How do I know this? A little bird told me.

Individual types of bird have more specific meanings. I was in the land of the Rio Oja or Oca, the land of the goose. We had crossed that river, walked on and climbed the Montes de Oca, the mountains of the goose, and entered its forests of oak and pine and fir. These particular forests have long been regarded as a dangerous place where the pilgrim may easily come to harm and may wander lost and imperilled. In medieval times, and long after, this was notoriously the territory of bandits and wolves. A Dantean and Conradian dark wood which contained the threatening powers of nature and its ruthless values. Here I had encountered a dangerous snake, and felt that confusing power, while swallows, markers of summer's strength, had congregated around me, above. In a clearing in the forest was San Juan, where I found a celebration in progress, was feted, presented with a fish, and encountered an elemental peace.

Believe me, San Juan is a very special place. But it must be apprehended through a training, which consists of the entire walk to reach it, of the feelings to produce an active symbolic awareness.

The goose is the paradigmatic bird of pilgrimage. It is migratory and succumbs to some deep instinct to travel and be gone, as does the pilgrim. It is traditionally regarded as following the sun, as does the traveller to Santiago, each day tracing the motion of the sun Westwards to the horizon. To see a skein of geese is to witness an omen of good-tidings, for they gain some strange, secretive knowledge in the land of the setting sun, the place of death.

The goose is the original Christmas bird, preceding chickens and turkeys. It is the bird of celebration, of feasting. Furthermore, it is eaten at the year's deep midnight, the critical time of the death of the year, when, at the lowest ebb of its power, it renews itself and embarks on the regeneration which will bring the summer and its swallows.

The man, San Juan, after whom the place is named, was a devotee of St. Nicholas. St. Nicholas is Saint Klaus, is Santa Claus, is Father Christmas. Events were bundling up and making sense, a fool's sense. For hadn't a child mistaken me for Father Christmas in Viana? Father Christmas is a popular embodiment of the bounty of natural love, of boundless giving at a time of paucity; a figure whose only role is to give and that in abundance.

And, to cap it all, here we were offered the eggs of rebirth, and given fish, Christ's symbol. Why, even his name was the first thing I heard at the door.

So San Juan is a haven of ancient peace, an oasis of primeval tranquillity reached through a risky encounter with nature's potency.

I had almost forgotten Margaritta & her instruction that I should try to find the five special places on the way, using only feelings & intuition. Now the memory came flooding back.

142

I had found the second Special Place.

After San Juan, I knew what I was here for, and what I was seeking.

Chapter 18

On the Way to Hell

We left in mid-morning when the mountain mist had cleared. The four of us; Claudio, Bienvenida, Kes and I, walked quietly down a dirt path through oak forest, the scrunch of our footsteps on dry leaves echoing off the silent, sentinel trees. Even the black redstarts made no sound. The path led out onto a plateau of parched grass, shrubs and a few trees, then down to the village of Agés; a dilapidated place, the buildings patched with ill-matching repairs over many decades. We were greeted by an Alsatian dog at its margins, sniffing at a cow-pat. It bit into the cow-pat and munched heartily, thick green slime running down its jaws.

"Doesn't that remind you of Life?" said Kes, grimacing.

On the road towards Atapuerca lay a long, grey snake, I think a female viper. She appeared stunned, even slightly cooked, by the livid heat. Claudio lifted her gingerly and carried her limp body to the grass by the roadside.

The bar at Atapuerca was like a kitsch ranch. It was full of men in blue boiler suits tied at the waist by string, and old women in filthy housecoats. We ordered tortillas and beer from a scruffy woman who asked all the usual questions about Kes and gave him a Valiente. She ogled at him in admiration.

"And doesn't he speak good English for only nine years old," she enthused.

We turned off the road for a steady climb up a path with outcrops of white and grey rock. At the climax of the ridge were a few stunted trees like oaks but with spiky leaves, and some gaunt, malnourished gorse. Wheatears flitted about. Here the three of us rested in scanty shade and took some very warm water. Kes made himself a raw garlic and Tabasco sandwich.

Bienvenida arrived, and sank softly to the ground, in a flurry of flesh, just in front of me. She spoke at length in Spanish, finishing with the word 'Michael' in an inviting, carressive tone while simultaneously slipping one strap of her vest off her pristine shoulder and pointing it towards me like an offering. The soft, rounded flesh lay exposed before me, deliciously pink and unblemished. She stretched her shoulder as if the muscles were weary and thrust it towards me. Sweet Jesus, she wanted me to massage her! I raised my hands in homage, prepared for the laying on of hands.

Then she leaped up and screamed, as if stung.

"I didn't touch her," I yelled, "I didn't touch her, honest. I just thought about it!"

"She wants you to pass her the water-bottle," said Claudio, much amused.

The wind blew a melancholy note, like the call of the sirens, across the top of the bottle as I passed it .

Beyond the ridge lay a vast panorama of undulating, straw-coloured fields with the entire city of Burgos on the horizon under a dirty haze. We lost the path on the descent and headed for the village of Villalval. The fountain by the church had superb water, cold and sweet. Down the street, men did odd jobs wearing green boiler suits and slippers. One old woman, in a blue housecoat and a head scarf, sat outside her house sorting two huge piles of sheep's wool.

A string of small, sleepy villages lay down the little-used road. The bar of one of them was the dirtiest I have ever seen. There were flies everywhere; flies on the counter, flies on the glasses, flies on the customers, who, like the Landlord of the Flies, didn't even bother to brush them off. A sordid sense of lethargy and hopelessness prevailed. In the midst of this filth, a young woman fed her infant with some brown gunk in a jam-jar. The men decided to teach the snotty-nosed, fat child to play dominoes. However, they didn't actually have any dominoes, or couldn't be bothered to get them, so they just imparted the basics, which consisted of bashing the flat of the hand down on the table while shouting a guttural and very loud cry. The kid soon got the hang of the skill, amid much amazement and immense general approval.

We emerged into the heat of the day, so hot it caught the throat as we breathed. A dreary, weary walk to the bar at Villafria, which means, ironically, Cold Town. The television showed live motor-racing at Brands Hatch; there was torrential rain under a grim, grey sky. We had an ice-cream.

Just over the bridge across the motor-way, lay a barracks designed like a fortress in the desert of North Africa, or a prison for the pathologically dangerous. Behind its barbed-wire, bored and restless young men stood on its corner-turrets playing idly with their guns.

The long walk into the substantial town of Burgos was terrible. Appallingly hot, road all the way, a constant roar of heavy traffic amid turgid fumes and the occasional stink of a putrid factory. The glare hurt the eyes, the hard surface hurt the feet. We passed another barracks, its sentries toting automatic weapons. Next door a school was being demolished. Two more military establishments further along.

We reached the city centre completely frazzled. The tourist office directed us to the cathedral to locate the refuge. There, vigilantes stood at the door checking people for excessive display of flesh. What they considered objectionable was completely arbitrary and seemed to depend on whim. Bienvenida was, naturally, turned away. We inquired about the refuge and were directed to the tourist office.

We hovered in the square outside the cathedral in a state of indecision. Then a cry caught our attention and Otto, the Norwegian pilgrim and his wife who we had last met, what seemed like weeks ago, on our first day in Spain, came pushing through the crowd. After some hearty greetings, we explained our predicament. Otto was staying in a hotel but the city was full of monasteries, convents, seminaries; why there was one almost opposite his hotel. We would stay there, he asserted firmly.

He took us to the Seminario Major San Jerónimo. It was huge; a massive building, looking more like the Ministry of Defence, or the international headquarters of the Foreign Legion, than anything religious; a high wall, then a car park like a parade ground, twin towers flanking the entrance, and either side row upon row of anonymous windows, like something in Whitehall. We trooped up the imposing steps into a vast foyer. It was empty save for a receptionist. Here Otto launched into an impassioned account of what he thought of a religious institution which could not accommodate a few wandering pilgrims. After much heated debate, we were each given a room upstairs down a long echoing corridor behind identical doors. Kes moved his mattress into my room and laid it on the floor, then we went to get some food.

We took our purchases to a park to cook. When I opened up a tin of meatballs it stunk. I explained to Kes that continental food often contained herbs and spices strange to the English nostril. But when it was cooking it smelt so foul I had to admit that the meat was seriously off. We had breathed in the foetid fumes. My stomach felt distinctly queasy. We decided to forgo dinner till later, much later.

We turned in early that night, and after some restless, light sleep I lay awake, and I stayed awake well into the hot night, rampantly celibate, troubled by an obstinate, massive erection. I tried to lay back and think of England: Salisbury Spire, the Post Office tower, Blackpool, Big Ben. In this tense state, I heard the door quietly click, and swing, eerily, ajar. The lithe shape of a slim young woman in a flimsy negligée slipped in, and stood irresolute, silhouetted in the moonlit window. The gentle light slid through her diaphanous night-dress delicately touching, and revealing, her dainty figure. My skin was electrified.

"André?" she whispered in a soft, shimmering, breathy voice. Very French.

I slipped my mouth beneath the blanket and mumbled, muffled, feigning sleepiness: "Oui?"

I began to wonder whether André had a beard.

She hesitated, as if the voice was not quite right, decided it was near enough, and began to glide towards the bed.

Then she tripped over Kes' mattress.

Kes responded with a shortened, but expressive, version of his impression of the rutting grunt of the Vietnamese Pot-bellied Pig.

Now, I'm not absolutely sure what this nymph expected to find in my room, but, whatever it was, it wasn't a Vietnamese Pot-bellied Pig on a mattress on the floor in rutting mode. She appeared flustered, stepped back, and swayed exquisitely.

"Oh, oh, pardon," she said, and left swiftly.

I stared at the lump on the floor that was Kes. There are times when the joys of fatherhood elude me.

****

There was no sign of a glass slipper on the floor in the morning; no trace of fairy dust, no fragile vestige of the shed skin of a nymph, green and translucent like a lacewing. Only Kes, snoring slightly, sleeping like a hog, dreaming of Mars bars.

I had a quick coffee and went out to see the cathedral. The concourse before the church was thronged with conmen and shysters, selling postcards and lucky heather and peacocks' feathers, and flyboys hanging around, looking shifty. The space had the feel of Kings Cross station with its dubious men loitering ready to accost the wide-eyed young girl, new to the big city, fresh down from the North, naïve and vulnerable. There were beggars at every church door.

The vigilantes had already started their day's quarrels with the underdressed. They glowered and argued and disapproved; a picket of snarling conflict and ill-feeling. I edged past them trying to keep out of it.

The cathedral tried too hard to impress. Like so much Spanish architecture, it is over-decorated, smitten with growths and subgrowths, like barnacles on a jetty. I'm a Cistercian at heart.

In a chapel was the famous Santo Cristo; a crucifixion with a wounded and bloody Christ supposedly covered with human skin (more likely a cow's) which was supposed to require a shave once a week. Several dark side chapels, and one in particular was dimly replete with the glint of silver and gold, jewels and lapis lazuli; stacked with elaborate reliquaries, each harbouring a filigree snippet of a saint, once priceless, now stored like last year's fashionable Christmas gifts in the basement of a department store. Lost treasure in the recesses of this model of one mansion of the psyche.

We have not outgrown the concept of the relic, merely seek them elsewhere. Elvis' wart is a collector's item. The impulse to obtain something from celebrity, even a signature, is alive and flourishing. Lest thou mock, oh reader, examine the trivia of your own hobby-horse; what would you give for, say, the pen of Keats, or the steering wheel of Fangio, the baton of Klemperer, the trowel of Gertrude Jekyll?

After the death of someone, all their possessions, from the most intimate to the peripheral, from an entire house to a matchstick, become charged with them and bereft of them; both at once. A fountain pen or a paper clip will be imbued with the presence of the lost person. Each thing becomes transfigured with death; and yet, the living presence has gone out of the objects as surely as if they themselves were living and had died. They are like absences in the world, as if they were made of some strange other matter unnatural to this place.

I recall once seeing the tea-pot with which Mrs.Thrale consoled the morbid Dr.Johnson; a rotund, homely, capacious grail of a pot, commensurate with his immense need. Someone, rightly, saved and treasured it, and it enlivened the man and his relationship.

And once, in Ayrshire, memorably, I saw a small, wooden spoon lovingly carved from a toilet seat upon which Robbie Burns had once sat. Now there's something to stir your tea with.

You may laugh, but do you not keep safe and secret, in a recess of loft or cupboard, some mundane and worthless trinket once intimately in contact with some long lost lover, or father, or daughter? A cigarette that bears a lipstick's traces?

I sought out the main post office to collect our mail. I recited the sentence the phrase book recommended, and displayed my passport to the testy young man behind the appropriate counter. Without moving from his place, he assured me there was nothing. Thinking he had misunderstood my dreadful Spanish, I went through the whole charade again. He irritably skimmed through the contents of a pigeon hole and then ignored me & wandered off. I was irresolutely wondering what to do, in the street outside, when he came out of the building and hurried away, scowling. I went back in and tried again with the young woman who had replaced him, and was rewarded with a satisfying bundle of letters.

In the symbolism of the Camino, Burgos is the Gateway to Hell. It is the portal to the Meseta, the severe core of Castile; an endless, almost waterless, plain, hot, bleak and testing. The Pyrenees incarnates the pilgrim's resolve to turn away from the comforts and securities of domestic life. Thereafter, there is the reward of the realisation of the riches of the simple, and glimpses of the Holy City and its enlightened state of mind. Beyond Burgos comes a more demanding trial, things get more serious.

Back at the Seminary I refuelled Kes with Mars bar and coffee and settled down to read my letters, precious links to another world. I took stock and tried to count up how far we had walked. I made it only 165 miles, scarcely a third of the distance to Santiago. A long way to go. I repaired my rucksack, took the straps in a bit and moved my belt along a notch to allow for the loss in weight.   Kes watched.

"Fat going down, eh Dad?"

"This is not fat, Kes."

"What is it then? It looks like fat to me."

"It is a gesture of Solidarity with our Pregnant Sisters."

"Well, other people call it 'fat'?"

Claudio came in and presented us with some cakes. They were a parting gift. He had received a note from the film crew, I had forgotten all about them, summoning him to San Juan for some filming. He would be cruelly missed. Bienvenida had disappeared. Presumably she had left early. We never saw her again.

Chapter 19

Patterns in Time

Kes and I left Burgos alone, following the spacious Rio Arlanzon beneath the shade of horse-chestnuts and crossing it over a wide bridge. The last building on the edge of Burgos is a prison. On the road to Tardajos a group of tattily dressed kids with a couple of scrawny dogs caught us up and tried to beg some money. I shook my head and the eldest said a few rough words and one of the dogs slunk up behind me and bit me in the groin.

Good water in Rabe and then the path began to climb. Trees got scarce and then disappeared altogether, just a very few stunted shrubs, no shade; the blazing sun directly ahead making us squint. Across the vast, parched landscape ahead we could count a few trees near the horizon. The grass by the cart track was like straw. Even the weeds were dying. We crossed a dusty ridge to see the village of Hornillos below us.

Then my ankles finally gave out completely. I'd been taking double the recommended dose of pain-killers for some days. Now my ankles had locked, I just couldn't bend them in the right places to enable me to walk at all. I sat where I stood and then dragged myself over the dust towards some shrivelled scrub. I couldn't get all of my body in the skimpy shade, just the top half.

Kes was understandably very concerned.

"What are we going to do, Dad?"

"I don't know."

The landscape was empty in both directions.

"Do you want some tea?"

"OK. Maybe I'll feel better after a bit of rest. You all right in the sun there, Kes?"

"Yere, it's not so bad. I'm a bit tired though."

He set up the stove, and brewed some tea.

I took off my boots and socks to get some air to my feet and rubbed some lavender oil into my ankles. The backs had swellings like walnuts. I reluctantly took another pill.

After about half an hour, and some more tea, my ankles seemed to loosen up a little and Kes helped me to my feet. I hobbled, very slowly, down into Hornillos.

A group of villagers sat on the shady side of the single main street. I asked them the way to the refuge. A man, his face dark with stubble and from working in the fields in the hot sun, said something I didn't catch and they all laughed. I repeated my request. Again I didn't understand the reply fully, something about building a new one, but it was clear there was no refuge available.

I took off my rucksack and rummaged in it for my Spanish phrase-book. They all waited and made a few comments and laughed again. I found a suitable sentence and asked if there was a room in the village where we could stay; a pension perhaps.

More laughter.

"They're laughing at us, Dad."

Kes was plainly right. Though perhaps 'sneering' was a more accurate description. They looked poor, maybe they resented a new refuge being built for the relatively well-off pilgrims endlessly passing through.

I thanked them, bowed slightly, and made ready to move off. They found this quite hilarious. I limped away, trying to keep my dignity. A gale of laughter followed us down the empty street. The houses either side were very simple and basic and all shut up like blank faces. A dog with enormous dugs, looking like a wolf, loped past. A shepherd brought in a herd of goats down the street, bells round their neck tinkling. I nodded greeting. He ignored us. Some sparrows mobbed a kestrel while a young man took pot-shots at them with an air-rifle.

The bar at the exit to the village was sparse and cheerless. The woman behind the bar seemed old before her time, all in black, a skinny body and a drawn face. She was immensely sad. The few youngsters lounging about seemed to resent our presence. I asked her for accommodation. She was much more sympathetic, but made it clear there was none. No shop either.

We walked out and into the empty landscape feeling pretty disconsolate.

"Where's the next refuge, Dad?"

"Hontanas."

"Is it far?"

"Nine kilometres, I think. Five miles and a bit."

I stumped along, awkwardly and slowly. Five miles would take us a very long time. Nothing but empty fields and an undulating path. I was even slower on the slight slopes. We rested often. The evening light was beautifully warm and orange.

"It can't get too cold at night. Perhaps we could make these straw bales into some sort of shelter."

But I wasn't sure if I could move one. They looked heavy. And, in fact, in this open landscape, under a totally clear sky, it would get quite cold at night.

I felt guilty. I should be looking after him. I ought to provide somewhere to stay.

We laboured on getting slower and slower. A building appeared off the path to the left. A very strange building, isolated amid the fields, it looked like a cross between a temple and a barn. It was only small, one room, but it had a dome. It became clear it was this or nothing. There was no other building in sight in any direction. We wouldn't make it to Hontanas, and it was beginning to get dark.

We turned off the main path at a sign saying San Bollo, committed to this place, and shuffled along the quarter of a mile to reach it. I even thought that if it was locked, I would consider trying to break in.

It was an oasis. The building stood like an oriental bungalow in its own patch of green. In the centre of the green, an open tank, like a miniature swimming-pool, of superb water, so cold it put the teeth on edge, was fringed by delicate willows.

The building wasn't locked. Inside its rough stone walls was a room like a stable; a concrete floor strewn with straw, a single window, glowing with the aftermath of the setting sun, wooden beams above. It was warm and dry. Home. This was better than any cheap hotel room. No electricity, no facilities at all, except just what we needed. We rested in contentment and gratitude.

I lit some candles for light and got the stove ready to cook. The candle-light made the place cosy and the smell was simple and homely. The candles kept the room warm too, as the sun's heat seeped away.

"What have we got to eat, Dad?"

"Frankfurters," I replied, waving a vacuum pack, "Not much bread though, I was hoping to get some in Hornillos."

"No matter."

"Oh dear."

"What's up?"

I offered him the pack to sniff. Definitely off.

"Never mind. This means the emergency sardines. Very filling, sardines."

The sardines were off too. The sell-by date was two years earlier.

I took stock. One Cuppa Soup, two crusts of stale bread, two tea bags, one cigarette. We shared it all, including the cigarette.

I knew Kes already smoked. You can't keep such secrets in a village. A neighbour had remarked in the pub back home that Kes had been seen puffing away behind the bus shelter. There seemed no point in pretending that I didn't know.

"I'm sorry, Kes."

"What for? This is the best place so far. We can hack it, Dad. I like it here."

"So do I."

"It's a great day for Scotland," remarked Kes, mysteriously settling the point.

We sat outside in the cool of the evening, peaceful and quite happy, alone in the landscape under a full moon whose soft light caused gentle, waving shadows of the young trees on the stone walls.

Bats skittered about and a barn owl flew by. The night was utterly quiet save for the endless supply of silver water tinkling into the tank.

****

In the morning I let Kes sleep late and busied about washing all our clothes, including those I was wearing, and laid them on the yellow grass to dry in the early sun. Then I washed up all our bowls and pots and pans. I enjoyed being domestic. While I was naked, I washed in the freezing water; and all manner of thing was good, very good.

I fixed things. The rucksack and my trousers both needed sewing. Both the camera and the stove were repaired.

Kes woke with the intrusion of the first troupe of cyclists around mid-day. They wore all the fashionable cycling gear and boasted about the distance they had covered already that day. French, macho types, slick with sun-tan oil, muscles everywhere, and solely concerned with using them. They posed by their machines awhile, photographing each other, and then raced off, jostling for position on the narrow track. Les Coqs Sportifs on the Tour d'Espagne. Competition is an ugly business.

Three Basque cyclists arrived. There were very keyed up, still with the rhythm of cycling in their actions, twittery, like blue tits. Three or four minutes of clipped sentences and they were away; exactly like a small flock of finches.

We prepared to leave at an easy going pace, refreshed in clean clothes, both feeling in harmony with the place. Our breakfast was water.

"How's your ankles, Dad?"

"Ankles?"

I had forgotten all about them, and the pain-killers.

"They seem OK this morning."

Back on the path, another gang of cyclists noisily zoomed past us followed by a van carrying their gear, bumping along the track, one man leaning out with a video camera recording the progress of the happy racers.

It looked like something out of a comedy film and felt quite insane.

The landscape achieved a new apotheosis of dust. I've never been in such an arid place. Nothing grew save in the irrigated fields. Green harvesters cropped barley in a cloud of dust. The countryside was an African study in shades of fawn. Behind us, on the horizon, appeared a single figure in a pith helmet with a gait like the back legs of a camel. We stopped in the shadow of some bales to allow Claudio to catch up.

"Hi, man, how was the filming?"

He settled between us and passed his water-bottle.

"I think it was maybe a mistake to make the film."

"Why?"

"Angel, the director, he makes a lie of it."

"What do you mean?"

"He has no script, so he makes up a story. I had to have an injury. Tomato sauce down my leg, I limp around San Juan. I had hoped that the film would bring more people to the Camino, but not with a lie."

"Never mind. How's that young girl?"

I had no idea why I had asked, why she came to mind.

"What young girl?"

"The one in the film crew that I chatted to in St. Jean Pied de Port. You know, curly hair and a blue anorak."

"She's dead."

He saw my look of horror.

"A motoring accident."

He shrugged.

"It is quite common in Spain."

"When! When did it happen?"

"I don't know. A while ago."

He looked at me intently.

"You seemed much troubled."

"She was the girl with the curly red hair like a child's doll."

"So?"

"Do you remember the lacerated teddy-bear in Navarette? At the roadside. You said that someone I know might have a violent death."

We stared at each other. There seemed nothing to say.

We moved off in silence through this shadeless land.

There was grit in the dusty wind. Grasshoppers landed, splat, in the powdered earth like drops of rain. The few butterflies here were as dark as their shadow.

"Where the hell is Hontanas? Surely we should have reached it by now?"

"That is Hontanas there."

He indicated half a church tower rising up like a barb in a lion's pelt.

"That's it? Half a tower?"

Gradually, as we advanced, it grew a base. Hontanas is built in a hollow, a dust bowl, and emerges when approached as if slowly jacked up, or as if the very earth was painfully giving birth to the village out of its own parched self. The low hills around were like tawny slag heaps, Hontanas was spawned from them, formed of dried mud and rust. We tramped through the deserted streets until accosted by a slab of the most vivid, shimmering ultramarine. It was so alien and unexpected that for a moment I couldn't recognise it. An open-air swimming-pool.

This was too good to miss. We walked through the entrance commenting on the stroke of genius responsible for building this incongruity in such a place. Near the entrance, beneath a large, colourful umbrella, sat a wiry man with a trim beard and a luxuriant crop of salt-and-pepper hair on his bare chest. It made him look virile, as if his body was using up an excess of energy. Two middle-aged women flanked him like a retinue. He called to us in English and introduced himself: Ed, a lecturer in Spanish language and literature from the University of Kentucky, doing the walk. He seemed very pleased to meet fellow native English speakers; the first he'd met on the Way. We sat down and ordered a beer. The conversation flitted in and out of Spanish and English. Claudio and Ed took to each other at once.

Kes and I left them chatting while we took a dip in the surprisingly cool water under such a hot sun. As we swam, swallows trawled the surface for insects. This was the life; it felt so luxurious; translucent blue, like liquid sapphire, all around; a vibrant, deeper blue above.

Claudio and Ed, I noticed, were locked in intense conversation. As locals arrived in ones and twos, loudspeakers began to blare obtrusive music. Soon couples were sunbathing on the grass around the pool. The women were exquisite, perfectly formed, confident, with delicious creamy-brown skin. I wondered, idly, how their companions could forbear to caress such beautiful arms, a promise of softness signalled by a smooth complexion.

An odour of grilled meat and garlic wafted around. We got out to order some food. There was no room at Ed's table, so we sat nearby. Claudio eventually came over to join us. He frowned over a blank sheet of paper.

"Are you drawing a picture?" asked Kes.

"No, I am trying to guess Ed's birth-sign," he replied.

My mind went blank.

"October 20th," I said, without thinking.

"A Scorpio? Yes, it could be. I was thinking maybe Libra."

"Don't ask me, Claudio, I know nothing about the signs."

"I will ask him."

He leaned over towards Ed and said casually, "Were you born in late October?"

"Jesus Christ!" he said, clearly startled, "how could you have guessed that? October 29 in fact."

He looked shocked, as if Claudio could peer into the recesses of his life and spout disreputable secrets. His reaction was far in excess of the success of a simple lucky guess, as if his view of the world was shaken.

Claudio turned back to me.

"How did you do that, Michael?"

"I have absolutely no idea."

"I think it must be your moon in Pisces. We must look at your chart."

"Mine too," pleaded Kes.

"Of course, yours too."

He turned back to Ed.

"And where were you born," he asked, his pencil poised over his pad.

At this moment the P.A. system launched into Bruce Springsteen and 'Born in the USA'

Ed's eyes went panicky. This sort of thing just could not happen! Despite his sophistication, there was something boyish about Ed, something likeable; a sort of wide-open readiness for experience, a vulnerability. Claudio and I both laughed, and Ed laughed too, his eyes visibly moistening.

Later, as we took our leave, he hugged us a bit too warmly for my repressed English sensitivities. I got the impression he didn't want us to go.

"Any parting words of advice?" he asked, "I know you've done a lot of walking."

"Find your own rhythm," I replied. "Always walk at your own pace. Take your time. Give the Camino a chance to do its work."

I meant it, but it sounded pretentious and I felt embarrassed.

"Will we meet again?" he asked Claudio, looking him straight in the eye.

"Maybe, it is likely. But if not you have my address. You will write."

We left, waving.

****

The walking would have been easy, down a level, powdery path like white sand, and then a tree-lined road, except for the plague of cyclists sweeping past us, dangerously close, every few minutes. As they passed most yelled a greeting, a dopplered 'Buenas Dias' or 'Adios.' At first I answered them in kind, but as I grew more irritated I yelled 'Sore Arse' instead, which sounded much the same.

Kes twigged.

"What are you shouting, Dad?"

I told him.

"You shouldn't do that, it's not nice."

"Bloody pests."

"You should be more careful. Things like that come back at you."

"Nonsense."

"You'll see."

The dead straight road went on for ever. A tractor stopped and offered us a lift, which we refused. We took a break in the first bar in Castrojeriz. Swimming from Sheffield was on the T.V. On a whim, I ordered a gin and tonic. The barman almost filled a tumbler with gin and added about half an inch of tonic.

"I think I might need that tractor," I remarked ruefully.

Further into town, a family, sitting on chairs and a make-shift bench outside their house, called us over. The father, a slim, swarthy man, still with the grime of the fields on him, offered me an implement which looked like something used to collect urine samples from a female rhino. It was a bulbous glass jar half full of red wine with a narrowing tube sticking out one side. Seeing my indecision, he laughed, and demonstrated its use, throwing back his head, holding it at a distance, and pouring the wine in a thin stream, expertly, straight down his throat. I had a ham-fisted try, much to the amusement of all. Kes declined. It appeared Castrojeriz was determined to get me drunk.

The refuge was in the basement of a house. The walls were covered with lurid, amateur murals of couples dancing. Some sort of youth club?

That evening, everyone staying in the refuge, except Claudio, went on a joint pub-crawl. It's all a bit hazy, but I recall hot, crowded bars, a fruit machine which talked to me, being introduced to a man on his 24th pilgrimage to Santiago, a student of English philology from Salamanca who knew more about English grammar than I ever will, and three young women from Barcelona, one very vivacious, who had studied English in Manchester and another, called Marta, who had the most beautifully deep, soulful brown eyes. To look into them was like falling out of an aeroplane.

I remember staggering back to the hostel, and descending the stairs with some difficulty to see a familiar figure sitting on the floor in the centre of the shadowy room talking to two young women. Roger, the Careers Officer from the college, who had also been affected by the lecture back in London enough to try the walk. A big man but normally quiet and restrained, even shy. He waved a bottle of red wine at me as if it were the most natural thing in the world that I should suddenly turn up like this.

"Ah, Mike, we need a philosopher here. Come and have a drink and join this political discussion."

"You're right," I cried, lurching down the last of the stairs, "we have nothing to lose but our brains."

The rest is a blank.

Chapter 20

A Fundamental Problem

I blearily read a note in the morning from Claudio saying he was walking on with Roger. Kes had a bad night, suffering from a sort of claustrophobia in the close cellar. He was wild-eyed & scared. A panic attack; I had to do an improvised meditation session with him to get him out of it.

We crossed the town, both feeling grim, and wandered out into a wide plain. Ahead loomed a huge hill, maybe a thousand metres high.

"We don't have to go over that thing, do we?" complained Kes.

"I hope not, but it looks like it."

I could see, through the binoculars, a long, irregular line of people with rucksacks, straggling up its slopes.

A hoopoe glided by and exuberantly looped the loop.

"Stupid bird."

Soon we too were laboriously toiling up a zigzag path: a stiff climb up a winding track of white stone with glints of mica catching the sun. We collapsed by a monument on top and took a long break. A refreshing, steady breeze blew up here. Several cups of tea were necessary and then we gathered bunches of wild lavender, breathing the scent deeply until we felt almost human.

Then a pleasant, meandering stroll over the high tableland and a steep descent into the thick heat of lizard-land once more. A solitary fountain, clearly visible on the horizon, drew us on. I found myself open-mouthed and panting, like a dog, in the stagnant heat.

Beyond the fountain and its tepid water, we ambled down a quiet road. Ahead, I could see that our road met another just before a bridge, and coming down that other road, exactly at a pace which would ensure we met at the bridge, was an extraordinary sight. As we converged I couldn't help staring and smiling. This walk certainly attracted eccentrics.

Tramping down the road was a tall, slim young man in his late twenties; dark-haired, clean-shaven, small features, snub nose. He was pushing a large, home-made cart by its long shafts. The cart was basically a substantial wooden box mounted on full-size bicycle wheels. In it was a hefty, shaggy dog, asleep. Above the dog, a makeshift canopy to create shade, and hanging from the canopy, a host of objects including various pots and pans, a fly swatter, washing, and a guitar; a blanket formed a curtain down the side facing the sun.

He explained that the dog had begun by walking, but the road surfaces were too hot for its paws and it had developed a limp, so the cart had been improvised to allow the pair to carry on.

We crossed the bridge over the Rio Pisuerga together, then the path turned away from the road to follow the river. The river bank was a perfect place for a break. A power of water flowed, the colour of pea-soup, behind a screen of willows, poplars and swaying rushes. We relaxed in the excellent shade. The dog went for a swim.

Our latest companion rolled a joint, stretched out on the earth as if it were some comfortable sofa, and told us about himself. He moved languidly as if motion was vulgar, or his limbs were filled with molasses. He sucked strongly on his joint, drawing up calmness from somewhere deep in the seventh dimension, his body swaying slightly to a slow, regular rhythm matching an inner oceanic swell, like a yachtsman ashore still rolling with the waves. It was hypnotic.

He spoke of his home the way sailors often do, nostalgically, vaguely, yet still a fixed anchor in an unreliable world. In Toulouse, apparently, he had a house and a wife. He'd been on the road nine years now. I checked it, suspecting my weak French, nine years all right. Yep, nine years. Where had he been all that time? Oh, up and down, here and there. Italy, he was pretty sure he'd been to Italy, maybe more than once. He smiled at some soft secret. And was he going to Santiago now? Probably. He'd been somewhere else, could easily have been Italy, when he'd heard of the Camino and had turned around towards Spain. Yere, just one morning, turned around. Wasn't that, like, so cool? The only way to live. He nodded slowly with satisfaction at this arcane knowledge he had mastered.

A kingfisher shot by, dead level, an electric blue bullet, low along the opposite bank.

There, you see? That confirmed it. Only way to live.

The willows rustled and whispered in a light breeze.

He admired our stove and lamented the fact that he didn't have one and couldn't afford restaurants. He prepared food over an open fire on occasion, but couldn't be bothered most of the time. He'd cook us a meal on our stove sometime, he promised.

We took our leave of Serge, as he looked set to remain on this pretty spot for some hours more.

The village of Itera de la Vega was a bland, brick and concrete place with some walls coated with sun-baked mud. By the central fountain, with its rearing horses, surrounded by palm trees, a small girl approached us and insisted that our friends were in the bar, and she would conduct us there. She was most insistent, and led us through the hot, empty streets to the hidden bar. Here were Claudio and Roger in a jovial mood, and very pleased to see us. I offered the child a few coins for her trouble which she indignantly refused.

Just a quick couple of beers and we were off again, leaving Claudio and Roger in the bar.

Through the village and out, over a road, and on down a wide track of dust and stones. The landscape looked wild, like something out of a Western. The path weaved between buttes; John Wayne would have fitted in well.

"I can't go on, Dad," said Kes suddenly.

"I know it's a bit bleak here, Kes, but keep going, it can't be that far to the next village," I replied, consulting my sketch-map.

"No, I mean I can't walk any more."

I looked at him. Nothing obviously the matter.

"What's wrong; blisters?"

His reply completely astonished me.

"No," he writhed with discomfort, "it's my bum."

"Your bum? What do you mean, your bum? What's wrong with

it?"

"It's seized up."

This reduced me to incoherent repetition.

"Seized up! Seized up! What do you mean, 'seized up'? How can a bum seize up?"

"The two halves have stuck together. One bit won't move over the other bit. It's seized up."

An appalling possibility crossed my mind.

"Kes, tell me, when did you last wash your bum?"

He looked acutely uncomfortable.

"Well, I washed it before we left."

"Castrojeriz was a bit sweaty last night, but it shouldn't have gone like that since then."

"No, not before we left Castrojeriz, I mean before we left England."

"England! England! Are you telling me you haven't washed your bum since we left England?"

He squirmed.

"Yes."

"But it's been weeks! And in all this heat! Seized up, it's a wonder the bloody thing works at all! You're not growing potatoes down there or something, are you?"

"I don't think so."

Then I saw the funny side of it, and staggered about laughing.

"It's not funny, Dad, it hurts."

"Sore arse! Sore arse!" I yelled, crying with laughter.

He grinned ruefully.

"OK, OK., Kes," I said, with some difficulty, one arm around his shoulders, "but you'll have to struggle on."

I gestured around at the barren landscape.

"We can't stop here, in the middle of nowhere. It will have to be washed. I haven't got enough water for such a big job. Why didn't you tell me before? Can you get along to that bridge? There's probably water there."

Michael Shearer

A few hundred yards ahead, a small slab of concrete constituted a tiny bridge.

He nodded, and began to walk along, knees apart, bandy.

The bridge crossed a narrow, but deep, irrigation ditch with water flowing steadily down it. By hanging over the side, with Kes sitting on my legs, I managed to scoop up some water using a bowl from the cooking kit.

"Here, you wash yourself in this."

I sorted out some soothing antiseptic cream.

"Dry yourself thoroughly, then put some of this on. You should be all right. You'll have to wash out that bowl. I ain't cooking with it now."

He objected when I took a photo of him about his ablutions.

"You show anyone, and I'll kill you," he yelled.

Once his moving parts were lubricated, we moved off, slowly.

Boadilla shimmered on the horizon through a heat haze, like some huge, outdoor chess-game for giants, abandoned in the landscape. There were no trees at all here. We passed a field of tall sunflowers, growing out of white earth which looked exactly like concrete. Hot air, like a soft pillow, pressed against the face constantly. A dust storm blew up, gusting grit into our faces, filling my beard. We fashioned masks out of handkerchiefs.

A few trees marked the edge of Boadilla. Here was a welcome fountain; a large, multi-coloured, metal wheel set flat in a wall pumped up cold water when turned. The old men of the village congregated here, their only entertainment to watch the passing pilgrims struggle with the pump.

The path skirted around the village to meet a tow-path by a broad canal. This was pleasant walking, the constant breeze keeping us cool, blowing the water into small waves, swaying luxuriant reeds.

A pilgrim shuffled along ahead of us, limping badly, so slow we eventually caught him up. He was a young man, thick-set and strong, one ankle visibly swollen; a teacher from Extramaduras, who spoke good English. He said that this heat was as nothing compared to his

166

homeland. People did little but sleep during the heat of the day in the summer months. He was cheerful despite his injury. I offered him an ankle pill which he refused. Then I realised that I hadn't taken any of these pills since San Bollo. The ankles functioned well, apart from the odd twinge.

He told us of another route to Santiago up from the South, but impossible to do, he thought, during the summer months, due to the fierce heat.

"Southern Spain is not really part of Europe," he explained, "it is more like North Africa."

We chatted about education until we reached Fromista.

Our friend inquired about the refuge and was told that we couldn't be admitted unless our passports were stamped by the local priest first, and he was at mass. So we joined a group of pilgrims waiting outside a church. One young man, waiting, twitted about neurotically like an injured bird. He had a serious nervous twitch. We waited for some time patiently. The priest emerged from the church as if it were Buckingham Palace, disregarding us all until called back by the Spanish teacher. The priest was haughty and full of his own self-importance, harshly demanding to see our pilgrims' passports and then ignoring them when produced. Down the street came Serge, with his cart and dog.

"Mother of God, who's this freak?" said the priest.

As Serge arrived he was accosted by a torrent of unfriendly Spanish from the priest; none of which Serge understood. The priest then interrogated Serge in staccato Spanish, which the teacher put into English, and I into poor French. Serge, not owning a pilgrim's passport, was banned from the refuge and summarily dismissed from the presence. The priest treated him as if he had some foul, contagious disease. Serge wandered off, saying there was always some place to sleep in the streets of a town.

I am attracted to Holy places but not, on the whole, to holy people; so many of them seem to have taken out religion like some sort of insurance policy.

Eventually, after much tedious, protracted formality, whose main function seemed to be to impress upon us just how powerful a man was this trivial priest, we were all directed to the refuge; a spacious, purpose-built hostel with lots of room. Here I insisted Kes took a shower.

In my dormitory, a Spanish pilgrim lay on his bunk like an effigy. Flat on his back, he clasped a purse, or a wallet, close to his chest. His knuckles were white, his eyes fearfully staring. He plainly saw thieves all around.

Later, taking a stroll around town, we bumped into Claudio.

"Aren't you staying at the refuge?" I asked, "It's a big place, plenty of room. Showers."

"No, too much trouble. The priest here is, how do you say, a hurt in the bum."

"A pain in the arse."

"Exactly. I stay in a private refuge."

"I didn't know there were such things."

"Oh, yes, many people offer accommodation to pilgrims on the way. But he makes his own rules. No alcohol, and I must be in by ten."

"A bit of a pain in the arse."

"Yes, but not as much of a pain in the arse as the priest."

"Could we change the subject. Kes is a bit tender in this area."

I explained what had happened.

"There's no need to tell everybody," Kes complained.

"There is a church here you must see."

"Not another one, Claudio."

But, as usual, Claudio was right. San Martín is not to be missed. I would be hard-pressed to cite another church as harmonious and well-proportioned, and it is built in a wonderful, warmly saffron stone. It stood entire and wholesome, glowing in the late afternoon sun like a ripe wheat field. It perfectly expresses an ordered mind at home in an ordered world. If you want to know what it might feel like to have an integrated psyche, where thought and feeling and action square with each other, and this whole matches a vision of the universe, go and stand before San Martín in Fromista.

That night a violent storm split the world around Fromista; the very texture of things flashed and crashed and shook, while rain scourged down like an endless volley of giant needles.

I kept thinking of Serge somewhere out there, taking refuge with his howling dog under the cart's canopy, strumming his guitar, smoking damp weed, keeping cool.

Chapter 21

Carrion up the Camino

A threesome once more, Claudio joined us for a long walk down a straight road out of Fromista through increasingly arid landscape. Where it was irrigated, barley grew, where it wasn't even the thistles were dried flowers on stalks like withered candlesticks.

We took a break at the hermitage of San Miguel; a quiet, green spot in a dry world. The simple rectangular building stood askew amid an oasis of willows. Lizards posed and scuttled on its creamy stone walls. Away from the building, the hermit's water supply still trickled coldly over stones at the edge of a baking field.

Off road soon after, down a long, straight dirt-track between endless sugar-beet. We passed a sign for a village called 'Revenge of the Fields.' Then the path grew more narrow and tracked a stream until returning to the road at Villarmentero. At an official picnic site by the roadside here, a pair of pilgrims on horseback had paused. One of the many motorists brought us a gift of melon while we were resting.

Further on, at Villalcázar de Sirga, Claudio insisted that we stop at the restaurant in the main square: El Meson de Villasirga. It was closed, so we knocked at its large, wooden door. It was opened by a sturdy, middle-aged man who had the comfortable confidence of the financially secure. Here was a man who had found his niche, and was content with it. He ushered us in. The room spoke of nature's bounty; the walls were hung with fruit and grain; and medieval decorations. A huge refectory table, sturdy like its owner, filled the length of the room beneath heavy, old beams. It looked as if it had been welcoming pilgrims for centuries. Everything was neat and put in its place with a domestic artist's eye for fitting harmony.

Pablo Payo called to the kitchen for soup and wine. He sat comfortably at his ease. He had plainly settled down snugly in himself and was content with who he was. Yet he clearly had enormous respect for pilgrims such as ourselves. This is uncommon in people with his sort of attitude. There is a type of person for whom it is unquestionably obvious that the purpose of life is to achieve a quiet contentment; to be secure and safe. Usually they find Seekers immature people who have not found their place, internal and external, wherein to dwell and be happy. What is the point of chucking things up, risking what you've already got, and going haring around the world looking for you know not what? The sport of ageing adolescents. Why rock the boat? Just strive to make the boat more comfy; perhaps a potted Jasmine in that corner and that pretty little mirror from the antique shop in Long Melford over there. Just the thing, let's get the place just so; make a hideaway, a nest. Never mind tempting Jesus with turning stones into bread, or to be master of all he surveyed, just offer him a thatched cottage in the country, central heating, furnishings of his choice, a regular, more than adequate, income and a cosy wife. That'll get him.

But Pablo wasn't like that. He had settled down, but lacked the disdain for the restless seeker. A rare mix.

He chatted to Claudio, with the inevitable questions about Kes, until the meal arrived: delicious garlic soup with little bits of bacon, fresh bread, peaches, and strong, red wine in portly brown jugs. He presented Kes with a chocolate brown cup, with the name of the restaurant on it, as a memento, and stamped our cards before bidding us farewell. He waved genially good-bye having helped another few on their way. The meal was free for pilgrims. Villasirga means something like 'town of the tow-rope.'

Thereafter yet another long, hot road straight enough to be Roman. We walked on towards the immense, white, grain silos of Carrion.

At the church of Santa María in Carrion, we were greeted by the priest and his tall sister, who reminded me of Virginia Woolf, and we were shown into the back garden; an idyllic place with a round table beneath a fruit tree amid rows of massive vegetables. Cats skulked among the onions. At the table were seated two pilgrims, one of

whom was a huge, muscular man resembling Popeye's enemy, Bluto.
They both gazed forlornly at a pair of enormous alpine boots on the
table before them.

"They are killing me," explained the large, thickly black-bearded
man, "I cannot understand it. I have walked many times in the
mountains with these boots, but here, nothing but pain and blisters."

"They're too heavy and stiff for the roads," I suggested, "very
hard on the feet."

"It is true," he said mournfully.

He was plainly taking it badly. Such a strong man, he was not
used to having his body let him down.

He picked up a bottle of red wine and swigged about a third of it
with gusto. He made a massive sandwich of cheese and very red
tomatoes, dipped it in olive oil, and ate heartily. He motioned for us
to help ourselves. Kes made himself a sandwich of sardines,
chocolate spread, and Tabasco sauce.

"Would you like me to get some paraffin for your sandwich,
Kes?"

"No, thanks."

"Or a touch of goat dung?"

"Well, if it's no trouble."

"I'll see what I can do."

"I will get more boots in Leon," interrupted Bluto miserably.

"It's a long way to Leon."

He took another hefty swig.

"I will see how it walks," he said.

Kes had taken some snippets of sardine and was trying to feed
the cats. They were semi-feral, and very wary. Often cats and dogs
here are not fed, but left to fend for themselves on mice and scraps
they find. Eventually a kitten snatched some fish from his hand and
scampered off into the vegetables to eat in safety. Virginia Woolf
thought this generosity of Kes charming, and brought her brother
out to see. Her melancholy look suggested that she would have liked
a child like Kes, but it was too late now. Kes was lying on the earth,

one open hand, full of fish, stretching into the cabbages.

Kes liked cats. We had four at home. The eldest had had trouble with her last litter. Kes, and his sister, had sat up all night while she was in labour. Most cats will not allow humans anywhere near them while they're giving birth. The runt of the brood had died in the early hours in his cupped hands.

In the evening, Kes and I went into a bar & bumped into the neurotic young man with the twitch who had queued with us in Fromista. In his twenties maybe, with a scrubby dark beard and one of those blemished faces which look as if they have been eroded by water in a ditch somewhere. He was short, emaciated and slightly bandy. His twitch was incessant, a jerk of the head to the side every few seconds. He wanted to know our names.

"Michael," I said.

"No Michael," he replied, shaking his head, "Papa Noel."

'Kes' was more difficult. Our new friend spoke no English, so we were reduced to mime and drawings. I drew a picture of a kestrel, wrote the word and crossed out the last four letters and gestured at Kes.

(In case you're wondering, Kes was born in Whipp's Cross Hospital, which is on the edge of Epping Forest. Things got a bit heavy while he was being born, so I stepped out for a breath of fresh air. Outside, a kestrel was hovering over the hospital. Kestrels don't often hover over buildings. When I went back in, Kes had found the right buttons to press and had got himself born. It was obvious he was a Kes. When I suggested the name to his mother, she readily agreed.)

When I asked our Spanish friend his name, he got up and stood in the middle of the bar and mimed it. He cupped both his hands and rolled them as if over a couple of oranges on his chest.

"Titania?" I suggested.

He shook his head and repeated the gesture more vigorously.

"Melanie," said Kes.

"Buster?" I tried, "Maybe, Chester?"

These were plainly wrong. He crouched slightly with his legs apart and knees bent and made a gesture as if throwing away something from his loins. Then he stood up straight, gave us a double thumbs up and rocked an invisible child in his arms.

"Jim?" said Kes mysteriously.

He gave up on us and wrote it down: Eugenio.

"Ah, I see. It comes from the Greek," I explained to Kes, "It means 'good birth.' 'Eugene' in English."

He approved of this and twitched a cracked smile while his restless eyes fearfully checked all around him for some unknown threat. If he hadn't already had a nervous breakdown, he was plainly on the verge of one. We walked together back to the church of Santa María.

It was early evening now & the refuge was crowded. There were bunks, Claudio had bagged one downstairs, but we had omitted to stake our claim and they were all full. Two inch thick foam mattresses covered the entire floor upstairs, each butted up against its neighbour, there was no space between them. I had Kes on one side and a beautiful French girl on the other. She was designed on Ferrari lines; aquiline facial features, exquisite streamlining everywhere else.

As I lay on my back, wide awake, I could feel the suffusion of warmth from her nearby body. My randiness was oppressive. I couldn't think of anything else. It took a long time to fall asleep. I awoke in the middle of the night to find her draped over me. Her slender arm crossed my chest, her hand lay, hot, on my naked shoulder, one of her legs overlay mine, her upper thigh in my lap. I gently laid my arm across her shoulders. She half woke with a start, and squirmed around with her back to me. As I instinctively turned on my side towards her, she executed an exotic jack-knife Karate blow with her bum, straight in my groin. A sudden resolution in favour of purity and celibacy came upon me. When I awoke in the morning, only her perfume remained.

Chapter 22

Meseta

Eugenio joined the three of us as we walked through the almost empty streets. We bought some sticky cakes for breakfast. Carrion has the feel of a pioneer town, the last chance saloon. Beyond Carrion is Hell. I suspect that Dante is right and the only way to heaven is through hell, most mystics seem to believe something of the kind. There had been much anxious talk of the flat plain of the Meseta among pilgrims along the Way. We knew of its reputation: the exposed furnace of Castile. The landscape becomes metaphysical; a world of basic, elemental categories: earth, sky, heat. No water. A diminution of the self unaccommodated; a poor, bare, forked thing creeping across Spain's equivalent of the heath. A cruel shadeless land where a straight path stretches to a featureless horizon, all day, day after day. Here a mind could turn in upon itself. No wonder Eugenio had joined us.

The four of us crossed the Rio Carrion together and plodded down a long, dreary, minor road. The small fields, looking like allotments, had pools of stagnant, scummy irrigation water. We were plagued with clouds of little black midges and the occasional mosquito whining like a Stuka. Kes tied his handkerchief around his mouth and we all followed suit.

The road became an apparently endless track like a straight, flat furrow through a bare and horizontal plain. No more fields. The scene was one huge field. Even my sketch map was almost devoid of features, it showed an "encina" marked a few kilometres ahead. I asked Claudio what it was.

"It means 'oak'. It's a tree."

The path had bulky nodules of rounded stones half buried in the ground, some edged green with moss or lichen. They were all shades of dull purple and pale blood, and shaped like fossilised kidneys and livers of extinct monsters. It was impossible to tread on a flat surface, and this hurt the muscles of the feet.

Conversation flattened with the landscape. Cloudless powder blue above, a level sea of golden stubble below. Not much else. The savage heat beat the words out of us. There was no sound save for the clunk of my staff on the stones.

We eventually elected to walk parallel to the path through the dusty, withered stubble. As we walked, vast crowds of grasshoppers rose from the earth, each in a long, jumping glide, spreading their wings to reveal patches of maroon, before plumping heavily into the ground in a tiny spray of dust. It was like walking through a colourful plague of locusts.

Claudio collected spearmint and watermint from in and around the ditches by the path.

We passed a sign for a village called 'Bustillo del Paramo' to our right. 'Small breasts of my Lover,' I supposed. Claudio taught me a new Spanish word: "uno muermo" – the same again and again, something excruciatingly boring. He also translated the name of the next village, Calzadilla de la Cueza, which was somewhere ahead over the horizon: 'Small path of the boiled.'

"Claudio?"

"Yes, Michael."

"While we are talking about Spanish, do you think you could teach me a Spanish sentence?"

"Just one?"

"I think so."

"What is the sentence?"

"I want to be able to say: 'Your beautiful brown eyes fill me with passionate desire.' Nothing personal, of course."

His rotting teeth appeared in his black beard.

"And what will you say after this sentence?"

"I thought I'd leave that to intuition. And body language."

"The sentence you want is, let me see: Tus hermosos ojos negros me llenan de deseo y passion."

I tried it. Claudio was very critical of my 'passion.'

"There is not enough passion in your 'passion.' It is not brave."

"Not enough 'oomph'?"

"What is 'oomph'?"

I jerked my right forearm up into the air.

"Ah, yes. More oomph."

I practised on the grasshoppers, bravely.

We rested briefly beneath the lonely oak. It was a poor specimen, a stunted and scrappy affair maybe eight feet high, but it was all there was, with a crowd of cheerful pilgrims lain beneath. We joined them in the poor shade, a little light-headed with the unrelenting heat, amid thousands of flies. Whatever the computation actually is, this lone tree felt like the mid-point of the walk; a marker, the stumpy axis of our world.

Kes sat at the edge of the shade with his staff held out into the sun.

"What exactly are you doing, Kes?"

"Fishing."

"What for?"

"Stones."

"Why stones?"

"It's all there is."

"Good, good. Any luck?"

"Not yet."

"Well, don't give up."

"I won't."

We emerged into an epiphany of heat to be grilled in the sun.

The landscape had became empty of people, indeed of life; even the birds had been incinerated off the face of the earth, devoured by the sun. Thoughts were burnt away, the past cauterised. Blanked by the fiery furnace, we could become otherwise now.

When the hamlet of Calzadilla, maybe two dozen houses, appeared ahead, it looked as if its roofs were metal melted by the heat. It glistered in the raw sun. Its few concrete streets were deserted as if cleared by a death ray. We filled our water-bottles from a tap sticking out of the side of a building. In the bar was Bluto, on the telephone to Burgos, arranging to be picked up. The lumpy path had proved to be the last straw for his tormented feet. They must have baked in their own sweat in his heavy boots. He was resigned, but determined to try again next year. He wished us luck, hobbled into the dining room, and sat down to a meal big enough for three.

Just beyond Calzadilla we were back on the tarmac. A van stopped just ahead of us and the driver beckoned. He had a plastic tub full of melting ice and cans of tonic and orange. He presented each of us with a refreshing drink.

About a mile further on a troupe of cyclists stopped by us and offered us water from a bottle wrapped in a wet sock. As they cheerfully departed we could see a figure pushing a cart along the road behind us. We sat by the roadside to let Serge, and his dog, catch us up.

Ledigos is a forlorn hamlet, mostly two-storey adobe houses looking as if they were made of chewed cardboard, and a few dirt or concrete streets. We were directed to the Tele-club as the refuge. This stood back from the road like a brick shoe-box. All the windows had iron grills. Plain brick entrance porch in the centre with a door at each side. Two rooms; to the right, a barren bar apparently filled with bored and bitter anarchists; and to the left, the old school-room now left for pilgrims. It was bare and filthy save for rickety desks around the walls and a voting booth like an impoverished confessional in one corner. Several windows were broken and the floor was covered with scraps of burnt paper. There was no water. No lights either for that matter, nor toilet. The drinkers went in the landscape.

I brewed up a cup of tea to cheer us up while Serge brushed his teeth with a tube of foot cream. While the kettle boiled, I found a broom and moved the dirt around a bit, then laid some sheets of cardboard, found outside, and stretched our sleeping bags on them. We sat around chatting till dark. Claudio talked of Astrology.

"It is not a subject or a system of prediction, it is a way of life. A way of life which lives in the grain of the forces of reality."

"And what is the purpose of the astrological life, Claudio?"

His shoulders lifted in the barest of shrugs.

"The same as every other type of life. The purpose of life is the death. A person must destroy themselves."

He looked despairingly gloomy.

"Yes," I responded, "but these things reflect each other, produce each other. An obsession with destroying the self emphasises it. It's just a sneaky form of egoism."

When Claudio began to prepare his Rice, Serge produced a bag of potatoes and announced that he would cook a meal for me & Kes. I gave him the stove and showed him how to work it. I lit some candles while he cooked.   He boiled the potatoes whole and when the meths reservoir ran dry they still weren't done. Several refills later they still weren't cooked and I'd run out of fuel. The dinner of half cooked, just warm potatoes, sardines and mussels, all mixed in, was the most disgusting meal I've ever eaten. Even Kes had trouble eating it. The dog refused it. We washed it down with liberal quantities of harsh red wine. Claudio and Eugenio had rice smelling sweetly of mint.

I retired to my bed, my stomach heavy, and queasy, with indigestible tubers. I began to feel ill and fluffy-headed. From the floor I watched Serge take out his guitar, tune it in the flickering candle-light, and play a mournful blues. Kes sat at his feet, transfixed. They passed a joint back and forth. I felt too sick to be concerned. The dog slept in the voting booth.

****

Eugenio snored like a sick outboard motor throughout the night. I slept badly on the hard floor. I went out at dawn to vomit.

I took a walk around the sleeping village. It was chilly, though the sun blazed low in the fresh, pure blue sky; it bathed the world in a cold light like incredibly diluted mountain water. The village cats ambled, sleepily, about, warily confirming territorial rights. Plants

179

stirred stiffly in slow response to their ruler.

Kes got up soon after, looking very pale. I packed, with my head blurry and full of cotton-wool.

With no fuel left I had to wait for Claudio to get up to use his stove for some tea. The Mars bar in my pack had melted in yesterday's heat.

"No problem," said Kes.

And he scraped it into a bowl, put it on the Claudio's stove, heated it up till it melted to a thick liquid, and ate it with a spoon. Then he went even paler, became very quiet, and sat in a corner.

Kes and I left ahead of the others. We were in poor shape and I knew we would be even slower than usual. The rest would surely swiftly catch us up.

The first hamlet, Terradillos, was scarcely more than a farmyard with a church. Chickens scrambled about its dirt street. The few further hamlets were much the same, perhaps smaller.

All road to the next town. A terrible road. The brilliance of the fiercely white sky hurt the eyes. At the horizon the dazzling sky merged with an earth as white as flour. We walked in the midst of a glaring white-out with a grey strip of tarmac down its middle, and, in the distance, short lines of poplars, like dark green toy trains, apparently floating in the air.

I periodically paused to be sick, even when there was nothing left to come up. Walking in such heat, when you can't even keep water down, is not funny. I began to dehydrate. Kes looked weak, but wasn't sick. I plugged on in a mental haze.

We reached Sahagun after crossing a railway line. It's a very odd place. I can't imagine anyone voluntarily living there, it's a place to be banished to, somewhere perpetually under siege; zapped with heat in summer, exposed and cold in winter; slapped down in the middle of a bleak plateau like a motley of second-hand condiments in the centre of a huge table. The feel of the place is run-down and forgotten; walls peel, brick cracks and crumbles, the main fountain had water that smelt of bad eggs, as if the town itself had gone off. My raw and empty stomach heaved with the stink of it.

Yet solid brick towers marked a clutch of impressive churches, substantial affairs with more than a hint of the military strength of Romanesque, foursquare and stolid like massive dovecotes. To the East of each of these towers, were blind apses, two or more stories of bricked-in windows to create, inside, a dark defence from the heat.

Sahagun has the feel of a town held like a fort against the surrounding elements. It's beyond the boundary of the safe, out in bandit territory where wolves might get you and the sun bleach your bones. A place where your church is a bastion, a retreat built to shrink perspectives amid a limitless surrounding space, and instil a little precarious confidence. I should imagine it felt much like Sahagun within the stockades of the US cavalry, deep in Indian country. Sahagun shouldn't really be here. The gritted wind has worn and grooved these embattled red-brick churches as if they were buttes in a desert.

We walked through the town, (I bought some meths for the stove), over the bridge, and down another straight, gruelling road. This became a stony track. Even my sketch map had little marked on it except the single black line of the path from the bottom of the page to the top. The mind had nowhere to go here. Dislocated with dehydration and fever, I sweated along grimly. Kes had tucked his handkerchief under the back of his hat to keep the sun off his neck. He walked steadily, head bowed, hands gripping the straps of his rucksack. We didn't talk much.

By the time I reached Bercianos, consciousness was a thin thread of a thing from which I hung. I was a blunt, wilful spike stumping along. I'd forgotten why. I'd been walking with someone but I couldn't remember who. I felt weak and my head burned.

At the entrance to the village was a stone fountain. I sipped its warm water and the liquid stayed down. I let the water run for a while, till it cooled a bit, and splashed it over my face. Then I eased myself wearily to the ground. My pounding head drooped and my eyes closed. The world seemed to roar as if I sat by a constant, crashing waterfall.

"You all right, Dad?" said a voice, and a mug of water appeared in my hands. I sipped some more. I sat there for some time while the world gradually rearranged itself around me. Someone had taken the mug away.

Much time passed.

Kes appeared coming down the main, dirt street. He had found the refuge. I rose shakily and he led me to it.

It was a large, rectangular block of a building, two stories, its red brick turned white in the sun's glare. Through a splintered door beneath a round arch, the cobbled ground floor was filled with debris like a building site. A stark, concrete staircase hung in the space. Upstairs were bare, wooden floor-boards and many bleak, dirty rooms. One had a grubby, horse-hair mattress on the floor. I sank onto it and into an instant, deep sleep.

When I awoke my head had cleared. Kes was asleep in his sleeping bag nearby, fully clothed. I went out for a walk. It was early evening. A shepherd was herding his sheep down the main street. A soft, russet light bathed the church beneath a beautiful, azure sky and lilac clouds. I watched the sunset. The azure deepened, first to indigo and then slowly to black while the yellow of the departing sun on the horizon mellowed to a suffusion of amber, then red, then rosé, then violet. Stars appeared in the black like a blessing.

Chapter 23

Hard Times

Through the night small, four-legged creatures scampered about just outside our room. In the morning I made some weak soup, scattered a little bread in it, and ate. It was delicious. I explored the other rooms and found a broken figure of Christ. It was what was left of a crucifix, though the cross itself had disappeared. Maybe seven inches long, naked save for a drooping loincloth. Thin streaks of blood dripped down his chest from the crown of thorns. One leg, and one arm, were broken off; only the stumps remained. The mouth hung slightly open, and the blank eyes stared in pain and shock. This poignant and mutilated figure embodied suffering humanity; hanging in there, clinging obstinately to a flickering and tenuous faith. I put it in my rucksack as a souvenir, wrapped tenderly in toilet paper.

Kes woke. He looked awful. A pasty face, like dough, and red, watery eyes. His forehead was very hot.

"You all right, Kes? You look terrible. You don't have to walk. We could take a day's break. Stay here."

"I'll try and walk," he said weakly.

A gritty kid.

He got ready to leave very slowly and had trouble lifting his rucksack. I took it and strapped it to my chest.

Down the bleak path into the immense landscape. Pretty soon there was no sign of human life in any direction, no roads, no buildings. We stopped for a break frequently. Kes had diarrhoea. He swayed when he walked and wandered across the stony track. As the heat built, he complained of the cold. Somehow he staggered on.

We reached El Burgo Ranero, only seven kilometres down the way, in the early afternoon. A village of fawn, adobe houses baked like biscuits. The refuge was the old town-hall; a dilapidated dump of a place. Pilgrims could stay upstairs in the old school-room. Several of the treads of the rickety staircase had rotted through. The bare, tiled floor upstairs was too filthy to sleep on and there was no broom. No water, no light. I pushed several desks together and made up a bed for Kes on top. He climbed awkwardly up and laid down, and swiftly fell asleep.

I went to find a doctor.

In the small, local shop I managed to communicate enough to discover that the village didn't have a resident doctor. However, one came once a week and was due in the morning. On the way back, I saw notices on every available post showing a skull and cross bones. I laboriously puzzled out their message. They were a warning not to drink any local water. It was contaminated. This scared me witless. I hurried back to Kes. He was still sleeping peacefully. I sat by his bedside and chain-smoked.

Through the long afternoon, pilgrims arrived in ones and twos, took one look at the place, and moved on. I went back to the shop for some food and bottled water. On the way back I passed a man in a blue boiler suit watering his dry garden with a hose-pipe. The water was light brown. He noticed the scallop shell around my neck and asked if I was staying in the village. His teeth were silver. I gestured towards our lodging. I must have looked dirty, for he indicated, with appropriate mime, that I might like to take a shower under his hose-pipe. I couldn't remember when I'd last washed, so I accepted, went back to check out Kes, changed into my swimming costume, found soap and towel, and went back and showered. OK if you didn't think about it too much. The man brought me out a bag of tiny apples.

Steadily, through the evening and into the hot night, Kes' breathing worsened. It began to rasp. Alone in the squalid room, the candles making flickering patterns of light, and changing the looming shadows, I became frightened.

No! Sweet Jesus, no! Not here, stuck in the middle of nowhere. I thought of running out and knocking on any door. There must be a telephone somewhere, and emergency services. Guilt seeped through me like a nausea. Gradually his breathing settled somewhat and I dropped into a fitful, exhausted sleep.

I dreamed I was falling and woke with a thud. Kes was still asleep and rasping noisily, wrapped up in illness. Early light streamed into the room.

When Kes eventually woke he seemed slightly better. We were sitting in the dust outside the doctor's surgery when she arrived. She spoke little English so I had to mime his sickness. I caught her suppressing a smile when I got to the diarrhoea. Food poisoning, I gathered, with a touch of asthma. We left with a prescription and soon had a bag of assorted medication.

The trip to the surgery had tired Kes considerably. I put him back to bed on the desks. I tidied up the sun-filled room as best I could. Through the morning I read, got my diary up to date, wrote letters home, wrote a poem:

The Stones of Santiago
There are stones on the way to Santiago.
There are stones all the way to Santiago.
But the stones are not pebbles,
the stones are not boulders,
the stones are not mountains.

The stones are a hardness of the heart
and are carried in the soul.

Every chance to take that's taken,
every chance to give forsaken,
these are your stones, pilgrim,
these are your very own stones.

I went for a walk. I looked at every building in the village, from every side. The bloke in the boiler suit passed me on a bike, carrying a scythe. He waved his scythe like a cheerful incarnation of Death about his business.

A group of about twenty cyclists arrived, looking fresh. All the fashionable gear on, all the same: skin-tight black shorts, thin red shirts with El Correo Gallego (Galician Post Office) printed across. They were a team. They tinkered with their machines, rubbed each other with various lotions, posed for photographs. In the midst of all this posturing, two middle-aged walkers emerged out of the forge of the landscape, flayed by the heat, frazzled out of their brains. Amid much consultation of watches, the cyclists moved off.

Soon after, another group of cyclists arrived, all dressed the same but different from the earlier group. They went through the same routine, but faster. Times were written down. It was clear that the two teams were racing.

I went back and took a siesta. Wrote another poem:

Alchemy
Take your gift of grief, pilgrim,
take your gift of disappointment,
take your gift of despair,
hold them close to your heart
and let it warm them into love.
This is the way to Santiago.

****

So the day whiled away. Kes slept solid.

In the evening, I walked out of the village to watch the sun set. The plain was springy with very dry, hardy grasses. I sat in the total peace and looked West, our direction, to a line of mountains on the horizon like lumpy grey cloud. Above them was a tremendous sunset of golden orange flushed with water-colour rose. Around me the light had a special quality of amber clarity. A marsh harrier swept silently past, quartering the planet.

Stars individually appeared, each a precise and gentle blessing. Slowly the massive master of the earth sank in the sky. The arch of gold grew brazen, became annealed to copper below the deepening cobalt of a sweet and easy death.

The brick and adobe buildings behind me gave back the sun's last fiery glow. Somewhere, amid all this aridity, frogs croaked. Then the world grew utterly still, and sacred.

****

Back in the village, huge trucks were rattling through, lights ablaze like fabulous undersea monsters. This place is a cross-roads; juggernauts from another time roar down a road from South to North, an intermittent straggle of pilgrims struggle on a medieval path of dust from East to West. El Burgo exists in a limbo between the two.

Cross-roads are holy places. They are out of this world, vibrant and dangerous with disorientating freedom. They are places of choice where the past is annulled, the old is on hold, opposites meet and a terrible beauty may be born. Oedipus makes the intuitive decision of his life at a place where three roads meet. At a fateful cross-roads Robert Johnson sells his soul to play the blues and is pursued by hellhounds ever after. Janus and Hecate and Hermes haunt here. Suicides were buried, criminals hanged, crosses and gallows erected at the spot where routes were unclear and ordinary rules failed. Hang a god from the cross of your gallows and you could spawn a new religion. The cross is the paradoxical intersection of logical opposites, the vertical of the male and the horizontal of the more earthy female, the crossed hairs in the seeker's viewfinder which enables a truer aim.

Back in the refuge I sat in the dark listening to Kes' easing breath. I made myself a platform of desks, lay me down as if on my own tomb, and slept easy.

In the morning I was headlong falling again. But I didn't wake with a jolt of fear. I let myself fall and fell into an extraordinary state of mind. I was on my platform, the room all around, but there was no me. I was conscious and undoubtedly awake, but with no consciousness of myself. I didn't exist, an astonishing selfless consciousness prevailed: light and airy and spacious and burdenless.

It was blissful. It went on and on, endless.

In this ecstatic cloud of unknowing a fear formed: how long could this be sustained? Might it be lost? At once I was down to earth with a shock and my own pathetic self again. I tried to retrieve the rapture but the effort shrank it utterly. But I felt I had been vouchsafed a promise. It had felt like the mildest, the most minuscule, silken brush with death. And this aspect of it was entirely banal, no big deal, like being offered a cup of tea, friendly:

"Oh, hi, fancy seeing you here. Would you like a quick cup of death?"

"Oh, yes, I could do with a break."

"Fine, I'll fix it then."

"Wait a sec, I'm tempted but I've got a few things to do. Eventually, I've got to write a book, I think."

"It's no trouble."

"No, it's good of you, but I think I'd better get on with it."

"Some other time then?"

"Sure, no problem."

"Bye for now."

"Bye, be seeing you."

****

Kes was much better when he awoke. He ate some bread and soup and I could see him in his eyes once more. My own eyes moistened with relief & gratitude. He was still weak and looked even skinnier but he wanted to walk on. I put the two sleeping bags in his pack and everything else in mine. We emerged into the sun tender as the newly born.

The day was fresh and clean, the path as stony and straight as before. Here the swarms of grasshoppers flashed wings of cerulean blue. Down the way was a shallow pond. Frogs plopped in as we arrived. Vivid blue dragon-flies hovered and idled over the surface like police patrols. The leaves of the trees around lifted and turned individually in the slight breeze; mirrored beneath, the water shimmered green in the dapple of their shade. A slim wheatear posed proud on a stone. We rested.

Further on, Villamarco, off route to the South but visible from the path, was on fire. Flames and dark smoke rose in the sky as a church bell clanged frantically.

On down the Way. Still no shade. After a while we grew desperate for a rest but to sit in the sun would be like laying two bits of bacon under a grill. Finally, I made a makeshift shelter by leaning the two packs together to make a sort of open wigwam, and we lay one each side with only our heads in the poor shade. So we rested like one strange beast with its rucksack head in the middle of its body, two legs sticking out in each direction, one pair notably shorter than the other. It was still hot and stuffy in there; heads side by side, each face apparently upside down. An odour of Kes' dirty socks, like rotting cabbage, oozed from his rucksack and hung in the close air like a fiery evil spirit, partially decomposed, fresh from Hell.

"I think I'll be a rock star when I grow up, " mused Kes.

"You've got some of the right habits."

"I've decided."

"What's your policy on the knicker question?"

"Knickers? What do you mean?"

"Well, Kes, apparently girls and young women gather in vast hordes solely to throw their knickers at rock stars."

"Really? No kidding?"

"It's well known. Knickers flying through the air. It's a health hazard."

Kes did not reply. Face upside-down, his eyes, apparently weirdly above a hairy chin, closed in meditative bliss and a subtle Buddha-like smile appeared in his forehead.

He dozed off and snored softly. I got out, unpacked my wet-wear jacket and put it over his legs to stop them burning; then joined him once more in smelly hell.

"Bit boring this bit," announced his awakening.

"Yep."

"Same all day; day after day."

"Yep. It's like Sisyphus."

"What's that?"

"He was Greek, and cursed to roll a large stone up a hill, but he'd almost get to the top when his strength would give out and the stone would roll to the bottom and he'd have to start again."

"Over and over?"

"Eternally."

"That's worse than watching cricket," said Kes.

"What do you think he should do?"

"He should try to really get into stones," he said, turned over and went back to sleep.

Kes snored.

My legs were getting hot in the sun. I turned over onto my side. With my legs in Spain and my head in hell, I urgently, actively waited for the next thought.

I thought of Kes' remarks about rocks and how they might be connected to his comment on stones; that thoughts were not isolated one-offs but had predecessors and were portents; that they were stitches across time that bound things together; bits of something greater; symbolons. They are not just fusions of fragments from the past; they are trans-temporal visitors, like a bird flying through the mind from utterly elsewhere. They are accompanied by a distinctive, recognisable feeling as unique as the taste of pomegranate. They are migrating items of a single puzzle, stretched across a person's life.

Yearning for meaning is a sort of love; a wish to know the pattern which joins, and to be part of it. The pattern criss-crosses minds and joins objects like a secret poetry.

I lit a cigarette. If I flick my lighter, now, and see its flame, the image seeks its kin, forward and back. My consciousness exists in a meaningful suspension between past and future, held in a web of meaning. This is why so much that happens feels resonant; what occurs hearkens to its kind. Birds of a feather.

Kes' inverted face stirred.

He awoke, rose and walked apart a little.

"One day there will be a huge tree on this spot," he said, pissing forcefully onto the parched earth.

Chapter 24

After Hell

On down the way, a railway line sloped up to the trail from the North. We crossed the tracks into some better shade and found the Light of India, asleep beneath a tree, his makeshift turban by his side. We let him lie.

Shade was rare round here though, and too good to miss, so we stopped for a break and brewed up some tea just next to him, talking in whispers. We were munching some doughnuts, which tasted of aniseed, when he eventually awoke. He nodded greeting, and produced some plums to eat.

"The people give me," he explained.

"Do you have a job back in France?" I asked.

He smiled.

"I do no work, only the spiritual work, you know."

The juice of the plum ran down his chin.

"But I 'ave the thought, you know," he continued, " of doing the carpenter."

"A carpenter. Why a carpenter?"

"Well, my third master, she say I am good with the 'ands. The carpenter is a good work, you know."

"So I believe. At least history is on your side."

"I do not live by the 'istory. I live in the moment. I live the spiritual life. But I 'ave not the religion, you know. I have the 'appiness only."

He was beginning to irritate me.

"Do you carry water?"

"Yes."

"Are you thirsty?"

"No."

"Then you don't live in the moment. You plan ahead."

He looked on me with pity. I did not understand the spiritual truth.

I sipped my tea. Why did he annoy me so much, this harmless twit?

He made a great show of gazing round the landscape, living in the moment. He was like a caricature of my aspirations. Didn't I aspire to become wiser? I too wanted to make spiritual progress. Is this how I appeared - an absurd, pretentious fool? I resolved to be more circumspect in future. We often dislike people who present our self in an exaggerated and simplified form. I suppose the experience is a sort of gift. A hint not to go that far.

We packed up our gear and moved off, leaving him to his fruit.

"I hope he's washed those plums," I remarked.

"Why?"

"Well, Spanish fruit doesn't usually get washed before it reaches the shops. It still has insecticide all over it. If he hasn't washed them, living the spiritual life, doing the spiritual work, he'll get the spiritual diarrhoea."

The next village, Reliegos, had a bar. Inside was a collection of stuffed animals and birds, dusty and moth-eaten, and a poster of an all female football team.

Through the village streets a group of kids spied at us from doorways, disappearing into back-alleys, reappearing further down, chattering excitedly. Eventually, a little girl plucked up the courage to ask me if I was Papa Noel. I said I was. Then they insisted that I take their photo and two of the girls wrote their names - Yesica and Beatriz - shakily in my notebook, so that I wouldn't forget them at Christmas time. They assured me they were very good little girls.

Just beyond the village we were plagued by tiny black midges. We walked, slowly, down the straight path, past fields of stunted, drooping sunflowers, towards a small town with a backdrop of distant mountains. With relief we entered the town of Mansilla, and so out of Hell.

We had crossed the Meseta.

****

It was market day in Mansilla with a plague of traffic like ground-based midges. It felt unfamiliar and bizarre. Market stalls had people buzzing round them buying cheese, garlic, bacalao (dried and salted cod) and fruit. We took a break in a busy bar for some coffee and croissants. The doctor who had treated Kes in El Burgo came in, greeted us warmly, and gave him the medical once over on the spot. She pronounced him weakened but well. In the garden was a mural of golden tulips breaking through a road; the hard way yields the flowers, up from the dark.

Parked by the straight road out of town was an open-topped sports car in British racing green, British number plates also. I strolled a little faster towards it. A middle-aged man with a jowled face sat in the driving seat, his wife beside him, pastel peach-coloured two-piece suit, single string of pearls, very Sussex. They sat side by side and miles apart, looking blankly ahead like test dummies awaiting a crash. A Harrods bag, staid olive-green with gold letters, reclined on the back seat like a badge of respectability.

My countrymen, my kin; I spoke to them with some eagerness. They seemed tired & fed up, although they had visited Santiago and Leon, and were en route for Burgos. He was tetchy, as if they had just had a polite row. I spoke to them of the Camino and its magical effects. They were unimpressed. As I warmed to the subject, relishing the ease of speaking English, I began to feel quite affectionate towards them. Leaning over the driver to address the wife through the urban noise around us, my arm, draped over the back of the driver's seat, naturally slid down onto her husband's shoulders. As I was talking to her, I became aware of the shoulders beneath my arm stiffening in resentment.

Oh dear, I had forgotten, the insular English do not touch. I glanced down at him to see that his stiff upper lip had spread, like a poison, all over his face. I raised my arm warily as if extracting it from a snake pit.

We said our good-byes, and all his social training could not mask his plain sense that the proprieties of good-manners had been inexcusably breached, he needed to convey to me my vulgarity. He drove away hastily from this embarrassing brush with the uncouth.

I watched the car merge with the traffic. Not, perhaps, my kin after all. They toured Spain, and saw it through the plate glass of their nationality, safe and untouchable, and profoundly bored. They were embalmed in their culture like fossilised grubs in amber. Doubtless, at this very moment, he was expressing his distaste.

Six kilometres of dreary road next, although the world nonetheless grew greener. We left the road near a petrol station.

On a road you walk on the surface, on an insulating skin. After the third step off a road everything changes. Earth underfoot makes the world softer, there is palpable depth.

We climbed a dusty hill. On the edge of Arcahueja stood Claudio, talking to a young woman by a massive, stinking tip of domestic rubbish. He was laughing.

"What's funny?" I asked.

"I said that there was a lot of rubbish. She said, 'Yes, we are very filthy here.'"

"That's surprising. That's the best lavadero I've seen."

Nearby was a public open-air laundry the size of a double garage. A communal building for washing clothes. Inside were two pools end to end like long, sleek steps; the upper slightly milky with soap; the lower crystal clear and very cool. Flat, sloping stones flanked the sides. A plump, grey-haired woman stood bowed over the slab, rinsing clothes.

"I think I'll do some washing," I said, shedding the rucksack with relief.

"I think I'll do some shade-bathing," said Kes.

"No you won't," I replied, "I'm not washing those socks. I could catch something foul, some fungus unknown to science. My fingers could drop off."

"They're not that bad."

"They are that bad. That's why you never get bitten by

mosquitoes. It's chemical warfare. Nothing smaller than a goat can survive anywhere near your feet."

I insisted, and showed him how to do it. By the time he'd done two pairs of socks, I'd washed everything else, and laid them in the sun to dry. His socks didn't look any cleaner but at least they bent a bit.

Beyond the village, the path returned to the road, which grew ever wider and more busy as we approached the big, modern city of Leon. It loomed ahead like an oppressive problem. Soon Claudio was way ahead of me, and Kes ambled far behind. A slip road came off the motorway and into the suburbs. There I took a seat outside a bar to wait for Kes. After an hour, it was clear he wasn't coming. I walked back down to where the slip road split from the main road. I could see miles down the way we had come. Tarmac to the horizon. I scrutinised the length of it with the binoculars. There were no walkers at all and certainly no Kes. This was worrying. Losing him on the outskirts of a village was one thing, but a big city was something else. Still, he'd coped well last time.

I hurried through the bustling suburbs to the town centre, found the tourist office and got a map with the refuge marked on it. It was on the other side of town, near the bull-ring. The refuge turned out to be a large college, set in extensive grounds. Claudio was there, and two of the girls from Barcelona we had met in Castrojeriz; Cristina and Marta (with the deep brown eyes); also Eugenio, the guy with the nervous twitch; but not Kes. The place was being run by young Christian volunteers, bright and eager. I told them the problem and they contacted the police. Soon patrol cars were out all over the city looking for Kes. After three more hours, I was frantic.

I paced, mind thrashing like a blender.

"I'm going out to look for him," I told Claudio.

"You won't find him. He could be anywhere in Leon."

"I know, but it will give me something to do. I'm too restless. I can't just stay here and wait."

I hurried out and wandered the streets, walking swiftly, scanning every side street. My brain was a whirr. I couldn't think. I made no attempt to decide which were the most likely places to find him. I walked randomly, turning here and there as the feeling took me, giddy with worry, obsessed. My whole mind was solely concentrated on finding him, everything else was irrelevant. I scarcely noticed the people, the traffic. I was soon utterly lost, small and smaller streets; till there, down a long, narrow vista, was Kes on a corner with two girls.

I yelled and waved like a maniac.

"KES! KES!"

As I hurried closer, I increasingly saw two young women with a child. I mean, it was Kes all right, but he was deflated. He'd lost his mettle, his crispness; he was shrunken and limp, like an old lettuce. Just this kid. He was subservient, secondary, in someone else's hands wholly. Details focused as I finally reached them. Head down, he looked ashamed, unnerved. Eyes puffy and reddened. He said nothing.

I gushed with thanks to the girls and they left. Kes and I began to walk back. He remained silent. I glanced frequently sideways at him. He looked pathetic. I felt deeply uneasy, then a painful truth broke in me like falling through rotten floorboards. I had never seen him as a child. I'd always treated him as an adult, spoken to him as such, even from before he could talk. It wasn't true that I didn't want Kes on this trip. It had never been true. I needed him, always had. Something in me wanted a pal. Something in Kes had responded to that. Part of his eagerness to be here was to supply what he felt I wanted. I didn't let him drink and smoke out of some laudable desire to avoid hypocrisy; it made him appear more adult, more of a companion. I'd always treated him as an adult to train him up to be the friend I needed; and that was why he was so precocious and apparently mature. He'd had nine years of constant reinforcement by my attention and approval.

Back at the refuge, which took some time to find, Claudio greeted Kes warmly, and hugged him. Kes grimaced at first, then smiled awkwardly. Cristina and Marta made a fuss of him. Eugenio twitched like a car's indicator.

I left him in these good hands and took a shower. Hot water! The luxury of it. I couldn't remember the last time.

Afterwards, I suggested a celebratory meal out, and Kes brightened.

Towards the centre of town we found a restaurant on a corner. Next door was a ladies underwear shop. Half a shop really, long and narrow, like a rectilinear grotto. Right at the back sat, silent and immobile, like some oriental idol, a short, fat chap with a vacant face and sloping shoulders. He looked as if he had shovelled food in trying to fill some inner emptiness and remained hollow; he was soberly dressed in a cheap, grey suit and a plain yellow tie. All around, and suspended above him, were festooned an array of knickers, hanging as in Mother Shipton's cave.

We went in to the empty restaurant next door and sat down. Cheerful red chintz tablecloths. Small wicker baskets on the tables.

The cook appeared in the kitchen doorway; a thin, dishevelled man with a thick, ill-cut, black beard. He leered at us like some madman out of Dostoevsky.

"I have something for you, special, very special, for you."

He turned, walked into the door-jamb, reversed, tried again, and fell through the door into the kitchen. He was totally drunk.

Kes grinned and relaxed a little. I took the opportunity to tell him my story about what had happened on the road into Leon. He told me his story. Instead of going straight on down the slip-road into the town centre, he had kept to the by-pass, curving around the city. Only when he realised that the road was leaving Leon behind did he become convinced of his mistake. Then he turned back and took the first turning into Leon. So he arrived in a different part of town to me. Leon is big, it was unlikely that passing strangers would know where the pilgrims' refuge was, but he asked around anyway. They didn't know.

He kept his head, wandered about awhile in the forlorn hope of bumping into me, then headed for the nearest church. A service was about to begin. He went up to an old woman and tried to explain. She didn't understand, though it was obvious he was distressed. He burst into tears. After some debate, the congregation threw him out. The service had been delayed. They had to get on with worshipping God.

Still disturbed, he stood on a street corner and wept.

A small crowd gathered, concerned, but he was too upset to find a way to communicate. A delegation was dispatched to find two local girls known to speak English. When they arrived, they were kind and sympathetic and decided to take him to the police station. They were on their way when I spotted them.

The Chef de Leon reappeared with two plates. With impressive concentration, he negotiated the flat space to our table with startling and awkward speed, as if juggling with chain-saws. He crashed down the plates and beamed like an imbecile. He had a sort of brittle gaiety, as if he had got drunk in reaction to some appalling trauma, and the alcohol had fuzzed the pain, made him into a tatty and torn rag doll. His grin was desperate.

His speciality, his gift to us, was prawns in some sort of sauce and not bad. We theatrically mimed excellence and he scuttled off like some wounded puppet.

He returned half an hour later to take our main order.

"I'll have the lamb Salamanca," I said.

He rattled off a great deal of Spanish in revolutionary fervour.

I looked blankly at him.

"It's me," he said.

I looked blankly at him.

"It's of me," he said, "my own creation."

Teeth appeared in his beard.

"What you having, Kes?"

"Chips," said Kes, with resolution "and lemon ice-cream."

I translated for Raskolnikov.

Teeth disappeared into the beard.

He lurched back to the galley.

When my lamb appeared, it turned out to be breast of lamb swimming in a sea of grease. I don't know about Salamanca, it was more like Bert's Caff, Slough.

"How's your chips, Kes?"

He was dipping them in the ice-cream.

"Great, really good."

"That's nice."

I ate half of my drowning lamb and retired hurt.

Outside, we passed once more the shop of the Knicker Man. It was late. In Spain the shops stay open very late, nevertheless all the other shops nearby were shut; but not the Knicker Man. He hadn't moved, delicately held in a skimpy trap like a fat fly in a web.

"It's handy really," said Kes laconically, "just in case someone realises, late, that they've forgotten their underwear, out they can come for a quick knicker."

"You're right. It's a public service."

The Knicker Man of Leon looked despairingly melancholic, as if the knickers were a constant, distressing reminder of past conquests. No new trophies would ever be added now. He stared sadly, blank-eyed, into a fading memory.

Chapter 25

Leon

The following day we took a rest day. I slept late and woke to a dormitory empty except for Kes. There was a small table in the corner of the room beneath a window streaming sun. After coffee, I sat by it to write.

About mid-morning Kes stirred, I furnished him with his Mars bar and returned to my work. After a while he chatted, through chunks of masticated chocolate and stuff.

"What are you doing, Dad?"

"Writing my diary," trying to put him off and get on with it.

"What are you writing?"

"About Oedipus."

"What's that?"

"It's an ancient Greek name. It means 'swollen foot'."

It was obvious that he wasn't going to shut up. I turned to him.

"Would you like to hear the Riddle of Oedipus?"

"OK."

"The Sphinx asked this riddle of Oedipus. If he failed to answer it correctly, she was going to kill him. Throw him off a cliff. Many had already tried and failed and been killed."

He was plainly intrigued. He liked a touch of the gruesome.

"What's the riddle?"

"What is it that walks on four legs at dawn, two legs at mid-day, and three legs at dusk?"

"Octopus?"

"No."

He thought for a while.

"Did Oedipus get it right?"

"No. Well, he nearly got it right. Right enough for the Sphinx to throw herself off the cliff."

"Tough shit," said Kes, impressed. "What was his answer?"

"He said, 'Humanity', people."

"Why?"

"Babies crawl on all fours at the dawn of their life. We walk on our own two legs mid-way through life. Then, when we're old, we need a third leg, a stick, to get along."

"That's neat," he said.

Just then a middle-aged woman popped her head round the door.

"You English?" she asked.

"'Fraid so." I replied.

"Me too," she announced brightly.

But I could have guessed. She could have stepped straight out of the Lake District. A small, tidy woman in full hiking gear, including the same make of walking boots as mine. She looked dapper; corn-flakes and pure orange juice every morning without fail.

She felt like another species. I didn't know what to say to her. We swapped the usual information about starting point and distance per day.

"Good refuge this" I said desperately, in a silence.

"Oh, I'm not staying here. I'm in a hotel. I'm just visiting some friends I met on the Way. They said there were some English here. I always stay in hotels."

"I like the refuges," said Kes, plainly irritated.

"Me too," I confirmed, thinking of San Bollo "they're closer to the potter's thumb."

She visibly did not like the idea of anyone's thumb coming in her direction.

"Any sickness?" I asked, thinking of this neat little body going through the trials of the Meseta.

"No, I've kept away from the water, of course, and we took a train over that bit in the middle where it's hard to get bottled water."

I couldn't believe it.

"You've drunk bottled water all the way from France?"

"Yes, of course. Well, must be off. Lots to see in Leon. Good luck," she said cheerily, and was gone.

Kes and I looked at each other.

"She'll walk all the way and miss everything," said Kes.

"Everything that matters. You have to rough it. Give the place a chance to get to you."

"Washing is unhealthy."

"I wouldn't go as far as that."

"What we doing today?" asked Kes.

"Seeing the sights. Collecting letters."

"Letters first," he stated firmly.

"OK. I'll find Claudio and ask him to give us a hand."

I remembered the trouble I'd had getting our letters in Burgos. A native speaker would ease the problem. I found him in another room, also writing in his diary.

"Hi, Claudio, I'm just going for letters. Do you think you could come and give us a hand?"

"No," he said curtly, "I won't do that."

This was a surprise. He had always gone out of his way to be helpful.

"Right," I said, puzzled, "do you know where the main post office is in Leon."

"Yes," he replied brusquely.

I took out my sketch-map of Leon.

"Do you think you could mark it on this map, then?"

"No, I won't do that."

"Just mark the part of town it's in then?"

"No."

I couldn't make it out and left in a rage.

"Come on, Kes, let's go and get these letters."

"What's wrong?"

But I'd already rushed out and he scurried after me.

I charged along raving, railing at Claudio.

"He knows how important letters are to us. He could have made an effort."

"Calm down, Dad."

But I didn't. I hardly heard him I was so annoyed. I went on and on, words and motion with one cause, walking as a function of my anger, not looking where I was going, up here down there, fuming all the while. We had walked quite a way by the time the passion had burnt itself out. I sat down on a bench at the edge of a public park.

"Well, I suppose we'd better start looking for this damn post-office."

"What's the Spanish for 'post-office'?" Kes asked.

"Correos."

"Is that it over there?"

It was. With my mind blanked out with fury, I'd walked straight there.

Finding Kes, finding the post office, something was happening to my intuition.

We collected our letters with no trouble.

****

The sights of Leon got forgotten in the luxury of sitting about, reading letters, resting. I was laying on my bed (a real bed, the last before Santiago according to Claudio) completing my notes on Oedipus, when I glanced up to see Kes inspecting his boxer-shorts, holding them up before his face as if his fingers were pegs. A handsome garment, white, with numerous depictions of rampant, bilious green tortoises in the act of mating. Suddenly, and sharply, he crumpled the shorts and threw them in his own face. Then he did it again.

"Er, Kes?"

"Yes, Dad?" he replied, continuing to throw his underwear in his face.

"I hate to intrude on a man's private habits, but, if you wouldn't mind, I'd quite like to know what you're doing."

"Practising."

"Practising?"

"It's all in the preparation, you said."

"Practising for what, exactly?"

"All those girls throwing knickers at me when I'm a rock star."

"Oh, I see. Well, keep up the good work, Kes."

"I will, Dad," said a muffled voice beneath a pair of lurid boxer-shorts.

****

We never did get to see the sights. Monuments got forgotten. They hung in the air of the refuge like the threat of an onerous, unnecessary work. Weren't we in Leon? And didn't Leon have a wonderful cathedral and all sorts of other delights which must be seen? They were here and so were we. So they ought to be witnessed. We didn't bother. I'll see the cathedral when I have need of it.

The letters were very welcome. My mother told me the time of my birth, which I conveyed to Claudio for my horoscope. My wife said she was wearing one of my shirts as a night-dress, for company. Sweet.

It was a joy to get letters, contact with the Old World, but I'd crossed some inner Atlantic, so the mundane life they talked about compared oddly with the vivid presence of the Camino. Here be dragons. Learning family news was like visiting a moribund museum full of relics taken out of the stream of life, pedantically labelled, and isolated in glass cases. Was this trivia really part of my life? It read like someone else's history. There was something musty about them.

At home I had lost that direct knowledge of just how strange the world is; how weird it is to look at a tree, be conscious, have a thought, a feeling. In Spain slowly, imperceptibly, we had become casual as cats and sharp as panthers. I had taken up my bed and walked.

I packed away my letters wondering what I could say in reply.

Kes had left his diary open on his bed. It contained just one item for Leon; it said, "Dad and his big nose."

****

By the next morning we were quite eager to be on our way. We felt competent, we were doing it; 300 miles down, 200 to go.

The bustle of the town clattered on around us, alien as a gannet colony. We walked through the crowds, no part of this city, a little proud, into the Western suburbs and imperceptibly out of Leon and into Virgen del Camino, a village swallowed by the town.

We took a break at a home-made bar which lay back from the road. Everything about it was hand-made as if by adult children as a hide-away. It was built of irregular stone blocks with two blank, glassless windows like black-boards; the seats outside were tree stumps or fat logs; heavy shade was further cooled inside by the stone walls. Behind the stone slab of the bar was a woman, stunningly beautiful; high cheek-bones, long and silky dark hair, soft and sensuous brown eyes, a buxom figure in a low-cut dress with an abundant skirt. She was wholesome as strawberry, like someone out of a Spanish 'Oklahoma', and full and fine as a peony. Her smile could melt ice-cubes. I felt just like a lump of sugar looks when it has coffee poured over it. She stood behind the bar leaning slightly forward, her arms straight, hands turned outwards like feline paws. She surveyed me from above, proud, like a cat in a window. She took all my words away. I retreated with my beer outside.

" I'm ill, Claudio."

"What sort of ill?"

"A visitation from Aphrodite," I replied, gesturing at the bar.

"I see. Perhaps this is the time for your Sentence."

"What sentence?"

"Your beautiful brown eyes fill me with desire & passion. You remember it?"

"Oh, yes. Yes, of course. Let me see. Tus hermosos ojos negros me llenan de deseo y passion."

"Excellente!"

"But first I need another beer."

After four bottles of San Miguel, I ventured back inside, only to be smitten dumb and rendered as awkward and clumsy as an arthritic hippo. I blundered back into the sun. Claudio was embracing one of the girls he had met in Puente la Reina who had just now caught us up. She flopped down gracelessly and was introduced: Ibai, (pronounced eebye, as in 'eebye gum' in Lancashire) a Basque girl in her twenties, short and thin, with a weasel face and the character of a farm cat, wily and self-indulgent. She smiled a small, tight smile like a malicious traffic warden. I disliked her instantly.

I couldn't find the courage to enter once more the dark sanctuary of the holy bar.

We joined the traffic, plodded on down the busy N120; then crossed a clover-leaf intersection with a motor-way, cancelled into lower forms of life, like badgers, by the lethal, inhuman terrain. You could cut through the hot air with a machete.

From then on road and more road and a series of strip villages skewered by the road; one of the dullest sections on the whole route with only a dusty roadside path for occasional relief. At Valdeverde we caught up one Allison from Bury St.Edmunds. She was walking extremely slowly, weighed down by a pack fit to trek the Himalayas. It was plainly new and unadjusted, leaning away from her back at forty-five degrees. She lurched along like a ham-strung giraffe.

We sat on the patio of a bar, elevated above the road, roaring with traffic, for a drink.

"That's one hell of a pack you've got there," I said.

"I think I may have brought too much," she confessed.

"Everyone does that. Absolute minimum, that's the rule."

She looked at the pack, propped up on a chair, like a lumpish, inert enemy.

"What have you got that you can dump? You won't make it like that. Where did you start?"

"Leon."

"And already in difficulties. There must be something in there you don't need."

"Well, maybe the hair-drier."

"The what! You're planning to carry a hair-drier for 200 miles!"

"Well, if you put it like that. Seemed a good idea in England," she mused ruefully, "and perhaps the evening wear could go."

"Evening dresses? Plural?"

"You never know who you might meet," she affirmed pettishly.

"Parcel them up and send them home by the next post-office."

"I suppose you're right."

I fixed her rucksack, tightening the straps and pulling the bag closer to her back. We left her to choose her lunch.

Nothing much down the road except the bars so we went in the one in the next village, the Sol de Leon. Tiled floor, chrome and glass everywhere and a draught lager pump like a ceramic samovar. Behind the bar were English pint mugs, dimpled, with a handle.

"I must have one of those."

"Me too," said Kes.

But, filled with icy, and strong, Spanish lager, they drowned nostalgia rather than awoke it. I had three nonetheless, Kes two.

More weary road, dullness upon dullness. How could anyone live here? We focused on tiny details of roadside plants, piles of rubbish, anything. But soon the mind went into defrag.

What is important about the long, dull stretches is that here the ego cannot get its own way. Its plans and stratagems are cancelled. For a while it writhes in frustration; then it replots the future to fit its purpose; then it broods on the recent past and then the distant past and rewrites to suit; eventually it gives up and lays it down to rest; then, as nature seeps in and gets to work, the interesting inner revisions take place. Interfering rationality is stunned out of commission; the mind chunters away on its own business.

Beer was expensive in the Bar Los Picos in San Martin, a one moped village. On enquiry among the locals, Claudio discovered that mine host added fifty percent for strangers.

Thereafter, only periodic drainage ditches and canals relieved the monotony. In them swirled and bubbled green liquid like sap. They paralleled the dirt path and sometimes crossed it to run under the road like arteries, out to fields of alfalfa and succulent, tall, sea-green maize.

Here Kes gave up.

He had wandered into the squelchy, over-irrigated fields, humid and sweltering like a diminutive jungle, sat down on a fat tussock of grass in the open sun, and announced that he would go not a step further.

"I've had enough. I can't walk any more. I've been meaning to tell you for ages. I don't like walking."

"But you can't give up here. We can talk about it in the next village."

He sat coiled up in himself; sullen, silent and resistant, like some mollusc.

"Come on, Kes, we're well over half way. All those miles for nothing. Knowing you decided to fail will do you no good at all. It will have repercussions for years. Come on. It can only be about 200 miles to go."

He ignored me.

Claudio was sitting in the poor shade of what looked like an elderberry bush at the edge of the field. I stumbled over to him. Ibai had stripped completely to the waist and was lying, face down, in the sun nearby.

"What are we going to do? He won't walk."

"Have some coffee," he said calmly, unpacking his stove, "wait."

"This is terrible," I said hopelessly. The bottom had suddenly fallen out of my world. There was only the walking, the one stability.

I began to cry.

"Do you know what plant this is?" asked Claudio, pointing to something like an tall, over-active young cabbage with wrinkled, spear-head leaves.

"No," I said, in a wavering voice.

"Mandragora."

"Mandrake!"

"It is important for witches."

I looked around at this soggy morass of a field with its bone-dry edges. There were hundreds of mandrakes.

My voice faltered.

"Witches. Is that why this is happening?"

"No."

He passed me my coffee.

"This is happening because you are both drunk."

I mentally counted up all the beer so far today. It was true. I sighed and sat down heavily where I stood, unbuckled my rucksack and it let flop down behind me. I took my coffee, humbly.

Kes stewed, red faced, in the damp heat. He had taken some lemons from his rucksack and was morosely chewing the bitter flesh.

Eventually, I took out my other shirt and tried to sew on a missing button. It was as if I were wearing industrial gloves. It took a dozen attempts to thread the needle. I placed the button where it should be and stabbed at it from the other side of the cloth, trying to find a hole.

Claudio was much amused.

"You are a Virgo. Use your reason. There is another way."

Damned busybody. He had to always be right.

Eventually, Kes came over quietly and sat with us. Accepted some coffee. Ibai turned her head and leered at me, lasciviously.

There was no more talk of giving up.

Chapter 26

Coping with Others

The next town, Hospital de Orbigo is mostly bridge. More like a causeway, it goes on and on, cobbled, ancient, one wagon wide, it spans the flood plain of the Rio Orbigo. Something of a resort; from the elevation of the bridge we watched families sitting on the beach of the river, picnicking; splayed bodies, glistening with oil, searing like burgers; fat mums in tight shorts licking ice-cream; swarthy dads holding their bellies in, looking at girls in bikinis; kids squealing for whatever it was they hadn't got; queues at vans buying trash; people in the river with bars of soap, lathering themselves; a babble of noise.

We descended to the beach and a large bar like a bus station, crowded with people. It was raucous. Several hundred unsatisfied lives were erupting in noisy spleen. Raw faced, sun-burnt people with harsh voices shouted at whining kids, then slapped them. Some sat in over-heated sullenness, simmering a row. Everywhere were testy people without will; animate, irritated puppets. We picked our way by push-chairs and bulging plastic bags, over a floor littered with cigarette papers, tissues and toothpicks, and slewed with beer and spit.

While Claudio consulted the sweaty, over-worked and harassed bar-staff, we sat in a corner at a table covered with glasses half-full of stagnant beer. It was like sitting amid a road-works with pneumatic drills going full-pelt.

"Do we have to stay here," I shouted over the hubbub when he returned.

"The mayor owns the bar. The refuge also. We wait for the key. He is coming."

We waited an hour, getting drained by the chaotic energy all around. Claudio, apparently immune, wrote up his diary.

The key arrived and we trooped out with relief, then through endless campsites and caravan parks; people playing football, putting up tents, frying sausages; kids two-handedly struggling with huge plastic containers of water, dragging them along the ground; radios battled for the very air; until, leaving all this behind us, we reached a brick bungalow which was the refuge.

"Don't drink the tap water, it's bad," said Claudio.

We explored our home like newly weds in their first house. We had the place to ourselves. There were bedrooms with lumpy mattresses; a kitchen with much gritty, black wrought-iron; a living-room with some torn armchairs and an open grate full of burnt paper. An oasis of peace. It was wonderful.

Ibai dumped her gear in a room and sat on the shady veranda and meditated, the erect nipples of her flat breasts sticking into her T-shirt like crab's eyes, her mouth in a sexy smirk. I sat in the shade by the door, on a park-bench, like a maharajah at a railway station.

Eugenio arrived, limping badly, but twitching with pleasure to see us, like some malfunctioning clockwork toy. He'd strained some thigh muscles. I gave him an ankle pill.

By late evening it grew chilly. I gathered wood from around the house, and Kes and Claudio lit a fire in the grate. Idling on the veranda, having a smoke, I saw a meteor and marvelled at the clarity of the Milky Way; stars thickly strewn like the lights of a thoroughfare for galactic beings, a gash in space. I took a stroll down by the river along its sandy soil. The day-trippers had all departed leaving testimony of empty bottles and cigarette ends, and abandoning the bridge to the sky and the still night. Silent and secret it stood in the cold light.

I walked to the middle of the bridge, over the knobbly cobbles like solid, reptilian eggs, stood and smoked a cigarette in the midst of the quiet night, watched the beautiful, unfolding, dynamic curls of evanescent smoke, and mused.

Historically, this bridge is supposed to have had some mad knight, Suero de Quiñones, who wore an iron fetter around his neck to show his love for his Lady, but only on Thursdays. He jousted with a woman's blouse over his armour and challenged all who approached to mortal combat.

Bridges are dangerous places where the mind may go a bit peculiar and death may strike.

In medieval accounts of the Way bridges take a prominent place, especially one known as the Bridge which Trembles; obviously some fearful symbolic crossing. Bridges are narrow, there is a focusing. Wherever they appear bridges link worlds, of course. Shaped like half a vesica, they act like metaphors joining the disparate. A bridge is an incarnate leap, a frozen trajectory; a state of mind between. All forms of the Bridge are themselves empathetically connected: the arc, the ladder, the pass, the strait, the tunnel, the rainbow. Boats are bridges. All avatars of Hermes, God of translation, bringer of ideas. All resonant symbols are bridges. The whole walk is a bridge in a sense. The Camino is a long narrow way to enlightenment; a yellow-brick road, a snake to travel down, a dragon. A pilgrim is swallowed by the whale.

The Milky Way is the night's rainbow.

****

That night I dreamt of crushing strawberries over the breasts of a beautiful woman and licking off the fruit.

I woke to the sight of Ibai packing. It didn't take long. She had none of the practical objects necessary; no soap or towel, no toothpaste or toothbrush or shampoo, no knife, fork or spoon, no food, no water-bottle, no cup, no maps. She walked in an old pair of plimsolls with no socks. The rucksack was three-quarters full of knickers. No bras.

She embarked on an elaborate series of neck exercises, then gave herself a vigorous massage culminating in slapping herself on her skinny back.

Amazingly, Kes was not only up but washing. The massive sink in the kitchen had no plug. Kes had solved the problem by climbing onto the draining board and sticking his heel in the plug-hole.

"Morning, Dad," he said, splashing himself with cold water.

Extraordinary. Clearly, Orbigo was not only the place of the body, but powerfully so. A place called 'Hospital' must always have cared for the tired and torn bodies of pilgrims.

Outside, the morning was girding itself up to fry the day's tourists. Ibai had lain out on the brown grass to sunbathe. She had stripped to her knickers and rolled them down to reveal the absolute maximum of flesh. Even in my deprived state (some sheep and goats were beginning to seem attractively coy) this was not a pretty sight. She looked like a gutted herring.

We left in a group, passing campers playing tennis. Eugenio was free of muscle troubles and raving about my ankle pills. He went off to find a doctor to demand some of his own. Claudio disappeared to return the key.

We queued at the public fountain in the centre of town to fill our water bottles. Nearby a street vendor sold live young chicks from a cardboard box. They had been dyed vivid green, butter yellow and reddish purple. They skittered about like toys, drawing an appreciative crowd.

Nearby, an ice-cream van sported a map of the world which divided the planet up into flavours of ice-cream.

"Not much strawberry," remarked Kes.

"Too right," I replied.

Kes bought his favourite; Frigo Dedo, Ice Finger, a lurid pink ice-lolly in the shape of a hand. He sucked on it like some epicure cannibal.

A short track with deposits of rubbish like spoor; packages and plastic bottles, a rusty lock and a key which didn't fit, a scorched one-eyed doll, singed and maimed; then road, road and more road, stretching out from Orbigo like an asphalt nerve. Heavy traffic. The town was a single organism, people served it like corpuscles and bacteria, rushing down the roads like the water in the canals.

Ibai stuck to Claudio like a terrier, endlessly yapping. They pounded on ahead.

Kes and I made up new verses to well-known songs and taught Eugenio a modified chorus. Soon he was happily bawling:

"Wank tiddley-Daddy-O

There's whiskey in the jar."

After too many dreary miles we turned off the road into some thyme-strewn scrub and followed a line of crosses.

As we trudged down the path, a cheery voice called from some poor shade off to the side. Claudio waved, Ibai squatted by his side. She was naked to the waist and rubbing herself with a cucumber.

"Just in time for some food," said Claudio.

Claudio was mixing something in a plastic bowl. He showed it to me.

"Delicious. Want some?"

"What is it, Claudio?"

"Apple and cucumber."

"Not for me, thanks."

"Yum," enthused Claudio, sampling it, "Want some, Kes?"

"No thanks."

I could see from Kes' eyes that we were thinking likewise. I was wondering about the cucumber, and its previous intimate relationships.

Pasty green knickers soon appeared. Her painfully white flesh was slightly translucent, like a fish, or an abscess. Kes and I politely took our leave.

We climbed a desiccated slope to a climactic granite cross and an escarpment overlooking a far plain with, in its midst, all of Astorga on a hill. A twin-towered cathedral squatted on it like a fat dog with its ears pricked.

The first bar on the edge of Astorga was like a working-men's club; plain, with four-square wooden tables and chairs. All male; old men in black berets, and the unemployed, vociferously played cards and dominoes. The T.V. programme, a dubbed American film, was interrupted to announce the death of a famous bullfighter. He'd been gored. There was sudden uproar. The games were abandoned. Everyone stood and gesticulated and argued. The fatal accident was shown in replay. Then again, in close-up, in slow-motion; the sleek horn going in just above the thigh and up into the guts. Hoisted by the spike in his bowel and already dying, the sleek-haired corpse in its flashy suit of lights was tossed aside like a doll. Helpers with plush blue capes rushed to his side. There was blood on the sand.

The visceral aura of Orbigo reached to here.

We walked quietly on down the Calle del Perpetuo Socorro (the street of unending succour) and steeply ascended to the wall of the Hospital de las Cinco Llagas (the five wounds). It had obviously been almost destroyed by fire recently.

In town, I left Kes in a bar with the bags while I went to find some meths for the stove. I was directed to a chemist. The pharmacist was a gaunt, bearded man with a ravaged face, pits and gullies as if eroded by flash-floods of caustic tears.

"Alcohol de quemar?" I asked.

His empty eyes stared as if at some ghoul. I tried again. He looked puzzled, so I did a complete mime of cooking on the trail. I unpacked an invisible stove, set it up, got out the meths bottle, holding it up and pointing at it for emphasis, lit the burner, magicked up a frying pan and shimmied away, cooking imaginary sausages. A pretty convincing performance, I thought. He was obviously impressed. I picked up my non-existent meths and waved it at him. He smiled a tragic smile and popped out the back. He returned with a small box like those used to hold smart fountain pens. Surely this couldn't be right. He opened the box and displayed its contents. It was a hypodermic syringe.

"No, no," I said emphatically, and I wrote out the Spanish words.

Unperturbed, he fetched my meths.

The refuge was on the other side of town, on the outskirts. A large, residential school for the disabled run by two Dutch brothers. One of them was tootling around by the entrance on a bicycle, waiting to greet pilgrims. He showed us to a gymnasium. A motley of sleeping bags were already dotted about on the floor. We staked our claim.

At one end of the gym was a stage with theatrical drapes. When

Claudio and Ibai arrived they laid their sleeping bags on the stage behind the curtains. They retired early as Claudio wished to investigate the Basque language and needed to explore her transformational grammar.

I hung around in the morning waiting for Kes to awake. Claudio was up and doing my horoscope. One of my Leon letters contained the information of the time of my birth. He had found a table to sit and work at and was consulting ephemera and marking the position of planets on a chart. He sat with his back to me but I could see him shaking his head and loosely waggling his wrist in the Spanish gesture that indicated something heavy and troubling. I didn't interrupt.

Later, the four of us took a quiet country road out of town, heading straight towards scrubby mountains with orange slashes like wounds. A pair of magpies fought in a field, leaping into the air and squawking. We soon reached a hermitage called the Ermita del Ecce Homo. It looked like a cross between a Wild West saloon and a minuscule ranch-house; an amateur building of two boxes built of ill-matched stones with a simple, open belfry. The porch, like a lean-to shed, was smothered with friendly graffiti of hearts and arrows, initials and names in pairs; Pedro and Raquel, Amelia and Lucas.

At Murias de Rechivaldo we finally left the road, joining a dirt track of salmon-coloured dust through dry gorse. Soon our boots were coated with powder like stale pollen.

"Look at this thing, Dad."

In the vegetation was a preying mantis, dull green with an alabaster head and milky, evil eyes with each pupil a black dot of pure malice; exquisite, and alien enough to be from another planet. It stared at us with intense, malevolent concentration, waved its lethal, fanged arms and hissed like a snake.

"Now that's all weird," commented Kes.

Once we got an eye for their camouflage we could spot hundreds in the bushes.

Santa Catalina was mostly stone with some wood and thatch. The main street was a dirt track like a dried out river-bed, littered with stones, flaking in the heat; the irregular stones of the simple, square-cut, two-storey houses were sandy and grey and dark, dusty red as if condensed from the earth. The place would have been eerie in its empty silence but for Ibai. She chattered like a cicada on heat. By all that's holy, she could rabbit like a cuckoo on speed. A little, wizened prune of a woman, born old, who never stopped prattling in a non-stop porridge of Spanish noise. Smitten with a virulent anger, I went and sat in the church porch to try and wrest some control.

Then we were into moorland; wild and lonely heath, sweeping hills of tough heather, gradually becoming mountains, with clumps of oak in the valleys. The villages were increasingly forlorn; decaying streets, deserted houses collapsing back into the soil, thatch holed and weedy; a dilapidation that reached a melancholy dignity like ruined monasteries. Few people here, after a while it felt as if the country had been ravaged, wiped clear by hordes of pitiless preying mantids.

Ibai gabbled on like some demented sports commentator. She must have had some Basque accent because I couldn't understand a single word. The babble spoiled the silence. Normally, as we walked, we said little. I'd grown comfortable with the peace. But Ibai went on and on. It was like suffering a high-pitched, nasal DJ with no music. After a while, Kes deliberately slowed down and walked fifty yards behind. Half an hour later, I did the same. Gradually, the unending spate ahead of us receded in step with her words until it faded into peace once more.

"That's a relief," said Kes, as she disappeared over the horizon still chattering to Claudio.

We never saw (or heard) her again.

Chapter 27

How to change your Mind

This was massive country, bleak and rugged, immense curves gashed with valleys. The landscape felt broken; as a horse might be broken, broken in spirit. Entire villages were increasingly decrepit, run down, even literally falling down, abandoned. We walked on, alone, into the stagnant silence of the burnished afternoon.

Kes suggested playing a game of inventing proverbs. Mine were pompous things in pseudo-Confucian style. The only one I recall is: 'It is instructive for a Man of Method to stumble on a petal.'
Kes' offerings were more down to earth, like:
'Red sky at night.
Barn's on fire.'
We had trouble finding decent shade. Eventually, we cleared a space in a scrappy bit of oak scrub. Not a good spot but we were tired.

"Are there any dangerous animals around here?"

"No, I don't think so, Kes. There's wolves further West," I said, sitting down, and unpacking the stove.

"Wolves!"

"Don't worry, people have gone out deliberately looking for them, for weeks, found nothing but droppings."

"Any bears?" said Kes nervously.

"No, certainly not."

"This looks like the sort of place that could have bears."

"No, bears, Kes. Aargh!"

I leapt up.

"Aargh! Shit! Aargh!"

"What is it? What is it?"

"Cleggies! Cleggies! Get out of here, Kes! Get out! Don't stop, scram!"

Kes quit fast, ran into the open heather and stood wide-eyed as I scrabbled about collecting gear, rushing out and dumping it by his feet, belting back for more.

Eventually, we sat once more in the attenuated shade of a tall tree whose shadow reached to the golden, wiry grass of safe, open space.

"What's 'cleggies'? I couldn't see anything."

"Horseflies. Lethal bastards. Fly silent, and bite you right through your clothes. Nasty bites. Damn things attacked me in droves. That patch is full of them. You get bitten?"

"No."

"Must be your socks. If you could put your socks in a bottle, you'd make a fortune."

We had trouble getting started again. This place induced a restless lethargy. The same energy which was crumbling the villages was sapping our strength. Things slowed here, and something else got to work.

It occurred to me that my irritation with Ibai was somewhat excessive, a bit irrational. She wasn't that bad, yet I had been seething. The way here fuelled a simmering discontent.

On the road a tall, upright, vigorous-looking man in his sixties shuffled along barely moving, he swayed along with blank eyes and a beaming face.

"What's he on?" asked Kes.

"Mountains," I replied.

In the warm late afternoon the sun glared with a rusty mantid eye in a bruised violet sky. It had a predatory presence like mosquitoes, or a mesmerising snake awaiting its chance.

According to the map there was a 'mina roma', a Roman mine, in the mountains to our right. Only 700 metres off the route, but we were too tired to bother.

We reached the next village, Rabanal, by early evening. Even as we approached, it was obvious that this place was different, very different. Just another in the sequence of run-down villages by the look of it, but its feel was exceedingly odd and nothing like any of the others. At first I merely felt uneasy. Then the vulnerable sense of being watched. Then a whiff of paranoia, a sense of slippage. Of course, I'm stepping over a gully in the middle of this dirt street but it looks like a miniature landscape, a rivulet, tiny waterfalls trickling over white rocks, grass on its banks. These silent houses looking on are not places to live in, they feel commemorative like inscriptions, or inscrutable warnings. It's very odd to look at a door, see plainly that it is undoubtedly a 'door', and to know that the term 'door' is wrong. This whole place felt like that. It was profoundly not what it seemed. There was an experience of confrontation without knowing what it was that was being confronted; a face to face encounter with something completely other, something organised on different principles.

We toiled up its main street, scarcely more than an alleyway with a stream, which served as a sewer, snaking down its centre. The ramshackle streets were empty of people but full of this sense of displacement.

Imagine a small toy truck with a real twig as its load. The twig looks like a massive log seen on the scale of the model, and it looks like something made, fashioned, as the truck is; but it's natural and just this little twig. The mind becomes indecisive, doesn't know what to make of it. Rabanal was imbued with this feel of the ambiguous; a toy, a model, a façade.

I scanned the few side-streets nervously. It was an error to assume that a house was in the same category as the one next to it. It felt as if we were straying into territory which required special knowledge which we did not have, like walking, uninvited and unexpectedly, through a deserted nuclear power station, not knowing what it was. We were trespassers here, ignorant of its functioning, incompetent. It made me feel restless; a stranger in someone else's world.

By the time we had reached its earthen central space, splattered with cow-pats and goat dung, the feeling was overwhelming. It was as if I'd wandered into a film set; the ordinary world was somewhere else. This place was old; medieval, no, older. So old it needed to be conceived otherwise. It was like walking into a pre-historic settlement where everything was ordinary yet had some function that couldn't be fathomed. Was this a well or a sanctuary, was that a shepherd or a priest? Were all these concepts mistaken? I didn't belong here. It reeked of a pagan way of life; it had structures of thought and feeling which clashed with the way my mind worked. I felt radically challenged. There was a sense of emotional dissonance. I looked around and everything was peaceful and unremarkable yet I had no idea what I was looking at.

"What do you make of this place?" I asked Kes, as we approached a fountain.

"It ought to be a ghost town, but it's not," replied Kes.

A few locals wandered around like extras, or spies. I asked a surly young man for the refuge and he waved at a derelict building nearby.

We dumped the bags by the fountain and took a look. The refuge was a two-storied, disused school-house, originally whitewashed, but so many patches had flaked away that it looked like mould on rotting flesh. It was in a state of advanced decay. It wasn't so much falling down as decomposing. The ground had risen around it, so it was in a shallow basin as if sunk into the soil. We walked around the building and descended to the entrance. By the door-way was an external staircase with scarcely any stairs. It led up to a wooden balcony, with no floor, that looked as if it was going to fall off the building at any moment. It was precariously held up by two dangerously eroded, primitive classical columns.

Inside, through the doorway, we were greeted with a scene of invasion; nature was in process of taking back this building into itself. Humanity was being over-ruled. It was damp and smelt earthy. There was no ceiling, the upper floor was missing, only skeletal, fractured rafters high up in the roof. Most of the floor-boards beneath our feet had rotted away, leaving mouldy and splintered remains. The struts for the floor, the joists, were mostly intact showing bare ground between. More like a cave than a building; it was dissolving back into the land. The room had the fluid, transitional feel of a rotting tree-trunk, of life beneath the stone; a place of moss and wood-lice and fungi. Here unknown creatures might plant spore; stanchions might crumble with dry-rot: beetles and roaches ruled and a man needed antennae and the alien, ruby eyes of a moth to see it aright.

We fetched our gear.

The ground was too filthy for the rucksacks, so we put them on what was left of the window sill. They hung there like cocoons amid the spider's webs and cobwebs.

Another pilgrim arrived wearing a T-shirt with "Anyone can have an idea" printed on it in English. She looked around in silent disbelief, shaking her head, and went away to try and find somewhere else. No-one in their right mind would sleep here.

"Are we really going to stay here, Dad?"

"Yep."

"We'll wake up as zombies."

I knew what he meant; a place for metamorphosis, for subversive change, lower your guard and it would seep in and reformulate everything, as a maggot might become a fly. Here categories were confused, boundaries breached. Even the distinctions between artificial and natural, inside and outside, were unclear.

It was getting dark. I found a thick church candle, covered in dust, in a corner, brushed it down and lit it. It multiplied flickering, other-world shadows around the room.

I felt excessively tired. Sleep kept creeping over me, like a drug, as I brewed up some tea.

"There's creepy-crawlies wherever you look," said Kes, brushing beetles away from enough earth to put his mug down.

"Nothing that bites, that I can see. No mosquitoes. No cleggies."

"Do you think there's mice?"

"Probably."

"Rats?"

"Maybe. But if there is they won't bother us. They'll try for the food in the rucksacks on the other side of the room. But I don't think they would get anything. I'll strap the bags up tight. Don't worry, we'll be all right."

We spread our sleeping bags on the bare earth between the struts and laid down as if in shallow graves.

"Good-night, Dad."

"Good-night, Kes."

The last thing I saw, as I blew out the candle, was a large spider, a couple of inches from my face, scurrying into the shadows.

I was woken by music. It was still quite dark but there was a faint light, whether moon-light or the onset of dawn I wasn't sure. The room was grey and shapeless. The music was weird; a single drum and castanets beat in a unmatching, lopsided rhythm that continually altered. It grew close and moved away. People outside were walking through the streets playing eerie music in the middle of the night. It wasn't revellers. There were no voices, just this haunting, formless dirge sounding like the last pair of a defeated army in retreat. I heard bells and fireworks, then utter quiet.

I lay awake for some time amid the murky, unidentifiable, grey shapes of the room. Then more music started up, not moving, but steady. It sounded as if it was right outside; as if local people were playing strange music just for us. Some wind instrument now, maybe a recorder or a flute, and a single drum. I listened carefully. It went nowhere. It went on and on without pattern. It just unfurled, lonely, out of the dark silence. You got caught in it, like a web. It felt uncanny. My temples tingled.

Most music eventually reassures. It embodies the archetype of the journey, establishing a home at first, a security which allows a wandering away; there is variation and development expressing the need to get away without the total vagrancy of the dispossessed. Then it makes its way back, returns home to experience the familiar anew.

This music of Rabanal was not of that kind. It started arbitrarily, established no secure base, then it wandered on with no discernible pattern. You never knew where you were. It led you up the garden-path, up a creek without a paddle, into a musical void. Here the mind could find no order, no melody, no repetition, no bounded concepts. It was untethered and disconcerting. Although it lacked pattern, it wasn't a freeform mess but harkened towards form without finding it. It was haunting, creepy, the music of ghosts and the eerie; the music of lost souls, of minds between places, between concepts, with nowhere to go; stripped of location, direction, dimension; bereft of reference. The very air wavered with silent appeals and mute calls of the utterly exiled.

My half-asleep mind followed, lured out of itself, fascinated.

It was cold in the early morning when I awoke. Kes was still fast asleep. I went for a walk.

The air had a mountain's chill. It was dewy and pristine. A pretty young girl in a simple, one-piece black dress and no shoes drew water from the well. I smiled and she turned away shyly.

A cart drawn by oxen laboured slowly past. It was quite Biblical.

Rabanal still felt like another world, but I was no longer estranged. I'd been touched by it.

I sat on the low, mossy wall surrounding the fountain and lit a cigarette, feeling rested and at home; a quiet consummation. I'd been recognised, as if greeted by locusts.

It was obvious that here was another of the special places of the Way; one of the markers, a place which allowed a stage to be traversed.

The feel of Rabanal is quite unlike anywhere else on the Camino, indeed it is quite unlike anywhere else I know. It feels ancient; as old as rock. Its world is different, stranger, more intimate. Rabanal is akin to the mountains, spawned by them, serving as a gatehouse or portal; it is a place where the rules change. There are secrets here. It is a place for breaking; a place for dissolution. The mind's cohesion is loosened. Rabanal is Dionysian. Dionysus is the God of dismemberment. To create anew, the old order must be broken. Rabanal takes apart the sense of the safe. It unthreads composition.

Here the mind is in quicklime.

Since Orbigo I had been feeling increasingly agitated, irritated, unsettled. By Santo Catalina it had ripened into anger, a sense of threat. I'd blamed it on Ibai, but now it seemed clear that was an over-simplification; to some extent I had been anticipating the presence of Rabanal.

Enter in anger, go in peace.

****

A young woman approached, smiling, across the green. Her whole manner was welcoming. To look in her eyes was to make gentle contact, like a familiar squeeze of the hand. She introduced herself; Barbara, an anthropologist from Zurich, here to study the Camino, and especially Rabanal. She wanted a chat, to ask a few questions. It would help her research.

"Why are you walking the Way?" she began.

"That's not easy to answer. I think I'm trying to let the Camino tell me."

"And does it?"

"Yes, gradually, in bits, as much as I can take. But I'm too stupid much of the time; too fearful, too insensitive. Not worthy."

"What do you mean?" she said, in an encouraging tone.

"Well, I resist its working. The Camino is very special. It's a symbolic thing, it works symbolically. Symbols are real."

"Yes, it is very special. I have walked the way myself. But some places are more important than others."

"Yes, I've found it so."

"Which places have you found especially important?"

I didn't want to answer this. I wanted to find out if my own experiences had been confirmed by others. I countered with a question.

"Have you interviewed many people?"

"Oh, yes, hundreds."

"And what do they say are the important places?"

"The ordinary pilgrims who are here for the holiday or the sport, they talk of the big towns."

"No, they are irrelevant."

"That's what the proper pilgrims, like yourself, say. The real pilgrims speak of Puente la Reina and San Juan."

"That's right!" I said, grinning, "Eunate near Puente, San Juan and, of course, here at Rabanal."

"Yes, this is one of the secret places."

"What do the proper pilgrims say about Rabanal?"

"It isn't just Rabanal."

She waved her arm towards the hills as she continued.

"Many find the mountains here a place of tension. It is a place for rows and argument. Groups quarrel and break up."

"I have found it a place for anger," I replied ruefully.

She smiled.

"Storms are frequent here. What else?" she said, encouraging.

"The anger is an energy of transformation, I think. Does that sound pompous?"

"No, it is close to what many people say, though they more often speak of it in a negative way. They talk of a sense of death and impermanence and of being transported back in time."

"I've found that too. How can you live here and study here?"

"Oh there are many scholars here, not just me. The English are going to open a refuge which will also be a place of study."

She consulted her watch, "I'm afraid I must go now. I have an appointment."

She bestowed a smile of kinship and left.

I was immensely pleased with this little conversation. It was a confirmation. The Camino had convinced me, incrementally, that the notion of simple subjectivity was wrong; a person is a sensitive instrument in a given location. Once the debris of town life is walked off, the pilgrim is as much a recorder of the felt quality of place as a thermometer. The Way is a training in the empathetic skill, a negative capability, which is open to such things.

There is something deeply disruptive and disturbing on the road to Rabanal, and Rabanal is its epicentre; a peak of disorientation focuses on this village. I know it. It isn't just personal response. Rabanal is one of the special places on the Camino. It resonates with Eunate and San Juan. Across space, across time.

Three found, two to go.

Everyone has an intricate internal structure of concepts, propositions & theories. This structure is what we currently think we know & believe. It's what we are. When we encounter some new material, we process it using this intellectual structure. If we can do that, then we say that we understand this new matter. Sometimes we don't understand. Then we need to tinker with our comprehending structures. This may require a bit of study, research, questioning so that we can add some extension to our capacity to understand. Sometimes we have to demolish a part of what we know & rebuild to accommodate the new. Sometimes what we have to understand cannot be fitted into ourselves without transformation. The old structure is dissolved to enable a new self to form. This is what Rabanal does.

The secret places on the Camino are Way Stations that prepare & effect these changes. They must be experienced in the right order. Each must have its effect before the pilgrim is ready for the next. It would not do to tackle Rabanal unprepared by Eunate and San Juan. The time gaps between enable the preparatory consolidation ready for the next. This is why the Way has to be walked. The walkers' natural pace is needed.

The tall man in his sixties that we had seen shuffling along the road to Rabanal came limping across the square. He was obviously in pain yet his face was still blissed out. I asked him what the problem was with his legs and he told me that he had strained many muscles. I offered him an ankle pill, which he refused, saying that he didn't need help as God would provide. I flared up with annoyance. How did he expect God to provide, send an archangel? God <u>had</u> provided, sending me with an ankle pill. Silly sod. He benevolently gazed upon me with forgiving pity and went on his rapturous way.

Kes was stirring in the refuge.

"Sleep well?"

"Like the dead."

"Didn't you hear the music?"

"What music?"

"There was weird music. I had a troubled night."

"Mine was a bit troubled at first."

"Really, how were you troubled?"

"Kept dreaming of steak and kidney pie and chips."

"Pie and chips?"

"Yere, covered in salad cream."

"Naturally."

We got ready to walk on.

Chapter 28

After Rebirth

We left through the village, past the toy-like church, looking as if it had been built of stones congealed from stale blood and essence of straw. Redstarts flitted among the stunted trees in the churchyard of cobbles and scanty grass.

A short path, past more collapsing cottages, took us to a minor road which swept through immense mountains. We were emerging into space once more; massive, exhilarating space. It was difficult to believe in the constriction of Rabanal, my burial & rebirth in the refuge.

The world felt unmade here, as if it could have been otherwise. Perhaps not 'unmade' so much as in process of being made. The whole landscape had the rosy freshness of a baby's flesh; or the nascent green of new growth. The very light had mellowed, bathed us more gently. It took me a while to realise that what had changed was not the world, but me. I had been taken in by Nature as one of its own. I was the new born child I felt all around.

At a bend by the roadside water trickled through stones and weeds down a pipe into a small basin. Mystic symbols had been inscribed on the rocks. Here a broad-shouldered young man with very short hair was filling his water-bottle with the cool liquid. This was Luke, half French, half Chinese. Slanting against the fountain was the most substantial staff I had seen; six feet long, thick white wood, for combat. When I asked about it, he said it was to ward off the wild dogs of Foncebadón, the next village. He gave us a lurid account of dogs which sounded more like scarcely tamed wolves, which would attack pilgrims with ruthless ferocity and the cunning of a slavering pack. He strongly advised us to arm ourselves as best we could.

We walked on with him, stopping to search for weapons in every patch of trees. As we turned off the road to go through Foncebadón, Luke strode ahead of us, stick held horizontally in two strong hands, like a quarterstaff, ready to do battle. He looked like some belligerent friar, trained in martial arts; a French Samurai acting as our champion, a knight in shorts and T-shirt.

So he led us, like a protective escort, an advance guard, up the dirt track, dry as ancient bones, of the main and only street of Foncebadón. It was deserted and completely ramshackle as if devastated by some lethal virus which attacked its very fabric. Tilted, makeshift, wooden crosses, stuck in cairns in the middle of the track, had forlornly failed to ward off some incomprehensible plague. Long ago an unknown elemental energy had swept over the place and all but wiped it out. Not a single building remained intact. Walls had collapsed, roofs fallen in. It was the memory of a village. Only the insane could live here.

We nervously picked our way over the uneven ground, spread with the detritus of the wrecked houses. There was no sign of life of any kind, even insects had abandoned it. There was no sound. Voided of the ordinary, it was heavy with the possibilities of alternate realities. Common-sense did not apply here. We walked in awkward and tense silence.

When Luke reached the edge of the village up ahead of us, he turned to face us and waved silently, raising his staff in formal salute, turned once more and strode vigorously out into the landscape.

Beyond the village, life returned once more; insects hummed, butterflies flitted, larks rose, singing in an unending, liquid stream. The narrow path swung and curved with the contours. The road, up above to our right, was marked by striped posts like barber's poles, used to locate the route in winter and help gauge the depth of snow. We climbed at an angle up to the road and into another world. It was exceeding strange.

Here many cars were parked and their contents scuttled around like disturbed ants. The focus was a huge pyramidal cairn of stones and shards, rising high above our heads, topped by an oak pole and, ultimately, an iron cross.

The tradition is that the pilgrim carries a stone and adds it to the pile here. Symbolically, this is the place to cast off the stones in the heart that have been painfully forced out by the Camino; a place of unburthening. I threw my stone, which I had picked up in Foncebadón, on the heap

Children scurried up and down the slope. No animal is as unwarily noisy as the human child. I scrambled up over all the loose stones & surveyed the site from the top, all around there was squealing and shouting, posing for cameras, picnicking, football.

Tourists, ejected from cars without having gone through the slow acclimatisation of the walker, they suffered from a type of geographical jet lag; their spirits were still somewhere else and unaware of the feel of where they were. The town habit of avoiding contact, sustaining distance, prevailed. They remained in the groups which had travelled together, as if the packaging effect of the cars still maintained a ghostly presence.

People gauchely strutted about like ostrich in Piccadilly Circus. It was bizarre and insensitive, like unwitting sacrilege. When I nodded greeting to people we passed, they just fidgeted and looked away. We were odd, outcasts.

A man loaded three large dogs into the boot of a car, slammed it shut, and drove off.

We made our way to a plain rectangular building with overhanging eaves and rested in its shade. A family were taking it in turns to carve their initials in the wall, with hammer and chisel. They did it with exhibitionist pride, as if it were enterprising to think of bringing the tools.

A line of pilgrims on horseback arrived sedately. One rode his horse straight up the mound, scattering children like peasants. King of the castle, he stiffened his neck to be photographed. The horse shit copiously on the way down. Kids squealed with delight. As they passed us, a rider threw his cigarette on to the ground with the terse command: "Stamp on that." They were aloof, elevated above the ground and the experience, aware of their effect, their superiority. Faster than walkers, slower than cyclists, they must have travelled without meeting many others, missing the contact and the camaraderie.

A car had been left empty with all its doors open to cool the interior. A dust devil whirled fiercely around it, collecting all the nearby litter, blew the trash inside and slammed the doors.

Hordes of flies bothered us continually, attracted by all the picnics, I suppose. Nearby, a family had set up a barbecue and the father was frying chicken. Latin-American pop music blared from their radio.

Their reason for their being here, the Cruz de Ferro, the cross of iron, stood ignored in the background. It was a symbol of unity, of spiritual integration: a phallic pole in a mound of joy. A place to humbly cast off the stony hindrances within. Now reduced to something to play on, or to use to show off, to provide a background to a photo. This icon of sacred and holy union had become an excuse for an outing, a backdrop for beef burgers.

It felt callous and shocking, like Goths larking about in a sacred grove, or Vandals joking and pissing in a chapel.

"Same old monkeys in the shadows," I said.

"What?"

"Oh, nothing. Let's get out of here, Kes."

"Yere. I was thinking further back that it would be good to find someone to play with, but these are just kids."

"What do you mean?"

"They are kept as kids by their parents."

"We don't fit in here."

"No, let's go."

Four hundred yards from the last car, we were alone once more. The motorists strayed no further as if joined to their vehicles by umbilical chord. The car is a marker, a pod of the known, a link to home, a mobile room. Each group were invisibly tethered to its car, like donkeys.

Just a couple of kilometres to the next village; Manjarin, a strip village with the road running through the centre the only street. At first it looked like just another of the series of defunct places. Fewer houses were actually in ruins, but many were dishevelled and some were boarded up. We made for the fountain marked on the map, down an alleyway through the houses. It was like going through a façade. Here was a grassy platform with an extensive view over the dormant mountains. The fountain was a spring protected by a small stone hut like a kennel, with a slate roof, a shrine to water. The spring trickled into a stone box set into the ground. I sat and stared into its crystal-clear water. It was magical, a whole world peaceful and still, a fairy grotto. Lime-green spiky plants made a delicate, sub-marine forest in which reclined two exotic salamanders, immobile, glistening crimson and black. The incoming water fluttered with a gentle, fairy-bell tinkle while the inner walls flickered in consort with a lambent, dancing, watery light. Wasps flitted back and forth, sipping at its edge by my hand. Linnets came to drink at the narrow stream flowing away at my feet. The view beyond stretched gigantic in curving immensities of misty green mountains and soft, blue sky. I sat content at the bottom of my huge pool of translucent air.

"Can we move on soon, Dad?"

"In a while, Kes, I like it here."

"We've been here over an hour."

"You're joking!"

"No, that man having the picnic has a watch."

The man rose, smiled a greeting, and went to the water and bowed to drink, like a homage.

Soon we were traversing a roller-coaster dirt track over the backs of vast mountains. Walking amid mountains is not like just covering distance in an impressive setting. Mountains have presence. They feel alive, resting. Beneath our feet was unimaginable energy locked up in matter. You could feel it, prodigious and august, venerable and potent. I felt respect. There was a need to be wary of the empathetic sense; to be fully aware of all that power would blow all the mind's fuses at once. We were in the mountains, not on them. Thunder rumbled ominously in the far distance.

I paused to jot in my diary some notes of what it was like to be honoured with being here, as if in the infinite throne room of an elemental royalty.

Kes caught me up, paused, and gazed out into the titanic landscape.

"Looks like sleeping dinosaurs," he said.

"Bigger than that," I said, writing.

"Whales then."

"Bigger than that."

"What's bigger than a whale?"

"A God."

He surveyed the landscape, head slightly tilted, assessing his feelings.

"Mountains feel like stars."

"How do you mean?"

"Big and strange, and here and far away at the same time."

There was an expectancy in the very air; like a huge, crowded concert hall silently awaiting imminent music.

We took a break more out of reverence than need. As I sat, assembling the stove, a huge bush cricket leapt onto my knee and sat there unconcerned like an exquisite gem for the priestess of a lost, pagan religion. It was a slick and vibrant emerald with curving, delicate antennae swept back beyond its body over a fearsome ovipositor rearing like a rhino's horn.

"This world is so weird," said Kes.

"Sure is."

"Does it bite?"

"No. Well, it might give you a nip, I suppose. I'm not sure."

It chirruped like a bird.

"This one seems pretty friendly, though."

She walked off as if on stilts.

Soon we walked off too, over a great belly of earth, around stupendous breasts, eventually along a mighty spur like a colossal arm, before going over the knuckles of a precipitous descent towards the village of Acebo, whose slated roofs lay in the landscape below like some plated reptile. The main street was like one long farmyard with gaunt, grey buildings like rocky outcrops irregularly jutting with precarious wooden balconies. We enquired for a bar but there wasn't one, so the man we had asked brought us ice-cold beer, and sandwiches of English ham, from his house. We sat in the dust watching chickens scrabbling about in the dirt. They had nodules of their own shit stuck onto their legs like spurs.

Beyond Riego we entered an enchanted valley. The path twisted and turned, rose and fell between noble stands of sweet chestnut, like elders in the mountain's antechamber. Late afternoon sun invested the air with a rich, luminous miasma of amber. Here was a lifetime's delightful work for an entourage of court painters.

Then a narrow, rock-strewn, winding path embracing rounded bluffs before descending to the ancient and picturesque bridge of Molinaseca. The refuge was an old school set back from the main road. We were warmly greeted by the two Catalan girls from Barcelona, Cristina and Marta, we had met in Leon, plus Eugenio, still twitching.

That evening , the five of us dined out. Kes amused the girls by teaching them how to speak Essex:

"Yer well arht of order, bitch. Yer doin me ed in, big time. Ooze this right gnarly geezer? Ees abit of a nightmare, well sad. I'm totally narked off, genna chip orff dahn the pub and chill arht. Gotta git mellow n' sorted. End of."

That sort of thing.

Eugenio sat glumly and sulked, complaining that the women spoke Catalan to each other and English to us and he was left out. He grew steadily more sour, griping continually and consoled himself by getting very drunk on Kalimotxo; a strong mixture of red wine and Coca Cola. On the way back to our schoolroom refuge, he went on and on about how 'the Cosmos' was going to cure him of all his troubles. Marta walked on ahead, clearly fed up with him. When I caught her up, I wanted to say something to take her out of her irritation. In the clear mountain air, the milky way was a revelation of cool beauty, not just a swathe but complex with swirls and eddies of exuberant, scintillating stars.

"Just look at that sky," I said, "doesn't it feel close? Imagine, all that energy, those suns, made into such beautiful peace."

The plush hot black of the sky was enriched with stars like a fortune of jewels on an immense cushion.

Suddenly my arms were full of young woman. She pecked me on the cheek, and whispered into my ear, "Thank you, Michael, thank you for that." I could feel her warm breath.

And then I was bereft of her. It was like being struck by soft lightning.

Chapter 29

Living with an Open Mind

Back at the schoolroom refuge, my mind swirled with energy through the night as if sensing the mountains all around. I dozed in a sweat. It isn't easy to have your mind opened to the powers of Nature. The same force which forges stars, and through the green fuse drives the trees, clashed at my mind like crashing waves. I could feel nature as Van Gogh paints it. Only a thin shell resisted the pressure of the mountains. To relent would be a form of suicide. No one could take that raw force; it could burst the dam of consciousness as an ocean might shatter a window. I was too scared to sleep.

At dawn I sat and wrote long, frenzied letters at the schoolmaster's desk on a dais above the sleeping bodies. Afterwards the morning dragged on. I was frazzled with lack of sleep; all my energy frittered away by the effort to keep energy out. Listless, restless, desperately needing sleep and sleepless, nothing felt worth doing, everything was too much effort. I packed like a zombie.

The Romans called these hills the Mountains of Mercury. As always, I prefer the Greek original: the Mountains of Hermes. Messenger of the Gods is the over-simplified cliché. Hermes is the God of translation; the presence which announces a contact with something not previously understood and the opportunity of reformulating the mind to comprehend. A capricious force which will upset in order to enable insight. A joker, a trickster. He doesn't convey messages, but facilitates re-writing. It isn't easy to change your mind.

Everyone else still slept soundly.

When I saw, from the wide window, people leading laden donkeys down the main street, I went out to find some normality. I found a small grocery shop in the back streets that was open and already full of housewives gossiping. My presence quenched their chatter at once. I don't know whether it was my wild eyes or their respect for the pilgrim's scallop, but they insisted that I be served first.

Back at the refuge I forced myself to wash some clothes, and drank lots of coffee.

"Do me a cup," said Kes, from the floor.

"OK. Pass your mug."

I heard a tinny clunk and a sharp cry from Kes.

He was staring into his cup. In it was a vivid green preying mantis, leering with its bloated eyes at its green prison, serrated arms raised to kill. I threw it out of the window.

"People here have great respect for pilgrims, Kes."

"Do they?"

I told him about the shop.

He sniffed.

"When did you last have a shower?"

"Astorga, I think, but what's that got to do ..... Oh, I see."

I washed as best as I could, awkwardly, like a robot. My mind felt stale, jaundiced, fuzzy.

The whole walk was like a rainbow, a sequence of energies. Rioja, near the beginning, means red. It has red earth & deep red wine. Then came the orange & yellow of the stubble fields of the Meseta. At Rabanal (which means 'radish') the red of anger flares up again, cooling to the amber light on the way here. Would it ever revive to new-born green? And could that green intensify to the purity and depth of ultimate blue? Is there a pot of gold at the end?

Maybe I was going crazy, touched by the sun, out of touch with physical reality. No longer walking through landscape but hues of light, shades of feeling. Thinking was being washed out.

Cristina, Marta and Eugenio were stirring. I was too unsettled to wait patiently for Kes, so when Marta was ready I left with her. The others would catch us up.

Walking nervously down the road, I tried to chat to her through the muzz of my fuzzy brain. I could only manage small-talk. She told me of her family and that she attended Barcelona university studying chemistry. I became aware that she needed something from me, but my mind couldn't find the categories. It was just a feeling, a sense that I had something to give her. She spoke politely, with respect, as if I were a source of authority. I smiled weakly through my pounding headache.

We took a break in a cool bar on the pretty main square in the town of Ponferrada. She went off to get some shopping. I bought her some cold, freshly squeezed orange juice to have it ready for her to refresh herself when she emerged from the hot sun. When she returned, I went to get some money from the bank. It took me ages. They couldn't work out how to persuade their computer to recognise my existence. Back at the bar, Marta had been worried at my absence, thinking I must have had an accident to be so long. Kes and the others still hadn't turned up so we went in search of them. We found them in a bar by the iron bridge which gives this place its name. It was an effort to keep things together in this place, to get things working. It was a place to get lost, to lose track.

The route took us around the town, to the East, over slag heaps and around industry. There were smuts in the air, and a sense of contamination. I deliberately walked under a sprinkler on a lawn to wash it off and freshen me up.

The water at the baking fountain of Columbrianos was warm and tasted of aluminium. I dallied here, not feeling well, and the girls and Eugenio went on ahead.

Through fertile fields, tidily cultivated like allotments, Kes & I walked ever more slowly, my mind blurring with the familiar first stages of food poisoning; a dull, sulphurous haze. A farmer seeing us approaching, disappeared into his house and returned with two cupped handfuls of tomatoes, as a gift. I tried to thank him through the buzz in my head.

By Fuentes Nuevas, I couldn't go on and flopped to the ground in a tiny churchyard, my brain buzzing with sickness and fatigue. I must have dozed fitfully.

Eventually, I forced myself up & onward. Things got very vague after that. We limped on, resting every few hundred yards. I grew weaker. Purpose disappeared. My feet scuffed the dust like some bad actor in an old B movie, lost in the desert. I seemed to be on my own, I had no idea where Kes was. Eventually I sank to my knees and fell out of my rucksack, I just didn't care anymore. I left the sack where it fell, and wandered off up the path, instinctively seeking shade. Something in me found a tree on a knoll. I crawled, on all fours, up the incline, and passed out.

Consciousness returned with the sight of the top of my rucksack rising up the slope of the knoll. Beneath it was Kes, like a grunting, huge tortoise. He hauled himself up, leaning heavily on his staff. My orange rucksack, like an exotic carapace, stretched from above his head to his ankles. He'd found me collapsed, dumped his own rucksack beside me, and gone back for mine.

He sat with my rucksack up against the tree and wriggled out of the straps.

"Want some tea, Dad?" he said, softly, his eyes full of concern.

"OK," I said wearily.

The tea tasted cloyingly sweet but when I sipped it, it stayed down.

After a while, we moved on. My limbs were heavy, but I kept going, enduring the long path to the road and on through Camponaraya. The fields beyond were full of vines. We crawled beneath the leaves, close to the ground, to lay in their shade in the soft mulch of well-tilled earth. I tried to ignore the troublesome little flies.

A long haul to Cacabelos which was in fiesta. It was noisy. The streets were crowded. A rock band was tuning up. There was no way I could cope with this place in my state. We met Cristina and Marta coming out of a bar on the edge of town. When we explained that we were going on to Villafranca, maybe six miles further, they decided to go with us. It was already ten o'clock and getting dark.

The night fell swiftly down the long straight road. It grew cool and the walking was easy. There was little traffic. I unpacked my torch and made Kes do the same with his. We waved the torches whenever a car approached. For long stretches there was nothing but bats and moths, a stony silence and a superb sky. It was comforting to watch Marta striding ahead of me, young and strong and resolute. It seemed that she had decided to walk with us out of a sort of trust.

The night was huge and intimate around us, not just a lack of light but a presence. The night and the land are kin, communing after dark, awakening the mind's depths, creating a new presence; the extra person who walks invisibly by your side. Some of the darkness was mountains.

Marta slowed ahead of me and I caught her up. There's something about darkness that gives an extra charge to speech.

"It is nothing," she said quietly.

"What?"

"Have you walked at night before?"

"Oh yes, at home," I said, looking into the pale shadows of her face, I couldn't see her eyes, "I often walk out into the landscape at night. I like it very much, especially in the forest, when there's a moon like tonight."

She stopped. There was no sound at all. Kes and Cristina were some way behind.

"I have a fear of walking at night. But now there is no fear," she said, very softly.

"No, what is there to fear?"

"Nothing."

She sounded grateful, and exhilarated.

We walked on together, almost a couple. I felt proud of her.

A valley opened up ahead of us with lights on the slopes.

I was sorry when we reached the first lamp-posts of the town. It had been a privilege to share the night with Marta. Something important had happened.

"That was a beautiful walk," she said, her eyes shining.

It was gone midnight when we reached the refuge, a large tent over bare ground. Although it was late we were welcomed with some beer and hot food. Here was a proper community; people came and went but hospitality remained. The tent was home made, basically a forest of scaffold poles draped with tarpaulins and polythene sheets, the roof swagged down in great pouches. Objects hung down: strings of garlic, clusters of scallops, bags of water, baskets, dried herbs, a flat iron and a coffee pot. Strange carvings in stone were unpredictably placed. We could have been in North Africa, in a Taureg encampment.

It was very crowded, no room for four more, only two spaces.

Once the others arrived, Kes and I volunteered to go on to the overflow accommodation. So we went out into the night once more, a guide showing us the way up a track to a couple of huge polythene tunnels. A frisky, brown puppy and three little kittens greeted us, glad of the company. There was no one else. The guide returned down the path, leaving us to the night's immense silence.

We spread our sleeping-bags on a dirty, orange ground-sheet inside one of the tunnels. The puppy snuggled in with Kes like a child, two kittens curled up on my chest, the third crawled in with me. The last thing I saw before turning off the torch was the face of a pretty, ginger kitten staring sleepily into my eyes with a look of utter adoration.

****

I woke in mid-morning. The tunnel was huge like a hanger, maybe a hundred yards long, ribbed like the belly of a whale, space for several hundred. A long noose hung from one of the ribs. It was already hot. A green-house in Spanish heat; we'd have to get out of here soon or we'd fry.

Outside, it was a fine, clear day. No one in sight, mountains all around, sweet peace. I decided at once that this was a place for a day's break. The puppy romped around me, hysterical with joy. I fed him with Bovril cubes, and mixed up some powdered milk with water and sugar for the kittens. I brewed up some coffee and sat on a breeze block to drink it, watching a lizard, black with a red head, gulping in the sun.

I surveyed my domain. There was a big shed made of breeze blocks and a lot of horticultural refuse scattered about; large cans, thick plastic sacks, broken implements. I collected together some old bits of wood and breeze blocks and fixed a broken chair, and put it just inside the shed in the shade. Then I went in the green-house to fetch some things from the rucksack to find the puppy eating Kes' socks. Lots of protein there no doubt.

I sat in my chair and did chores. I mended the camera, sowed up the tears in my trousers, cleaned and sharpened my knife, cleared the holes in the stove's burner with a needle, and generally did the things a good scout does. I woke Kes up to stop him being roasted alive (the puppy helped by jumping on his chest and licking his face), fed him, and sent him down the hill to fetch drinking water.

I wrote letters while he was gone. He was a long time. Claudio had arrived down below, apparently. He should have been far ahead by now, but had been delayed by filming. I'd forgotten all about the film crew. He must have been popping off to film at regular intervals.

I washed my hair in a large flower-pot, then all our clothes. It was like an oven outside, I'd guess over a hundred degrees F, but it was like a furnace in the green-house. It was impossible to stay there very long, the heat was like a burning on the skin, you could feel it prickling, and it was hard to breath. The washing dried a treat under the polythene, very fast. The only way to get it in there was to strip to my underwear, grab a bit of washing, run in and peg it up quickly, then run out again for another item.

Kes was able to cope with the intense heat better than me.

"What's this creamy stuff coming out of your rucksack, Dad?" he shouted from in the tunnel.

"I don't know. Stay there, I'll run in and we'll bring the rucksack out between us."

I rushed in all but naked, the puppy enjoying this fine game, running alongside and barking vigorously. We ran out together with the bag.

The 'creamy stuff' was the candles melting.

244

"Better get your bag out of there too. If there's anything in it which can melt, it will."

The puppy had a great time.

I lazed about for most of the afternoon. Kes and the puppy disappeared into the hills. I heard distant barks and shouts from time to time as they ran about together.

When he tired of that, we went swimming. Down the hill, across town to an open-air pool. It was a popular place on this hot day. Beautiful, young women were everywhere and I had to take a swim in the cool water quite frequently.

I returned from one such dip to find a young man sitting talking to Kes. He was about twenty.

"The boy is with you?" he asked.

"Yes."

"He is very beautiful."

"Well, I wouldn't put it quite like that."

"Would you like to go for a walk into the mountains?" he asked Kes.

"No."

The young man turned to me.

"May I take him?"

"No."

"Just for half an hour. I'm sure he would enjoy it."

"Certainly not."

"Please."

"Absolutely not. Go away."

He reluctantly moved away and eyed Kes from a distance, regretfully.

"Don't think much of your one, Kes."

"Shut up."

"You're only playing hard to get. True love may strike at any time, Kes."

"How would you like a wet towel in your gob?"

"There's no need to be bitchy."

Kes threw the towel at me.

I thought it best not to go in the pool again. We got dressed in the same cubicle.

On the way back through town I phoned home from a public booth. I'd almost finished when Kes started knocking on the glass.

"Hurry up," he shouted.

"What for?"

"You see that man in the shell suit?"

"Yere."

"He keeps asking if I'm with anyone and, sort of, looking at me."

"You shouldn't lead people on."

"Stop laughing. It isn't funny."

"No, no, I suppose you're right. I think we'd better stick together in this place, Kes."

We walked back with my arm over his shoulder.

The dog practically killed himself, rushing backwards and forwards, leaping up, in his joy at seeing us again. The kittens came and rubbed themselves on our ankles.

Chapter 30

Home at Last

After a good rest we went back down the hill, and into town, to eat.

We found a cosy-looking place in the back streets and went in. We'd sat down and were perusing the menu when I discovered I'd forgotten to bring my Spanish phrase book. The friendly waiter, who was also the proprietor, didn't speak English.

"Are you hungry, Kes?"

"Starving."

"Me to. I'm famished. Haven't eaten today, didn't eat much yesterday, either. Well, it should be all right then. We're hungry enough to eat almost anything. All we have to do is order several things from different bits of the menu."

I ordered, and the waiter didn't seem to regard my choices as peculiar.

While we were waiting, there was a flurry of shouts from the kitchen, and a buxom woman, somewhat flustered, rushed out, across the room and out the door.

"Probably gone to get the fireman and the bishop's hat you ordered," said Kes.

Up came a massive tureen of soup about the size of a coal-scuttle. It had bits of cabbage and boiled bacon floating about in it and was delicious. We ate most of it.

"Do try to eat more neatly, Kes, you're such a messy eater."

"I'm not," he said with his mouth full of soup and bread roll, spraying it over the table cloth. He looked down at the mess, laughed, and tried to do a gesture with his bread which indicated nonchalance. However, he lost his grip on the bread mid-gesture which caused it to rise up into the air and clunk down into my soup. Most of the liquid leapt up into my face and dripped off my beard onto my shirt. I must have looked as if I'd been dunking my head in the tureen. Kes was helpless with laughter.

At this point the waiter returned.

Fortunately, his attention was taken by the nearly empty tureen which, it appeared, was intended to last for all other customers for the rest of the evening. He whisked it away from us, plainly displeased.

The meal was a great success. There was veal and some strange, shrimp like things, green beans, peas and lots of good red wine. But above all, we had both laughed & laughed helplessly.

On the way back, we popped into the refuge. It was crowded and the atmosphere was festive. Beyond Villafranca is Galicia, the final province, the last stage, almost there. People celebrated, like Christmas Eve. Round about midnight, what I thought was a bit of fun turned into a ritual. The warden, in black T-shirt and beads, had brewed up a strong punch in a tureen as big as a cauldron. Gales of laughter accompanied mock incantations as various fruits and spirits were added and the brew stirred. The potion was lit with a flourish, intense blue flames swirled around the bowl like playful demons. The warden, like some humorous magus, began to chant dedications.

"Here's to all the pilgrims of the Camino."

Everyone howled like wolves at a full-moon.

"Here's to all the poor, sore feet on the pilgrims of the Camino."

A long, loud, heart-felt howl went up.

"Here's to all the blisters on the poor, sore feet on the pilgrims of the Camino."

We all bayed to the roof.

"Here's to all the pus from all the blisters on the poor, sore feet on the pilgrims of the Camino."

Laughter and caterwauling like moggies at mid-summer. And so it went on, rhythmically back and forth, an invocation followed by a yowl to send it on its way aloft.

"All the pus goes into the bowl."

Heads back, snouts up, howl.

"All the sweat goes into the bowl."

Howl.

"All the blood goes into the bowl."

Howl.

"All that is seen by all the eyes of all the pilgrims of the Camino goes into the bowl."

Howl.

"All that is heard by all the ears of all the pilgrims of the Camino goes into the bowl."

"And all that is felt by all the hands of all the pilgrims of the Camino goes into the bowl."

Howl.

"And the lips."

"Si, si si!"

"And the other parts."

We cheered and laughed and raised our glasses and howled.

"Especially the other parts," I shouted, grinning.

"And all that is smelt by all the noses of all the pilgrims of the Camino."

"The noses!"

"And all that is tasted by all the tongues of all the pilgrims of the Camino."

"Tongues! Tongues!"

He stirred manfully, swirling the heavy, fruit-filled liquid, two-hands on the big wooden spoon; the last of the flickering blue flames licking the surface.

"Now drink! All must drink!"

The potent liquor was ladled out and passed around.

We all drank.

Late, the two of us toiled up the path to our polythene ark to sleep with the animals.

****

Remarkably, in the morning, Kes decided that he wanted a shower, down in the refuge. Down we went. He took a very long time; which was doubly remarkable.

For a while I waited around. The place was even more

atmospheric in day-light. The sheeting gave the light a warm golden glow, like airy whisky.

I shouted through the wooden door to him.

"I'm going to make a start, Kes."

"OK," he called, amid the splashing.

"Cristina will wait for you. I'll see you down the way."

"Fine. See you."

So I left with Marta. There are two routes out of Villafranca, though I didn't know this at the time; a short one, straight down the road; and the Ruta Romana, the Roman Way; a hard, long, looping path over the mountains. Without any conscious choice, Kes and Cristina went down the road; Marta and I went into the mountains.

We went through the town by picturesque back streets following yellows. Then we began to climb. We walked apart, concentrating on making way. The effort precluded talk. It was steep and demanding, unrelenting; head down, short steps, I flowed with sweat like a human well. It sluiced down my face, trickled down my back, exuded from the very palms of my hands. On and on we went, the path seriously steep, and I began to doubt if I could make it. This was harder than the Pyrenees.

The road became a track and the track emerged into the bosom of enormous mountains. We were above it all, liberated into massive space. It was exhilarating. We climbed further, to the mountain marked on the map as Cerro del Real, which means both 'Hill of the Real' and 'Hill of the Royal.' Once the path had levelled out and began to roll with the contours, we walked in a state of exuberance. It was heady and magical. I felt like singing. Energy gushed up through me like a spiritual oil well. It was special here. I knew it as surely as if there were a neon sign, yet there was nothing but the path.

Mystic symbols began to appear in the rock; the Star of David and Spirals primarily, others too, five-pointed stars, also the words 'La Luz', the light; hieroglyphs left by the informed. We met no other pilgrims. Few made it up here, those who did, and understood the place, confirmed each other by these encouragements. My kin had been here, were here still. I had been here before and left myself some signs. So it felt.

The sense of euphoria grew & grew. It took over until I was just one glorious bubble of bliss. It felt as if I'd lost location. My self had opened and opened & in had flowed the energy of the mountains & the sky. I was ecstatic.

The frequency of the mystic symbols, drawn by pilgrims on the rock, increased until we reached a height & a concentration of pure delight. I didn't need the symbols to tell me. Here was Home.

I'd reached the next Way Station in the succession of secret places; number four. Not a village or even a building, after Rabanal there can only be nature itself.

It seemed inappropriate to stop for a break here, like having a picnic in a chancel. So we waited until a small spur over the landscape below. As I was making the tea, amid this fabulous view, Marta asked me if I knew the meaning of all the symbols

Ah, where to start!

We sat on the dry, sandy earth beneath a single tree and I tried to explain some of what I'd learnt.

I've spoken of energy coming constantly into the mind. It's possible to experience this directly. It isn't easy. What prevents it is the fact that we use the bulk of this energy to sustain the structure of our own personalities. To have this special experience you have to stop using the energy in that way. You forgo your identity and let it rip.

The boundaries, especially, no longer apply, they don't exactly dissolve, it's more that they become transparent. The self becomes a glass castle. It feels like a great opening out, or opening up. And there, revealed, is the source of things, like the tender heart of some atomic pile.

This cannot be depicted, it's impossible, odd things happen to dimensions and time, but the mystic symbols are reminders of some of its features. A great deal is packed into those simple diagrams. They have multiple meanings in many areas. They are like visual metaphors, or rather, they are a reference to many, interconnected metaphors which themselves have reference to a further system, and so on. Mirrors in mirrors.

Symbols can do that. They point to wider things beyond a literal meaning. Literal meaning is restricted by the deep structure of language itself, as Quantum Mechanics is discovering. When Plato wishes to speak of the Form of the Good, he says it lies beyond words, beyond the implicit relativity of language. So he turns to a sequence of Similes; it's like this, resembles that.

The most important feature of the Star of David (to take just one), or the Seal of Solomon, as it's also known, is the hexagonal space in the middle. This is where the action is. It is the nothing from which everything comes. It is a depiction of creation & a representation of a state of mind. Both of these, and more, at once.

The central space is formed by the interconnection of two triangles: an upward pointing triangle and a downward pointing triangle. Together they make a star. The star is shaped like a flower head with six pointed petals.

The two triangles represent opposing forces brought into unity. It's a dynamic diagram; the triangles are in motion, sliding over each other. The upward pointing triangle is moving upwards, the downward moves down. Only at one moment of their passing does the star appear. This is the moment of insight, the moment of creation. It's possible to hold the two energy flows at that critical instant of crossing; held thus, a new energy emerges out of the opposition, in the central space.

There are many oppositions expressed by the triangles. In a sense, they are the fact of opposition itself, logical opposites brought into impossible union. Beyond language, beyond logic. Medieval philosophers called this the Conjunctio Oppositorum; the conjunction of opposites from which all comes. Jung wrote a fat, & difficult, book about it. In the East it is the Ying & Yang of the Taoist symbol, which we had come across in startling circumstances in Pamplona, now felt as a prefiguring. In physical terms, it is the

252

fact that something is not everything else. In union, this becomes the fact that each thing is defined by everything else. The stasis which holds the opposites together necessarily makes space, time and logic to hold them apart.

Let's shift into poetic expression.

Traditionally, particular instances of opposites have been emphasized. Thus the erect upward triangle is considered male, while the pubic downward triangle is female. Held in dynamic union, they produce the central energy: climactic ecstasy. Shiva & Shakti.

The upward triangle yearns towards the sky and its traditional, male gods, while the downward is drawn earthwards towards the goddesses, Mother Earth. This is aspiration on the one hand, and the desire for grounding on the other.

In terms of consciousness, upwards means outward, and downward means inward. So the outward (the upward) triangle is the bright and clear light of conscious awareness, while the inward (the downward) is the dark depth of unconscious process.

Considered as a state of mind, represented by the diagram, the inside & outside get merged; you lose yourself in the world, they are no longer different things. There occurs an inflorescence, an opening; the praying hands part, the mouth gapes in ecstasy, the mind sheds its layers, the rose unfurls, the jewel is disclosed in the lotus, the water burns, a universe emerges. A star is born, a star which includes and informs all other stars.

The wise mind intimates its source and follows this star to its own birth. Its central void, a black womb, whirls with creation, an invisible energy swirls in the empty heart of darkness.

In a nutshell, though the words are all wrong, there is a place in the mind, swirling with energy, which is the same place which makes the world.

****

What are we to make of this sort of thing? What on earth is going on? I am not of the persuasion that personal experience can directly show us reality, no matter how overwhelming & impressive it may be. Subjective conviction does not guarantee truth. Even when what happens appears to nullify the subjective/objective distinction.

The name of this type of experience, however, is clear. It is Nature Mysticism; mystical experience of unity in all things, triggered by nature. It is surprisingly common in all cultures at all times & is not necessarily linked to religion. In the ancient world, it is associated with the name of Dionysius. In philosophy, with Plotinus &, to some extent, Spinoza. In English Literature; George Herbert, William Blake, W.H.Hudson, Richard Jefferies &, of course, Wordsworth. Many others. In the East it underlies Dogon, Hakuin, Lao Tzu, Basho among many others & much Chinese & Japanese landscape painting & poetry.

I'll tell you this. However we interpret experiences of this kind, nothing is quite the same for the individual ever again.

****

We were above the vegetation in a tawny world, as if amid a pride of stupendous, reclining lions, regal and dignified. The landscape watched over us with a slow, sleepy, feline blink of confident power; a concourse of sphinxes. They allowed us to pass, admitting us to their presence. We weren't in these mountains, we were of them. Sharing their body-heat, their blood-heat, breathing their breath, of one flesh.

When we got up and walked on, Marta and I kept glancing at each other in confirmation.

We didn't speak.

My mood became disengaged. I was no longer a figure in a landscape. I was a function of this earth, a feature of it, as a tree might be. I became free of personal concerns. I had expected to be going down the road below, with its many bars and the occasional fountain, so I hadn't bothered to replenish my water-bottle. It was empty. It didn't matter. Trust was a fact. Not that the world would take care of me, no such arrogance, rather that whatever happened would be fitting. The route markers ceased. It didn't matter, I knew the way.

Chapter 31

Slow Living

We reached Pradela, meaning 'small meadow', which felt extremely remote; an eyrie in the hills. A woman opened her bar for us. It was underground; a cellar, functional, like a garage; bare concrete, produce piled up, a store. She served us silently, preoccupied, as if her attention were elsewhere, listening to secret orders from voices we could not hear. When Marta tried to talk to her, she replied reluctantly, in few words, as if speech were an effort.

Beyond the village, we freewheeled down a zigzag path with hair-pin bends, some road, some track, into trees again, chestnuts and oak. We took a break by a particularly fine old oak with a hollow trunk. Marta sat in the trunk like some beaming foetus in an arboreal womb. I took her photo.

Descending to the main road was a return to standard time and normal conceptions. Down here were trucks delivering coke, and places for people to drink it; there were electricians out to fix a fridge; tourists getting away from it all, looking for a beer.

A couple of hundred yards of madness down the road, then thankfully off on a minor side road. Fields were lush and green, the light gentle, the very air soft. People had time, paused according to impulse, lived by a different agenda, an agenda somehow in the grain of things, leading a cow down the street. Along the pretty Rio Valcarce was a series of villages set aside from any highway. They felt like those places that Captain Kirk finds on alien planets, a capsule of a culture which the viewer knows ends just off-screen. Except that here it felt as if the set was real and the rest of the planet wasn't.

We took a break in a field of mint on the river bank. Laying back on the crushed leaves, taking great grateful breaths full of mint, the scent suffused all, flushed the brain, cleansing it.

Then the second tough climb of the day. A path like tilted rungs of a ladder, zigzagging upwards over a slew of rocks the size of skulls, into Galicia.

More mountains, rounded like clouds. During the day's walk we had climbed into one range of mountains with the mystic symbols, then descended into the valley which carried the big, main road and then ascended the other side into more mountains, and yet these hills felt entirely different from those around Pradela. There was the domain of the lioness, here of the wolf. Here were mountains to instil paranoia. They felt grey, metallic. Above us appeared, through the mist, lines of real fire, like cryptic symbols ringed round a mountain. Ravens scouted for carrion. Unseen forces were grouping, tracking. A waxing moon rose in an ash-blue sky while a fuzzy smoulder of sun sank like a pink, smoky bruise. Darkness fell like a conspiracy. The world became cloaked.

Hidden in the cloak was Cebreiro, a village built from grey blocks of cold night, high & chilled. Big dogs barked, unseen. Its granite church and houses glinted like wolves' eyes. Each cobbled street concealed a phantom precipice, receding, never reached.

The refuge was a low, stone hut, circular and thatched. A place to hide from a night flinty with invisible arrowheads. I had to duck to get through the broad door framed by heavy white stones, inside, the room was full of straw. We slept on a mattress, four feet thick, of clean straw, shared with smaller creatures, deeper down, furtive in the rustling stalks.

****

Day light in Cebreiro was still grey. Fog seeped through the square window of the refuge. Outside, chill mist swirled. We were high in the mountains here. This was a place for furs, where animals were brought indoors to help heat the house. It felt twinned with the Atlantic and of kin with seals. Granite was in the air; an iron place like a hill fort, somewhere to hole up, hoping marauders would pass you by.

At the nearby hostel was Eugenio with a message from Kes saying that he was safe and well, and had stayed in one of the dapper little villages down in the valley. We moved on out, dawdling to allow him to catch up.

At Liñares, just a couple of miles along the road, we found an all-purpose shop selling boots and umbrellas, rat killer and food. We bought octopus, sardines, and tuna, and when we asked for lettuce, José took us out to his fields and pulled a couple from the ground. Back at the shop, he insisted we share a glass of rough red wine and presented us with some sausage as a gift.

We picnicked all afternoon, waiting for Kes, dozing in turns on lush grass down by a sweet stream. Eugenio insisted on being by Marta's side, sat by her, too close sometimes, so that she complained. He got up when she did, trailed her like some twitching terrier.

Onward, the landscape was a ground swell patched with small, well-tilled fields, straw and deep green, stretching up the flanks of the mountains with white tracks, like spaghetti, twisting around. Some of the fields were so steep, they seemed to be hanging from the sky like pegged up blankets.

The entire Way is a rainbow, there was no doubt we had entered a green land now, every shade was here, from pale olive to bright apple.

Neither Marta nor I had any sense of urgency or worry left. Eugenio was one of life's followers and took his cue entirely from us. It was necessary to wait, so we waited. I had no fears about Kes. He was with Cristina, I knew he would come to no harm, but he had no money and that would get awkward after a while. He also carried our shared towel. I'd left it with him when he showered at Villafranca.

We waited, content, and chatted. The talk was interesting; not that we ranged over topics so much, but rather that with no pressure on conversation whatsoever, we soon finished talking about the spot we were in and then there was nothing left but what needed to be said. We sat, in a sense, in a clearing of time, and talked around and around, like a spiral of words, approaching what was ready to be brought out. That there was something was plain, it was just a matter of who realised it first.

Sometimes what needs to said isn't just a one off. Not something just fitting the occasion, but something which we vaguely know, and know we need to know, but have never succeeded in expressing. Indeed, much of our time is spent in finding activities which will help us in avoiding the task of trying to express it. What we most need to know, we don't want to know. This is the situation of Oedipus, and, indeed, the rest of us.

Sometimes what needs to be said is not just deeply buried in one mind, which that mind alone works to hide and reveal. What needs to be said seems to float around waiting for someone to find it and say it. It needn't be some great traumatic revelation. More often what needs to be said is some much more modest thing on the way to that revelation, a small step. So here's a group of people and there's something which needs to be said for each one of them, now. There is the deep something which is almost certainly not available, and if it were said may very well not be understood.

There is an agenda written in the air, or so it feels.

It's just the same with events. There is something to be done, it's on the agenda. But there are other things which we must do, which we feel obliged to do, which we are paid to do, habitual things which we regularly do. Mostly these things get in the way and prevent us apprehending the thing in the air which needs to be done, the thing which will help us on our way. Often the blocking pressures of work and habit, and the cog activities which keep the physical and social machine going, are so thorough in preventing access to the agenda, that we grow restless, we want to get the hell out, to escape, take a break. Then we long to go on pilgrimage, though we might not express it exactly like that. We feel the need to throw off the restriction and begin the journey to what it is we are hiding from ourselves.

The Camino calls. The Camino is the agenda.

The first stage to a new thought is a new metaphor. The first stage to a new metaphor is a new feeling. The first stage to a new feeling is an arrested attention. These are our yellow arrows. This book is an unpacked moment of arrested attention which happened when I watched the slides of the Camino in London. That moment echoes back and forth in time.

So, as the afternoon wound on, this thing to be said was as much a presence as the mosquitoes, circling and dithering over the stream.

We decided to stay at the next village, Fonfria.

It consisted of a single dirt track flanked by simple houses. It had no bar, no shop and no refuge. People sat outside their houses, on ancient wooden chairs, in the cool of the early evening, unwinding from the day's labour. They were suspicious. Pilgrims rarely stayed here, there was no provision. There was much of the day left to find somewhere else. We weren't injured or sick. They were unco-operative. They resented intrusion.

We wandered up and down, it took less than ten minutes to walk from one end of the village to the other, asking for a floor and a roof. Nothing doing. Nowhere here. Go away.

Eventually, we were shown a tiny storage room. It was worse than filthy; bare earth covered in oil, broken machinery rusting; damp and smelly. It apparently served as an emergency toilet. It would take half a day to clear enough space to lay three sleeping bags. Nonetheless, we seriously considered it, before politely declining.

It emerged that one farmer would sometimes allow pilgrims to sleep in his garage. At the house, a confused, and plainly scared, old woman tried to put us off, and then said that only the father could give permission, and he was still in the fields. We sat around on a jumble of logs by the garage door. For several hours we waited amid the chickens, writing letters, bringing diaries up to date, completely relaxed and unworried. We weren't optimistic, just comfortable with waiting, though we had no food, no water and nowhere to stay.

Marta remarked that Fonfria meant 'cold fountain' so there must be good water here. Eugenio went off in search of it. He returned with full bottles of excellent water.

People were returning home from the fields all the time. A small herd of slow cows was shepherded past, stately and curious, and they walked through the front door of an ordinary house, into their quarters. More people sat outside, taking a glass of wine, watching the world go by. Marta went to consult them. They said that a new house was being built on the edge of the village and it might be possible to stay there. We found the caretaker, a friendly chap in an old, stained T-shirt and baggy trousers, with all the time in the world. As he directed us over the building site his wife appeared, squawking and railing furiously at us in a high-pitched, nasal voice.

He waved her away. "Don't listen to her," he said, "she's a dragon." She disappeared.

He took us around the back, and up bare, concrete stairs to the first floor. Cool, evening air wafted through the frameless windows. Some loose straw lay about, some bales, and a mattress. He slept here himself sometimes, he explained.

I collected some straw and laid my sleeping bag on it, hefted bales to make a bed for Eugenio, and brewed up some coffee. We had a home.

The front of the building had a sort of concrete shelf on the first floor which served us as a balcony. We sat and watched the street for Kes. The moon rose elegantly far to our left. More cows processed along the track, looking up with curiosity, ambled on. A shooting-star flared in the silence, then another. We just sat and watched.

Two young women came along below us who we had met much further back on the route. We hailed them and asked for news of Kes. They hadn't seen him. They were obviously very tired, and had walked a long way, down the dreadful, busy road from Villafranca, up the stiff climb to Cebreiro and on to here. We invited them up to join us and they did. They had food enough for two, and when they found out that we had none, they shared theirs with us; some soft chocolate, a few biscuits, a bit of bread and sausage, not much.

It was quite dark when Marta took a torch and went for a walk.

She returned with two plastic bags of provisions. She'd just knocked on doors asking if she could buy food. She had bread, cheese, ham, milk and cigarettes; everything we needed and more than enough for five. She was very pleased with her own enterprise, and that she had the gumption to act on her own idea. The proper meal was a celebration, a reward for patience. A short while before we had nothing, now we had it all.

Marta began an earnest conversion in Spanish with Eugenio which I couldn't follow. I went and sat on the concrete of our balcony and smoked a cigarette. Eventually, she came and sat by me.

She was restless and had something on her mind. She talked of her family, her unfaithful boyfriend, how it always seemed that other people were running her life. Even this trip had been the idea of Cristina, she was invited as a companion.

I listened with great attention. There was a long pause.

"Michael?"

"Yes, Marta?"

"I have something to ask you."

Ah, this was it. The time had come.

"What is it?"

She looked apprehensive.

"I am thinking to walk on ahead, on my own."

This was like a bucket of cold water. I had not expected this. I had grown very fond of Marta. I very much wanted to be with her. I would miss her dreadfully. My feelings cried out within me to object, to plead with her not to go, to stay with me. I felt I needed her.

The atmosphere was intense. Whatever was said now would strike deep. She awaited my response. I looked at her trusting face. I was being consulted. Reluctantly, I admitted to myself that I knew what it was that she needed. It was permission, confirmation, consent. I fought with my feelings and answered carefully, choosing the words.

"You must make your own decision, Marta."

"Eugenio says I must not go. I must stay in the group. He says terrible things will happen to me alone."

"No, he is talking of what he wants. You must decide. I'm sure that is important."

"How to decide?"

"Trust your feelings. Look inside your self and see how you truly feel. If it is clear to you that you need to walk alone, that is what you must do. Trust your feelings and have courage."

She looked deeply into my eyes. It almost broke my heart. I let her take what she needed. She turned her face away, got up and walked inside. I knew she would go.

I lit another cigarette. My contentment drained away. The concrete felt hard.

I turned in with a heavy heart.

I was lying on my straw, having just filled my ears with toilet paper to reduce the snores of Eugenio, when suddenly Marta was leaning over me. She embraced me warmly, kissed me gently and softly whispered, "Thank you, Michael." I held her for a moment, then she disappeared.

In the night a violent and windy storm flashed and crashed around us, blowing straw and sheets of metal about the room.

When I woke in the morning she had gone.

I felt deserted.

Chapter 32

Myth Returns

I sat for a long time stewing in self-pity. Nothing seemed worth doing. I tried to console myself with the thought of how noble I had been, but it wasn't much comfort.

Packing took an age. Eugenio seemed a demanding oaf.

I was sitting on the balcony, trying to summon up the motivation to go on, when Kes and Cristina appeared below me. How small he looked. I shouted down.

"Kes!"

"Hi, Dad."

Obviously pleased to see me. The closest father and son get to intimacy in English culture.

"You all right?"

"I'm fine."

"What kept you?"

"Pool."

"Pool? Have you been swimming?"

"No, pool. You know, like snooker. That big road had bars with pool tables. It was well good. We've being playing pool."

"I see, pool."

I grabbed my rucksack and went down to join him.

Kes had much to tell me about the delights of pool and how excellent the bars on the main road were. He chatted cheerfully as we went along. It was so good to be together again. I wanted to hug him, but when I moved to do it the unspoken messages of distress from him were clear and I backed off. Eugenio and Cristina moved on ahead.

Just beyond Biduedo, a middle-aged woman sat alone in some scrappy bushes. She rattled on at a great rate, talking to herself loudly, in a world of her own. She was unkempt, wearing a dirty frock, her hair unwashed, sticking out oddly. Her hands were awkwardly bent over at right angles, unusable. She had no fingers. As she babbled, I could see that she had no front teeth. The lower lip receded, and her canines protruded. Poor soul. It felt guilty to be relatively whole

We descended into a series of tunnel-like paths, overhung with shrubs and trees, rural back streets, alleys scarcely leaving one hamlet before the next appeared. An intimate place, close to the earth and the greenery. Dappled sunlight skittered through the trees above. It was like being cosseted, as if nature had put her arm around you to tell you something private. Scale was being reduced here, focused down to a human compass. A land for leprechauns, for Puck, and cheeky spirits of nooks and corners.

The people were introverted, turned inward to a local psyche; especially the men. It was the women who were in the fields, short, bulky women with muscles, mostly all in black, wearing wellies and hefting mighty wheelbarrows. I wondered whether the mad woman was the result of in-breeding.

Even the dogs were different, they skulked, not like the vigorous defenders of territory of the rest of Spain. Birds too were secretive, hard to spot, flitting, hidden in undergrowth; the land depicted in the paintings of Richard Dadd; a claustrophobic place packed tightly with intricate life.

We emerged from these alleyways into Triacastela, only a sleepy village but it felt like a major place after so many hamlets. It even had bus-stops and a bakery. An inhabitant said there was a refuge, but we could sleep in the town hall which was closer.

It was small and empty; a low dais at one end; dull, green furniture and a creepy atmosphere, as if past officials lurked in the air. It was cool yet felt chill. On a book-shelf was the complete works of Aquinas in Latin, bound in old, well-worn leather, as if he was consulted when making parochial decisions.

I washed our clothes in the nearby lavadero. It didn't seem to be used much; made of stone with the chilly feel of a cave. Moss grew and water trickled and echoed. Green light, filtered through leaves at the glassless window, hung like a presence. I climbed into the stone box and washed myself in the icy water. It was like being in a trough for embalming. There ought to have been frogs.

That night, we lay our sleeping-bags on the floor, in the unwelcoming council chamber, feeling like intruders. Something seeped into the mind here. Our washing hung around and wasn't drying, making the air damp. I kept looking behind me expecting to see someone. No-one else arrived; not visibly anyway. It wasn't easy to get to sleep.

"Spooky here," said Kes.

"You made me jump," I replied.

"Sorry."

"At least I know it's not just me."

"I wouldn't like to be here on my own."

"No, nor I."

We were talking for the sake of it; to put a bit of humanity into the tomb-like, shadowy space. Ghosts met here to decide their business. Here it was settled that a particular cow should be given a squint, that a farmer's milk would curdle in the pail, that some strapping lass would miscarry.

"Is there far to go?" asked Kes.

"Less than eighty miles. Maybe five days. We're going to make it."

"If we get out of here."

"It's not that bad."

"What's that!"

A loud creaking noise came from the door. I got up out of my sleeping bag reluctantly and checked it out. Nothing to be seen. I unpacked my torch and laid it by my bag. My knife also.

"Can't stab a ghost, Dad."

"What about hobgoblins or trolls?"

"Don't know. They don't tell you important things like that in school."

"I wonder if I should unpack the garlic."

"I'm not hungry. Tell me a story."

"You're a bit old for that sort of thing, aren't you?"

"No, I'm not."

"I'm not really in the mood."

"Please."

"I'll tell you about Oedipus, if you like."

"OK. That'll do."

"All right. Are you lying comfortably?"

"No."

"Then I'll begin. Once upon a time there was a city in ancient Greece, called Thebes."

"Thieves?"

"No, Thebes, City of Light. It was founded where dragon's teeth grew into soldiers."

"We could do with some light in here."

"You're right, I'll light a candle."

It wasn't much better. Our washing hung, stiff and unreal, like the mutilated corpses of criminals, or just their flimsy remains; the guts having been spirited away.

"Anyway, the King, Laius, and the Queen, Jocasta, had a son called Oedipus, which means 'swollen foot'."

"You've told me this. It's a funny name."

"It is, people would have laughed at him. It's like Ramsbottom, or worse, Glasscock."

Kes giggled.

"Are there peopled called that?"

"I'm afraid so."

"Poor things."

"Well, the king and queen took the new-born child to an oracle; that's like a seer who could predict things. They wanted to know the future for the young prince. But they certainly didn't want to know what the oracle told them."

"What did he say?"

"She."

"What did she say?"

"That when he grew up, Oedipus would kill his father and marry his mother."

"Shit! That's worse than Bradley Berigan!"

"Much worse. Well, they decided that the only way to avoid this terrible fate was to kill the child."

"That's not fair! Couldn't they just send him away to Thurrock?"

"They weren't that cruel, and besides Thurrock didn't exist then. It was a long while ago."

"So they killed him?"

"Not quite. They arranged that he would be dumped in the mountains to die, and just to make sure he didn't crawl off somewhere, they riveted his ankles together."

"Nasty."

"Very. They gave him to a shepherd to take to the mountains. However, when the shepherd got there, he didn't have the heart to do it."

"Good for him. What did he do?"

"He gave the child to another shepherd who came up into the mountains with his flocks at the same time. When it was time to leave, the shepherd from Thebes went back down the mountain on one side, the other man took Oedipus down the other side to Corinth."

"What does 'Corinth' mean?"

"I don't know. Want a cup of tea?"

"Yes, please."

I crawled out of my sleeping bag & started to brew up .

"The second shepherd took the child home and gave him to the king and queen of Corinth and he was brought up as their son. So, all went well until Oedipus became a young man, a young man with a limp."

"With a limp?"

"Remember the rivets in his ankles."

"Oh yere. They didn't leave the rivets in though?"

" Of course not, but he'd have the scars. Swollen Foot. His

name must have been a real irritation, like a taunt. Anyway, he was having dinner one day when he annoyed one of the courtiers."

"How?"

"I don't know, but the courtier, who was a bit drunk, said that Oedipus wasn't the son of the king, an insult. Now, most people would just shrug a thing like that off, the man was drunk after all. But it troubled Oedipus, and he didn't know why. He decided to consult an oracle himself. And the oracle, not the same one, told him not to be concerned about the King of Corinth because there was this other stuff that was far more important. The oracle said that Oedipus was going to kill his father and marry his mother."

"Bit of a nightmare."

"The worst. Well, Oedipus figured he couldn't kill the King of Corinth, who he thought was his father, if he went away, far away."

"Not to mention the other bit of the prediction."

"Quite."

"There's a rude word for someone like that."

"True. So, to avoid being the rude word, Oedipus left Corinth. Guess where he went?"

"Thebes?"

"Exactly. But as he was walking there, at a place where three roads meet, he came across a procession with an old man in a posh carriage. As the old geezer in the carriage passed Oedipus, he leant out and hit him with a whip. Oedipus lost his cool and attacked the man and killed him.

"Pretty violent guy, Oedipus."

"Yep, and the man in the carriage too. Guess who he was?"

"The other king?"

"Yes, Laius, his real father, so the first half of the prophecy came true. Oedipus went on towards Thebes and met the Sphinx."

"We've done this bit."

"Some of it. What I didn't tell you before is that the Sphinx had brought plague to the city which wouldn't stop until someone solved her riddle. You remember the riddle?"

"What is it that walks on four legs in the morning, two legs at lunch time, and three legs at night?"

"Near enough."

"And Oedipus said 'people' because they are babies, then they learn to walk, and they need a stick when they're old."

"That's right."

"And you said Oedipus got it wrong, but you didn't say why it was wrong. What's that noise?"

"Just the wind, I think."

I sipped my tea.

"Got any biscuits?"

"Sure."

Kes dipped his biscuit in his tea. The soggy biscuit broke off on the way to his mouth and fell into his sleeping-bag.

"So why was he wrong?"

"Think. The riddle was the story of the life of Oedipus in a nutshell. Oedipus, who, as a child, had his ankles riveted and could only crawl on all fours around the mountainside. Oedipus, who, when he's a young man, walks on his own two feet to find his fate at a place where three roads meet. Oedipus, who, when he finds out what he has done, will blind himself and have to tap his way out of Thebes with a staff, into the wilderness."

"Serious shit!" said Kes, spitting biscuit everywhere.

"Yes, indeed, now think a bit more. Lots of people had tried to solve the riddle, and had failed, and been thrown off the cliff by the Sphinx. They died."

"So what?"

"So no-one, except Oedipus, returned to tell what the riddle was. So we only know one riddle."

"Each person got a different riddle?"

"Well, we don't know that for sure, but I think so. They each got their own. So, the question is 'Why did Oedipus succeed when all the others had failed? Why him especially? What was it about Oedipus which enabled him to know the answer?'"

"It was his life story."

"Yes, but presumably they all got their own life story in their own riddle. The question is how did he know it was his life story?"

"How do you mean?"

"Well, he was very young when he was brought to Corinth but he would have to recall it enough to recognise that part of himself in the riddle, and he would need to know his own future, well, vaguely anyway."

"This is a good story, Dad."

"I think so. I've thought so ever since I found out about it at school. It was our school play one year. It's by Sophocles."

"I'd read it if I could read better."

"You should. Everyone should."

"So what happened next?"

"We haven't finished with the riddle yet. It was a sort of test. Could Oedipus recognise himself in the riddle? Could he dredge up enough of his own past, and foretell enough of his own future, to be able to say to the Sphinx 'I know who that is, that's me!'?"

"But he got it wrong."

"Only just. Instead of saying to himself: 'Oh, that's me, Oedipus' he veered away from the full truth and said to himself, somewhere inside, 'Oh, that's me, a person.' He got it nearly right. Enough for the Sphinx to know he was the sort of person who could predict, the sort who could know the past and the future and put it together so it made sense."

"He was an oracle!"

"Not quite, but he could be one, with the right sort of training, he had the right sort of mind. You see how it was a test?"

"Yes. He passed it."

"Yes, unfortunately, he'd shown he was the sort of person that could be aware of the gods. The gods could use such a person."

"Is that bad?"

"Usually pretty bad for the person themselves, they get hung on a cross or something. The gods work through them for the benefit of the rest of us. Good for everyone else, though."

"That's not fair."

"Maybe not, but a hero pays with their suffering for the knowledge the rest of us get. They give their lives for us, it's a sort of gift."

"It's a bad deal. Have we finished with the riddle?"

"Enough for now. So the Sphinx held up a mirror for Oedipus to see himself. But he didn't see very clearly, not yet. Nevertheless, the Sphinx was dead, she jumped off the mountain, and the plague was at an end. Oedipus went on into Thebes where the people were very grateful. They wanted to give him some reward. Of course, the king was recently dead."

"Oh no!"

"Oh, yes, someone who could defeat a Sphinx and cure a plague was just the sort of man to have as your king."

"So they made him king?"

"Yes, and, of course, the queen had been left a widow, so he married Jocasta, his mother."

"Didn't she recognise him?"

"That isn't an easy question. She didn't on the surface, maybe, but perhaps deep down."

"Why deep down?"

"Well, she had a lot to make up to someone. She'd dumped her son in the landscape. Not a nice thing to do, not very motherly. She might very well have a deep need to mother someone in place of her lost son; and Oedipus would be exactly the right age, the age her son would be if he had lived. He would even look like her son, had he grown to be a man. In a sense, she couldn't make it up to a better person. Something similar goes on way down in Oedipus. He is someone who has a dim awareness of his own past. He had been abandoned by his own mother. He'd missed out. It sounds weird, but it's sort of natural that he should look for another."

"This story is like really deep, man."

"Deep it is."

"Go on. Any more?"

"Lots. They had children."

"With his mum?"

"No less."

"That's disgusting. You'd have thought they might have known."

"Why?"

"Well, she was old enough to be his mother!"

"That's right. And it's worse than that when you think about it. They should have known."

"Why?"

"Think about all that they <u>must</u> have known. Let's just take Oedipus. He knows about the prediction that he will kill his father and marry his mother. He knows he has killed someone. He knows that the someone he has killed was an old man, old enough to be his father. He knows that the person he killed was an important person. He knows that the King of Thebes was murdered just before he arrived. He knows that he is married to the wife of the dead king. He knows that she is old enough to be his mother. He knows that someone in Corinth thinks that the king and queen of Corinth are not his real parents."

"It's a riddle! The whole story is a riddle!"

"That's right! Very good, Kes. And remember, Oedipus is good at riddles. He can see a story hidden in a few facts."

"He must know."

"No, that's too strong. He <u>should</u> know. With all that evidence, any reasonable person would put two and two together, as it were, and at least suspect what has happened. Even more so when you add all that his wife must know. I could give you a similar list for her. She ought to know too. And if they compared notes .....talk about why he limps, for example, or if either mentions the prediction."

"They can't talk to each other."

"Obviously not, not about this anyway. They'd have to carefully edge their way round the topic whenever they got close. People find ways to tip-toe around things that need to be said, but which they are scared of thinking about, especially couples."

"Doesn't she ever ask him why he came to Thebes?"

"She couldn't have, it would all come out."

"Why doesn't she ask?"

"That's an excellent question."

"She must know that she shouldn't ask."

"Yes, indeed."

"So she does know."

"Not exactly. Somewhere deep inside her she must have some idea or she wouldn't avoid the topic. But she doesn't know on the surface. The truth would be well buried."

"Why?"

"That's obvious."

"Too horrible?"

"Disgusting, you said."

"She doesn't want to know."

"Who would."

"Him too."

"Him too. But he's a bit different. He's the sort, remember, to put things together, to dredge things up from deep down and make something of it. And he's got all this crap in his head which doesn't fit with his life. He's admired. He's a king. He's got status. People look up to him. He saved them from the plague."

"He doesn't deserve it?"

"Not completely, but he's got something on his mind which is fouling everything up. There's much that he can't think about, thoughts he can't follow up, feelings that have to be ignored. His mind would have to veer away from all this. Not much space left in his head to live in. He needs to get it all out."

"But he can't, it's disgusting."

"Right. So he has a desperate need to cover it up. It depends which need is stronger."

Kes yawned.

"I think that's enough for tonight, you're tired."

"No, no, I'm not tired! Finish the story!"

"OK. Just the simple version then."

"What happened next?"

"So Oedipus has all this muck deep inside him, and it's not doing him any good. In a sense, he's ill. And when a king is ill, his kingdom is ill too. The land is sick. The plague comes back."

"But not the Sphinx?"

"Not the Sphinx. And the people ask their hero to rid them of the plague, as he did before. Oedipus consults the oracle to find out what's wrong, and the oracle says that the killer of Laius has not been found. There's a murderer on the loose in Thebes. Oedipus becomes detective and sets out to find the killer. He finds him."

"He finds himself?"

"He does. Jocasta can't stand it and hangs herself. Oedipus takes the broaches from her dress and plunges the pins in his own eyes, over and over, till he's blind."

"Je-sus!"

"Then they throw him out. After all he is disgusting now. He takes a staff and taps his way out of town into the wilderness."

"Like a pilgrim."

"Yes, except he doesn't have a Santiago to aim for. He wanders in the wilderness. He lives in the landscape, becomes part of it, finds his way by intuition, until he reaches the place he's looking for."

"Where's that?"

"The place where he must die."

"Is that the end?"

"No, that's the beginning."

"I don't understand."

"Some other time, Kes. That's quite enough for one night. You can hardly keep your eyes open."

"I don't want to be a hero."

"Who would?"

"I'm glad I'm not Oedipus," he said sleepily.

"So am I. Though you're like him in a way."

"I don't want to marry mum!"

"No, I'm sure you don't. I didn't mean that. We don't have what Oedipus had hidden, that's just his personal problem. No, I meant that you, and me, and everyone else, have deep secrets that they hide from themselves which they sort of know and sort of don't. That who they are deep down doesn't fit who they pretend to be; pretend to themselves to be."

"It's a great story, Dad."

"The greatest, Kes."

"Good-night, Dad."

"Good-night, Kes."

"Good-night, Oedipus," he said to the echoing room.

Chapter 33

Greener and Wetter

I woke still thinking about Oedipus & his riddle. I recalled my strange feeling back in London that I had somehow already walked the Camino, not in some other life, but in the future.

Can someone be in a state of mind that is aware of the future? I notice that, increasingly, neurologists don't talk about the human perception of time, but the mind's representation of time. What happens if that manner of representation changes?

The two biggest problems in contemporary philosophy are the nature of time & the nature of consciousness. My feeling is that the two problems are connected.

Past, present, future. Maybe there are echoes back and forth. Somehow a person's life exists all at once like a landscape, a path; unrevealed in its integrity. We traverse it and get it in bits. Yet there are moments which imply the whole, worm-holes threading through across the grain of time; an invisible skeleton liquidly present, like a law of nature in a tree.

Outside, the morning in Triacastela was dull and overcast, heavy with grey clouds. It looked like rain.

Kes slept late. After his coffee we discussed our route.

"There's a choice from here , Kes."

"What sort of choice?"

"Either over footpaths through the mountains to Sarria, or along the road to Samos."

"Are there bars along the road?"

"I don't know, probably."

"And along the footpath?"

"I don't know, probably not. Just a few small hamlets."

"Road then."

"I can't play pool, Kes."

"I'll teach you."

We went down the road. It kept to a gorge with steep sides

covered in dark green forest. We took a break in a pretty glade, green and damp, with a small stream with stepping stones; a place where unicorns might come to drink. We sat on a mossy shelf like a couple of gnomes, at the foot of a steep slope, protected from the drizzle by an overhang.

"Good place for fishing," said Kes, watching the rippling water.

"Not really, it's too shallow. Anyway, it's raining."

"I like the rain. Is there somewhere I can go fishing?"

I consulted the map.

"There's a river at Samos."

"Can you make me a rod?"

I scouted about for a switch of whippy wood, stripped it of bark, tied a length of our washing-line at one end, and added a hook made from a bent safety pin. Kes was very pleased. I showed him how to cast, and we sat practising hitting particular stones in the stream. This was awkward from the ledge, so we were soon out in the rain howling with laughter as we hooked trees, slid on the slippery rocks, and, in my case, fell into the stream.

"Are you good at anything in this world, Dad?"

"Would you like a quick summary of St. Anselm's version of the Ontological Argument?"

"Not a lot."

"Well, anytime you're wondering whether your axioms are consistent, just ask."

"I'll do that."

I stripped off, shivered briefly in the cool air, and changed into dry clothes and we went cheerfully on our way, singing Buddy Holly songs together.

The refuge at Samos was a monastery. In fact, it would be more accurate to say that Samos was a monastery with a few other buildings nearby. A tractor was parked outside. The monastery was a massive cluster of dour and serious architecture like huge fungi, heavy and forbidding, austere grey with high, blank windows which were an invitation to suicide. It was locked and no-one answered the bell. We decided we were simply too early, and went off to do some fishing in the nearby Rio Ouribio; the Golden River, I think. Our equipment couldn't catch anything, but it didn't matter. We crashed about up and down the river bank most of the afternoon. Exquisite ultramarine damsel flies skimmed the surface in the emerging sunlight.

Samos, the monastery, has been put together by an amateur surrealist. The main entrance was around the side and would have been quite imposing in a pretentious manner, with it's stiff, florid, classical style, except for black stains, mottled moss, bird droppings, and the fact that it had lost its upper stories. The building promises to soar with more grandiose decoration, but just stops, as if some passing giant had lopped it off with a two-handed sword. The side which faced the road was a petrol station. It didn't have a petrol station attached, it <u>was</u> a petrol station; the attendant was a monk.

Later, when we were allowed inside, a monk showed us around. It was full of the same odd contrasts. Everywhere was immaculately kept; clean, dignified, tasteful. Cloisters and corridors and ambulatories and passages, peaceful and still, cream barrel-vaults and sober grey piers in harmonious proportions, except for embarrassingly bad murals in clashing colours, incompetent and sentimental. One solemn space led into the main church which was a riot of lurid colour: gold everywhere with glaring reds and brash blues like a fight at a fiesta. Up above were garish depictions of the Fathers of the Church, including Aquinas, and St.Anselm wearing, what appeared to be, a hefty pair of incongruous sunglasses. A tasteful building with tasteless decoration.

But, above all, in the centre of one staid quadrangle, amid the neatly pruned, pink roses, and tidy gravel paths, was the most astonishing fountain. Holding up the main basin were four mermaids with enormous breasts; real Baywatch jobs, so heavy the figures tilted forward. The sculptor had got so caught up in his work he'd forgotten their arms. Kes was most impressed.

"Look at that, Dad!"

"I can hardly miss it, Kes," trying to be reverential in front of our guide

"I've never seen anything like it!"

"I should hope not."

They loomed over us like trees with an extraordinary fruit.

"Most unsuitable for a monastery," I said critically,.

"Fine for a dairy," said Kes.

I struggled to appear dignified, thankful that the monk didn't understand.

At the end of the tour we were invited to buy souvenirs, which included liqueurs made on site. Someone had decided that a suitable name for a monastic liqueur was Pax, peace, but there was also a stronger version called Super Pax. We bought some of each.

We were shown to our quarters; a sedate room with real beds and a fine writing desk by the window. Yet on the wall were cheap religious prints; at one side, the virgin, garlanded in red roses, in a red robe and blue cloak open to reveal a flaming heart of light with a dagger through it. Facing her, at the other end of the room, Christ, with a split and bleeding heart and a garland of thorns.

Our guide seemed reluctant to leave us and was very curious about Kes.

"Does he walk all the way?" he asked.

"Yes."

"And can he tie his own boot-laces?"

"Of course."

"Does he sleep by himself?"

"If necessary."

"And wash himself?"

I was about to do a mime of Kes' troubles with his sore arse when I caught his eye and changed my mind.

"Mostly."

I went to try the showers. My high-pitched cry reverberated around the hills as I discovered they were icy cold.

"I think I'll give the showers a miss," said Kes, as I vigorously dried myself.

****

In the morning, we waited for the bank to open to get some money, then had breakfast in the sole café which seemed only to serve huge chops and chips with generous carafes of red wine. Fodder for hard-working farmers, and very cheap.

Very late, we waddled, stomachs full, down a road smeared with slurry, amid thick, deep green forest, below a sky completely covered with opaque clouds whose lower mists reached to the hill tops.

We soon reached Sarria. We climbed a hill towards another monastery, passing an ancient cobbler's shop where the cobbler sat making shoes, all his implements hanging around him. Further up, a church with a wedding in progress; some guests had climbed onto the porch roof ready to pelt the newly weds with rice as they emerged.

Next to the monastery was a small town of tombs in black and white marble. Each monument had an oval photograph of its occupant, formally posed in their best clothes. Despite the sun breaking through, the marble was smoothly cold. A grim place; the vignettes of children, smart in their Sunday best, especially poignant.

A dapper little girl, all dressed up, insisted on escorting us to the refuge, and ringing the bell for us. We were shown into a function hall spread with foam mattresses and equipped for table-tennis. Kes insisted on playing, and beating me, at Ping-Pong. My boots were heavier than his.

We rested for the remainder of the day. In the evening, the monks presented us with some huge tomatoes and an elaborately decorated, and very sweet, cake.

I spent most of the night being sick.

By morning the washed-out feeling of food poisoning had set in, yet again, augmented by the exhaustion of lack of sleep. My mind was a dull brown fudge.

I recall little of the landscape down the way except that it was a medley of open farmland connected by tracks through dense woodland. Yellows petered out. Instead were blood-red crosses with a sharpened base like daggers. The paths were muddy. It rained frequently here. Just beyond Mercado we passed a herd of cows wearing raincoats.

Kes slipped in the mud and strained the muscles in his hand trying to save himself. In a bar by a road the woman of the house insisted on making an omelette for Kes, sending out to a farm for fresh eggs. She did it out of concern. There were no 'Valientes' for Kes in Galicia. He was looked upon with pity. When they found out that he had walked more than four hundred miles, the commonest response was "pobriño"; 'poor child'.

A little further on, in the midst of an oak and chestnut wood, Kes sicked up the omelette and announced that he couldn't go on. I was feeling decidedly shitty myself. We lay down beneath the trees and slept.

When I woke I felt worse; sapped and weary, with a queasy stomach and a raging headache. No energy at all, no drive. Kes, dead asleep, looked pale with very flushed cheeks. His forehead was fiery. I had no heart to go on. I couldn't muster the will-power to continue. Gradually, I formed the conclusion that we would give up. I couldn't walk another step. Things would be very difficult with both of us ill. I felt dejected through the fuzz of the illness. So close, maybe seventy-five miles to go, but I knew I couldn't manage the odd five. All this way to end like this. I consulted my sketch-map, my limbs heavy, tears forming, mind like mouldy meat. There was a main road maybe half a mile ahead. I made up my mind. I couldn't inflict any more of this on the 'poor child.' We would struggle to the road and hitch the rest of the way. Completely disheartened, I waited for Kes to wake to tell him my decision.

I could hear some people coming, and over a slight rise down the path came Ed, the American we had met at the swimming pool at Hontanas, weeks earlier, appeared, walking with two women. He hailed us with enthusiasm.

"Hi, hi," he shouted, getting close, "Mike! Good to see you. You remember me?"

"Yes, of course."

I could see how ill I was reflected in his face, though he tried to be cheerful. I explained our position.

The women looked tenderly concerned and plied me with questions. They decided it was a salt deficiency. I'd lost over two stones by now and must have sweated out a lot of salt. Ed found me a couple of aspirins and the women gave me some salt tablets. I chewed the bitter aspirin but the salt tablets made me feel sick so I quietly dropped them into the vegetation. They decided to fix me some fish stew and set about cooking it. It smelt like glue and looked as if it had been eaten once already. When it was done I tried to sip it but it was impossible, and I surreptitiously poured it away.

Kes stirred and woke and rubbed his eyes.

"Hi! Kes! How's it going?" asked Ed.

Kes, seeing company, responded appropriately.

"Would you like a liqueur?" he said.

Ed was nonplussed.

"Hell, why not?"

So Kes rummaged in his bag and poured some Super Pax into an enamel mug.

"Well, I never thought I'd be sitting in a Galician forest drinking a liqueur," said Ed, sipping his drink.

When they began to pack up, we did so too. They were our only hope. We wouldn't make it alone. We chatted as we went along. I had trouble keeping up with his pace.

"Quite a coincidence, you coming over the hill like the US cavalry. I never expected to see you again. Your timing was impeccable," I remarked.

I told him I had decided to give up. If they hadn't have turned up exactly when they did, we would have packed it in. I had no doubt of it.

"I think you're exaggerating our importance. You'd have made

282

it."

"The Camino works in mysterious ways, its wonders to perform," I replied.

Ed told me about his book on Hemingway, and talked knowledgeably about bull-fighting. I leant on the conversation like a pilgrim's staff.

Thus we reached Portomarin.

****

The town lay beyond a wide valley, over a long road bridge, up a steep hill. Along a main street flanked with shadowy classical colonnades was a central square focused on a stone church like a fortified shoe-box. Here we sat and watched the world go by while I tried to assess the odd atmosphere of the place. It had a new type of unreality; a non-place, a place that wasn't a place. The architecture had some style and dignity, I could see that, but it still felt wrong; lifeless, dispiriting, as a toppled tree feels. Soulless. A camp for displaced persons, or that final space in an airport beyond customs yet before the plane. A nowhere place. Somewhere to wait, not to live. It induced lethargy.

We sat, apathetic, for over an hour before enquiring about the refuge; a low, grey building with a classical portico like a morgue for emperors, a stone's throw away. We contemplated it, inertly, for half an hour or so.

Inside was a gymnasium with many pilgrims sitting about. An official of some kind arrived in a filthy mood and began to harangue me in virulent and incomprehensible Spanish. I shrugged, uncaring, and the resting pilgrims laughed. He turned on his heel in fury and went off to bully kittens or stick pins in leeches.

We felt well enough to eat by evening and dined out with Ed. A stray dog slunk in and sat beneath the table by Kes, who smuggled chips down where they were sloppily swallowed whole.

"What's that in your beer, Dad," he said, reaching down, trying the dog with a bit of Spanish omelette.

In the froth was a perfectly formed fish.

"It's a sign from the spirits of plaice," I said.

"Got anything for the dog?"

I secretly passed him a chunk of veal.

Ed was explaining that the town had been transported, stone by stone, up from the valley when it was flooded to make a reservoir.

"That explains its character; rootless. It shouldn't really be here," I remarked.

The waiter discovered the dog, and threw him out.

After the meal, Ed went off to his hotel while we retired to the gym. It had filled in our absence. The entire floor was covered with sleeping bags. People sat and chatted, smoked, ate. We wandered around and joined in where we could hear English, which wasn't much. The general mood was subdued, like refugees from some disaster. Instinctively, the talk was low, almost in whispers. The conversation lacked energy, silences were long, people looked down at the shiny floor, thoughts failed to form.

I went out for a stroll. Groups of kids sat clumped disconsolately in the main square and the shadowy arcades, plainly bored, vaguely threatening, like convicts in an exercise yard. A depressing aura of the dispossessed damped down the place.

I went back and escaped into sleep.

Chapter 34

News of the Future

The gym was almost deserted when I awoke. The air was cold and damp; it seemed to congeal in the large, empty space. All the sleeping bags had receded like a tide, leaving Kes and I beached like seals in a chill dawn.

Outside it was grey and wet. It had rained in the night. We left with some speed as if eager to quit Portomarin. We walked at some pace through the dreary town, over road and path, over a narrow foot bridge, and up a steep slope the other side of the valley. Fat, slimy, immaculate black slugs, slow as a meditating monk, sleek as spivs, were out in the wet, as were small yellow snails. When Kes wanted to pause to appreciate spider's webs festooned with dew like exquisite sculptures of pure water, I hurried him on impatiently. I wanted to get on once more. The lessons of taking time weakened, as if the magnet of the end, now close, pulled more strongly, like approaching death revving up a fever, drawing back the energy it had lent out, it burned through me. The landscape sped by almost unnoticed. I stopped taking notes, I recall only a small dead fox by the roadside; its bloody nose, its swollen tongue protruding grossly, slug-like, its ears still laid back in shock at the swift and horrific vehicle which had killed it.

We circled hillsides to Hospital, crossed a main road, and then plunged into a warren of paths and walled lanes. We gradually slowed as we made distance from Portomarin and the grey cloud cleared. As the sun emerged, the way became magical; narrow tracks through shrubs and tall trees, dappled greens and yellows, a tunnel of glinting jewels, and, as the raindrops evaporated, a musky incense of Eucalyptus, heady and invigorating.

On a mossy platform in a patch of pine, stretched out, like a bearded version of Alice's caterpillar, was Claudio. We embraced warmly. I brewed up some tea.

"English tea is very good," said Claudio appreciatively, "it is much better than Spanish tea."

"I know, I've tried it."

"In Spain it is thought of as a medicine, for the sick."

"Well, if they weren't sick before they drank the stuff, they would be afterwards."

Claudio went quiet and looked serious.

"What's wrong, Claudio?"

"I have finished your chart."

"My horoscope?"

"Yes."

"It's not that bad is it?"

"There are some bad things. You will need to be careful, to go along with the changes and not to resist them. You have a double transit of Pluto in the next year, in the early part."

"Is that bad?"

"It can be. It is a time of great change."

He looked me sharply in the eye as a doctor might, sizing up a patient to see if they could take the worst.

"There are good things too. You have a good analytic mind and always will, good intuition also. Sun in Virgo and moon in Pisces. They are in opposition. It is the most important feature in your chart."

"Is that the bad bit?"

"No, it just means that your main life's task is to harmonise the head and the heart, the reason and the feelings."

"I thought that was everyone's task."

Kes started collecting old, dried Eucalyptus leaves and shredding them into a pile.

Claudio watched without seeing. He seemed decidedly troubled.

"You must use these things in your chart," he went on, " to solve, or help to solve, your problems."

"What problems?"

"There will be a challenge to your marriage, and your job. Perhaps illness, physical illness, chronic illness, and a trouble for your sanity; psychological problems. There is much need for a strong emotional base. Pluto is a slow planet. The effects will last about two years."

Claudio looked at me with some tenderness, as if apologising. I didn't know whether to believe him.

"I will show you, in your chart."

Kes had spread his Eucalyptus shreds in a cigarette paper and rolled it up. He lit it, and sucked the smoke in, trying to look at the end to see if it was alight.

"How is it, Kes?"

"Disgusting," he replied, inhaling deeply.

"Would you like to know when you die?" asked Claudio.

"I thought astrologers never told people things like that."

"They don't. But it is always the first thing they check, for themselves, when they are learning. When I learnt about my death it was terrible. I thought of going far away, on the other side of the earth to see if I could change it. When I did your chart it was like that. I know you are very important for me. I don't know how, but I know it is like that. We are like brothers, more than brothers. So do you want to know?"

The forest was still. The sun shone steadily now. Eucalyptus and pine was vivid in my nostrils like a tonic. My brain felt clarified.

"Yes," I said firmly.

So he told me.

A strong, young Spaniard came striding through the wood. Claudio called a greeting and he stopped.

"Would you like a cup of tea?" I asked.

"But it isn't five o'clock," he answered.

"Pardon?"

"The English have tea at five o'clock."

"Well, it must be five o'clock somewhere. Which would you like? We have Tesco's Premium, Spanish (not recommended), Camomile, or Linden?"

"Or peppermint," added Claudio.

"You carry five sorts of tea?"

"Naturally, doesn't everyone?"

He giggled.

"It's just like the 'Good Soldier Schweik'," he said inexplicably.

"Well, which would you like?"

"You could have coffee if you prefer," offered Claudio.

"Or a liqueur," added Kes.

Kes offered me a drag of his Eucalyptus joint. He was right, it was foul. It went straight to my head.

"Would you like some Eucalyptus," I said to our bemused friend, "we have no hookah, I'm afraid."

Claudio was preparing lots of little bits of bread with snippets of sardine on them, like tapas. He offered them on an aluminium plate from my cooking kit.

"Be careful from which side of the plate you choose," I said, enjoying myself, "if you eat from the right side you will shrink into yourself and strengthen your separate identity, but eat of the left side and you may expand and lose yourself in the Great Space."

"Er, I'm not very hungry," he said, embarrassed and very puzzled.

"I will eat of both sides," I said theatrically, "for I have sun in Virgo and moon in Pisces."

I raised my tea in a toast.

"Death and Eucalyptus," I said.

"Mars bar and Tabasco," said Kes.

"The road and a blanket," said Claudio.

Our guest showed distinct signs of wishing to leave. Claudio asked him to take a photo of the three of us, which he did, and he made his escape.

"Poor man, " said Claudio grinning, "he will think about this meeting for many days."

"And talk about it in the bars of his home town."

"He will. Crazy people on the Way. He will say there was a strange Englishman as fruity as a nutcake"

"Just so. I remember going into the Gents in a pub in Poplar," I related, "and reading a graffiti on the wall. It said, 'I am neither Hamlet nor a suspension bridge.' I've never forgotten it. No idea what it means. Same sort of thing."

"Red sky at night, trip on a leaf," said Kes.

"Exactly," I replied.

We packed up and went on our way.

Villages emerged out of the increasingly bushy woods, and the labyrinth of paths, every few hundred yards. A few simple houses made of ill-fitting stones by a dirt track, carts filled with compost, haystacks like sheds, grain-stores on pedestals like tombs, chickens scampering in consternation, dogs hiding in the shade, sometimes a porch overhung with vines. Rest after work and reach up and pluck a grape. Kes sat, like a blond owl, on the single shaft of a wooden Galician cart with solid Celtic wheels with metal rims and pointed sticks to hold the crop in, while I took his photo.

We came upon a weather-worn woman of indeterminate age casually driving a herd of goats along the path. She paused to chat with Claudio in heavily accented Spanish. She talked with him while looking at Kes and I with undisguised admiration. I warmed towards her. Suddenly, Claudio laughed.

"What does she say, Claudio?"

"She says it is very wonderful that you do the walk."

I gave her a modest smile of acknowledgement.

"Very wonderful, father and son, the son so young, the father so old."

The smile checked itself and I felt a decided need to move on.

Eventually, we descended a gravelly path, past a football stadium, into Palas de Rei; a bland place, almost deserted. Claudio was supposed to meet the film crew here, and went off to find them. The refuge was at the priest's house, a shed-like building in his front garden. He greeted us warmly, as did his dog, a small white terrier scampering about in excitement. The priest's elderly house-keeper plainly disapproved of us and scowled behind his back. Give her a few more years and she would stop this pilgrim business.

Our room, like an attic, upstairs in the shed, was used for storage. It was full of the detritus of the ecclesiastical life: broken chairs and a lectern, a crucifix and various crosses, bits of vestment, stubs and shafts of candles, long tapers, some dented plate, sheet music, dusty leather-bound books in piles; an odour of incense and foxed books.

I propped my rucksack in a corner, sat on the floor and took up a book from the top of the nearest pile. It was an odd volume of liturgy. A book-mark fell out; slightly bigger than a credit-card with a calendar for 1969 on one side and, on the other, a picture of a very pretty young nun, sensual lips and long eyelashes, holding a full, red rose in her left hand. She stood in profound contemplation of it, held gently in her slender fingers, the thorny stem trailing down her palm. Behind her was a round-headed arcade with slim pillars, open to the scene of a mountain village in winter. She held the rose so that it was framed by an arch and given emphasis by a background of snow. 'Santa Rita de Casia' it said, 'Granada.' I put it in my pocket.

I had a wash in cold water at a basin downstairs while Kes played with the dog. Then we laid out our sleeping bags and had some tea before going off to find the film-crew and Claudio. They were treating us to a meal on their expense account. The food was fine and the atmosphere friendly, but conversation was almost entirely in Spanish and we felt left out of it. Kes was intrigued by the whole filming business, it was arranged that he would get a lift in a van with Claudio and the crew the next day and they would spend a day filming here and there, & meet up with me in Arzua. They would call for him in the morning at our refuge. Claudio was staying at a school at the other end of town.

Back at the refuge, a group of six French, Catholic girls arrived, young (late teens, maybe), tender and delicate like a bowl of newly picked peaches. I suggested that Kes and I vacate the room for them but they wouldn't hear of it. They were fresh and lively, enthusiastic and enlivening. They bustled about, thrilled with the whole adventure. We sat on our sleeping-bags and watched as they took turns to go downstairs for a wash, the musty room rippling with excited chatter, shouts up and down the stairs, girlish laughter. Soon they settled down to pray. They all knelt, a grove of girls, eyes closed, devout, their fervent, young voices carressive in the holy peace of the room. The ecclesiastical debris all around helped the sense that more than two or three had gathered together to make something more. A sweet moment.

Then they began to undress for bed. They had no modesty. When they got down to their underwear, chivalry got the better of me, and I went out into the quiet garden, in the cool of the day, for a cigarette. I returned to find them all tucked up, cosy. There was a chorus of innocent "Good-night's." Kes, I discovered, had stayed put. He sat on his sleeping-bag, goggle-eyed, in a state of shock and babbled about the removal of what was, apparently, a particularly fetching pair of blue, nylon knickers.

Chapter 35

Meeting & Parting

I woke in the morning to the sight of the French girls packing, barefoot and talking in whispers so as not to wake us. They waved gracefully, in silence, and left. I shared a cigarette with the priest in the garden. The dog shook hands with me. Claudio arrived to collect Kes. I equipped him with the necessary, medicinal Mars bar and took my leave, pleased to have a day's walking alone.

Through the town, the route passed by a children's playground. One wall had murals, two teddy bears, three feet high, each with a plume, in the form of a rainbow, spurting from the heart. El Oso Amistoso, 'The Friendly Bear', was written beneath.

Down the first proper path, out of town, I came across a German girl, sitting with one boot off, removing a stone. I stopped, and sat, and chatted. We talked for quite a while about the Way and its effects. A figure appeared down the path, coming from Palas. It was Marta. I had thought she was far ahead by now, but no, she had been behind, and if I hadn't have stopped for a long chat, we might not have met once more. We were both very pleased to meet again. I offered to let her walk on alone if she wished, but she wouldn't hear of it. It felt intended.

"Eugenio was in Palas," she said, as we took our leave of the German girl and walked on together.

"Oh, yes."

"He was looking for you."

"Really?"

"Yes. Going around the town asking people if they had seen a pilgrim who looked like Father Christmas."

"Oh dear, we were in the priest's house. How is he, anyway?"

"He has given up."

"No! So close."

"His feet were very bad."

I felt responsible.

"It's my fault. I knew how much he was leaning on me. I forgot all about him. He would have made it if I'd have stayed with him."

"No, I don't think so. He was a bit crazy in the head."

"I know."

"He told me that all men are very bad, that they think with their prick, that the Cosmos would cure him. He was very loud, I was frightened. He said he had lost his nurse and couldn't go on now."

"I was his staff. He depended on me."

"Did you notice his staff?"

"Yes, of course, who could miss it, it was enormous."

"He never touched it to the ground, just carried it. He made a burden of the things that can help him."

"Poor Eugenio. We could have helped him."

"He asks too much. He asked me to tie his boot-laces."

"No sense of self-worth. He needed you to show you cared."

"I am not his mother. You are not his father. He must learn for himself."

"I suppose so."

The patches of forest were growing thicker, introspective. The villages in the clearings looked poor; plain houses, tough granite churches with slate roofs, muddy paths for streets, primitive carts and ploughs, solid women, grizzled men in black berets, no children. We saw just one girl about Kes' age, already into the mould; black dress and wellies, a weathered face, huge bundle of kindling on her head.

In the middle of one densely wooded patch, marked on the map as Casanova, stood a lone, defunct school-house; many windows broken, those intact with Stars of David drawn on them, smears of mud down the walls. Inside, a bereft silence, shards of glass and fallen leaves on the floor. On the green blackboard, three hearts with arrows through them with 'LOVE' printed in English beneath. More stars on the door.

Out of the wood, in open farmland, we were passing a lone farm-house, when a woman rushed out and nervously asked if we wanted coffee. We followed her into the farm-yard. We could have

been following her into the thirteenth century; it was like something
from a Book of Hours; ancient farming implements hung
everywhere, all home-made of wood, leather and beaten metal. A
large table was impeccably laid piled with home-made biscuits and
cakes. We sat on a bench and were served. There were flecks of milk
solids in my coffee. The woman noticed my minute hesitation and
deferentially asked if 'Sir' minded. When I said, casually, that I didn't
really mind, but I preferred coffee without, she ran across the yard, all
of a bustle, and was smartly up an external wooden staircase. She
returned swiftly with a woven, cane strainer, and filtered out the
flecks. The coffee was excellent.

The woman hovered, eager to serve, and apologised for
interrupting our walk but they only had one cow and the harvest had
been poor, and the winters were so bad here, and times were hard,
sometimes she didn't know what to do.

Suddenly, Marta laughed.

"What did she say?"

"She say we are a fine couple and are we married. I tell her we
are good friends who meet on the Way."

The cost was modest so we left double what she asked, still
cheap. She protested that it was far too much and came out onto the
path to wave us good-bye and stood long, her sad, brown eyes
watching us walk out of the life of poverty which had assembled and
settled around her, and within her.

In a section of open farmland we climbed a low fence and took a
break in a field. Farmers waved cheerily as they passed. In the
distance a forest was burning. Overhead, an immense, ponderous
flying boat, like a fat-bellied duck, passed over us, laboured onwards
towards the fire and dropped a stream of water on it. It made no
perceptible difference. Half an hour later, it returned and did the
same.

We crossed the medieval bridge at Furelos and soon entered the
town of Melide. In the main street, octopus was being cooked by the
roadside in great, two-handled cauldrons, rosy-pink tentacles

bubbling away as if for some witches' feast, dead flesh from the sea in a ferment of boiling water.

We didn't pause in Melide.

Santiago felt close, though still some thirty miles. The impulse to hurry along was powerful, it simmered in the mind like a child's excitement on Christmas Eve. What goodies awaited, what would Santa Claus bring?

Beyond the town, in the farmland and forests, people were woven into a past which stretched for generations, born and bred and part of the place, roots going so far back, tendrils of identity, a selfhood grew which would scream if ripped out. The forests and the people were of a piece. Escape meant burning a past. Claudio had told me of a tradition of burning an item of clothing worn on the route, a shirt say, on the beach before the open sea, at Finisterre; the trappings of the old self consumed at the earth's end.

There was something immobile about Galicia; a place with old and binding traditions, to stay was to be enmeshed, as shoots snaked out of the social soil and twisted through the mind. People stared, sullen and trapped, through a thicket of their own psyche, like faces amid the interlacings in the margin of a Celtic book. It was easy to become ensnared. Thus the urge to snap out of it, tear the web, sheer away, move on, skitter down the path, make hot haste. Static and dynamic, rush and repose were held in tight tension here.

Galicians, like the Irish, export their population.

Dense forest of eucalyptus, pines and oak around Raido, lonely and still. We took a break among the tall trees, sitting on soft, dried leaves. I fried Frankfurters and onions. Then Marta took a nap, curled up like a cat, her sun-browned skin matching the fallen, golden leaves. I watched over her, settling into peace. The slim, elegant eucalyptus boles soared seventy, maybe a hundred feet. They swayed slowly as the wind surfed gently through their matt-green, scimitar leaves, high up, hanging idly. From time to time I could hear the thud in the distance as an acorn dropped unseen. As eucalyptus leaves fell around me, they turned swiftly on their own axis, twirling down like

Tibetan prayer flags. Violet flowered ling, and bracken were in patches on the leafy floor. The pungent scent of eucalyptus suffusing all, like earth's own medication, a soothing balm.

Down the path, in sight through a break in the trees, came a pilgrim in shorts and singlet, carrying a big pack, running; head up, eyes ahead, the rucksack lurching and clomping against his back. I called greeting and he waved and grinned and pounded on. I laughed aloud.

I packed up quietly. When Marta awoke I was ready to go and hoisted my rucksack.

"I go one moment pissing," she said, retreating into the bushes.

The path met the road at a fine fountain, blessed by a stone cross, in Boente de Riba. We stopped at the intersection, filled our water bottles and sat awhile. Cars belted down the road. Up the track came a pair of oxen pulling a wooden cart piled high with grass. A herd of inquisitive cows were driven slowly past, their rumps flicked idly with a thin switch by an ambling boy. An old man with a stick, and a neat, grey beard, walked, stately and dignified, to the fountain and sat on its low wall. He waited, leaning on his stick, watching the oxen. After a while, a child came to the fountain to fill a pitcher. The man spoke to her, sedately, holding her arm gently, and she scampered off into a nearby house to return with a glass tumbler. He thanked her politely and bowed his head, and took a drink from the fountain.

At Ribadiso was an extensive scout camp. They invited us to eat, and share their tents. Marta declined and we went up the road and into Arzua.

The refuge was over the main church, through a green side door. Inside was a wooden staircase to the left with a tiny toilet and washbasin in a minuscule cubby-hole beneath the stairs. Upstairs, a long room with bare, wooden floor boards paralleled the North aisle, leading to a snug annex with two real beds. We claimed the beds with our sleeping bags and marked our ownership by brewing up some tea. We had the echoing place to ourselves.

Although pilgrims were massing on the Way this close to Santiago, no-one else had arrived by the evening, when Marta cooked some spaghetti. I arranged a desk with chairs either side and we sat and ate in the peaceful room; with a candle burning softly between us, we broke bread together and drank full, red wine.

****

"Oh, here you are."

"What? Oh, hi, Kes. Where did you stay last night?"

I sat up in bed.

"In the gym. It's huge. There's hundreds of pilgrims. I'm in the film."

"That's nice."

"I'll go and get my rucksack. You have to get the stamps in the shoe-shop. Do you want me to do yours?"

"OK"

Marta's bed was empty.

****

We left late in the morning, and despite what was marked as a straight and obvious black line on the map, got thoroughly lost. We came upon a lone farmer and asked him the way; a short man with very black hair, a long face and a mouth which hung open and dribbled a bit. He didn't seem very bright and looked at me blankly. He would show us the way, he said, the path was not far from his house. He offered me a Spanish cigarette which I accepted in the spirit it was offered, a token of friendship. It was made from black tobacco, strong and cheap, and tasted as if it were mixed with the shredded remains of the unwashed underwear of incontinent sailors.

His family sat outside his simple house; three women, one old and two about his age. They were a distressing threesome. They were plainly seriously mentally retarded. The old woman, all in black, appeared already three parts dead. She sat immobile, eyes like stones; gaunt, striated face, blotchy and heavily stubbled. To her right a young woman stood and waved her arms, her upper lip stretched unnaturally upwards on one side as if hooked, the skin round her eyes seemed pulled back making them protrude as if starting away from the terror in her mind. Seeing us, she gabbled in panic. The edges of her mouth jerked back, stretching her lips and pulling them open. A smile. Her face was worked by hooks and spasmodic pulleys under the skin. Her sister had stumps for legs, fish eyes, and very little hair; a lump of humanity dumped in a tatty chair. Our friend pointed out the way to the correct path, sucked strongly on his cigarette, and ground it out with his boot. He seemed lucid and competent by comparison.

Back on the path, in a clearing in a eucalyptus forest, was parked a motorbike, a startlingly attractive woman lay draped along it. She leaned backwards, supported by her elbows, head tilted back, eyes closed, long, midnight-black hair cascading, her full breasts were raised by her pose like a homage to the sky, plump young buds offered upwards. Sun streamed down through the clearing like nature's spotlight.

"Is it far to the next village, Dad?"

"Don't interrupt when I'm studying Art."

"What Art?"

"The woman, on the Kawasaki."

"What woman? There's no woman. You're hallucinating. You're in a bad way, Dad. Them blue knickers have gone to your head."

"Don't confuse me, Kes. This is the moment for my Sentence."

"What sentence?"

"Your beautiful dark eyes etc."

Kes sat down to watch. I strode forward with confidence. This was fate.

As I got close to the bike, a bald head rose from behind the machine. Beneath it was a massive male torso, somewhat resembling a gorilla, clothed in a dirty yellow vest. A long arm with a spanner on the end of it appeared.

I asked the way to the Camino and he indicated, through grunts, the path I had left.

"It's most important, Kes, to retain sexual energy to use for spiritual purposes."

"Oh yere?"

"Yes, when you have meditated more, many hours of practice, you will gain the control over the body which I have painfully acquired."

"I'll look forward to that."

"You have to watch the world carefully for these little lessons, Kes. Meeting a girl on a motorbike in a eucalyptus forest is very good for the inner being."

"Really?"

"Yes, excellent for nasal congestion. Now, let's be on our way."

"I learn so much, being with you, Dad."

"Thank you, Kes. That's what teachers are for."

"You mean to make a pratt of themselves in public?"

"Exactly. An embodiment of error, Blake called it. A noble calling for which I am unusually fit."

"Too right."

The path met the road at Salceda. A bar was visible down the road slightly off route. The bar was bare wood and sparse. A crusty old woman, sour faced, served a shabby, unshaven customer who looked as if he'd spent the night in a ditch.

"Be careful of the dog," shouted the woman.

Two disreputable, indistinguishable white terriers scanned our ankles with interest.

"One doesn't like children and bites them."

Both dogs showed their teeth in a snarl.

"A bottle of lemon, please."

"No lemon."

On the wide shelves behind the bar were four dusty bottles, one orange, one mineral water, two tonics.

"Beer?"

She looked at me as if I'd asked if she knew any nice young poodles, preferably French, interested in nasal sex.

She went to a fridge, glancing behind her often to check if I was attempting something disgusting with the dog that bites children.

There were four bottles of beer and a tin of sardines in the fridge. I asked to buy the sardines. She placed them on the counter. The colours of the cardboard package were faded. She rested her forearms either side of the sardines like a dog with a bone, leaned forward, and glared at me, defying me to buy them. It became a matter of principle. When I asked if she had any bread she started to shout at me. We took our beer and sat and drank it outside.

We fed the sardines to an eager Alsatian at the edge of a forest down the way.

As the sun began to set, we turned off the way where the path met a road, and walked into Arca. The refuge was the old post office. The front door was locked, but a side door was open. Inside was a wide, filthy room with a concrete floor like a garage, with graffiti everywhere, some pious, some obscene. A washroom next door had basins smeared with excrement and dog-shit in one corner. A third, doorless, room was completely tiled, brown on the floor, glaring white on the walls; a place to sluice down alcoholic tramps. No windows, a single, naked light-bulb slashed out a harsh light. Mosquitoes played around a ventilation grill. I found the door against the wall in the washroom and fixed it back on its hinges. We lay our sleeping-bags on the cold, hard floor.

I left Kes to set up the stove while I went in search of food. The village had a small shop where I got some white beans, a tin of meat-balls, cheese, oranges and red wine. Back at the refuge, Kes was playing with a frisky, young Retriever. It had wild eyes, a lolling tongue, and flecks of foam round the mouth. I thought of rabies.

"Be careful with that dog, Kes."

"It's all right."

"No, it isn't, look at its mouth. There's something wrong with it."

"Maybe he wants some water."

Kes filled a bowl from the taps in the wash-room. The dog

lapped up the water with astonishing speed. And the second bowl, the third and the fourth.

"That's one thirsty dog."

"In all that heat today. It's a wonder it didn't kill him."

We gave him half the meatballs and he was our friend for life. He sat at the door and guarded us all night.

When the light was switched off, the mosquitoes swooped in to feed. We slept with the light on.

Chapter 36

Santiago

Ten miles to go. Almost a formality. We got up late, strolled down the path which soon entered a maze in a damp coniferous forest with a thick undergrowth of bracken. This went on for hours till we emerged by Santiago airport, huge planes coming and going every few minutes.

We reached Lavacolla, which means, something like 'The place to wash your bum'. No doubt there was much need for this stop as the unwashed neared the sacred end of their long journey, but, like everything on this route, it seems, there would be a symbolic reason also. It is difficult to approach purity. On the Camino our own impurity is emphasized, brought home to us. The greater the purity, the more the slightest fault appears heinous and filthy. For the impure the presence of the Holy would be Hell. All traditions of preparation for spiritual experience involve long programmes of purification. This is self-defence.

Nonetheless, not all the medieval pilgrims stopped for a total sluice at Lavacolla. In Santiago cathedral itself, the practice arose of having a huge incense burner which was hung from the crossing & swung by ropes all the way from the roof of one transept, down on a fiery arc, & up to the roof of the other transept. Necessary because of the pong of the ripe pilgrims. This theatrical display is still done, despite improvements in habits of hygiene.

Just two or three kilometres down a minor road to Monte del Gozo (Mound of Joy); a modest hill from which Santiago Cathedral can be seen in the hazy distance, lain in the town like one of yesterday's dogs.

Here was Claudio and the film crew. Angel, the director, was doing his bit.

"Ah, the child, just what we need. You see this doll?"

He waved a pathetic-looking, rag thing apparently borrowed from a smiling mother, looking on.

"Yes," answered Kes dubiously.

"You want it," Angel stated factually.

"No, I don't."

Angel ignored him.

"You ask for the doll. You really want it."

"I don't like dolls."

There was a lengthy consultation in Spanish with Claudio.

"He says you must be more child-like. It is needed for the story."

The scene was shot, Kes whined for the doll, doing a fair impression of an infant.

"I thought this was supposed to be a documentary about the Way?" I asked.

"It is. But Angel has invented a story. He makes it up as he goes along. It's all lies. It's the usual thing," explained Claudio.

"I'll never trust another documentary as long as I live."

"The Camino is more powerful than Angel."

Cristina and Marta arrived. We said our farewells to the film crew and went our way.

Busy road through the outskirts of the city. We walked faster and in our eagerness, got lost and wandered through a romantic scene of colonnaded walkways; entrancing, picturesque empty streets; a place to stage a mannered drama; until we finally reached a spacious square with the Baroque façade of the cathedral rearing up, theatrically, on one side. We climbed the tiered stone staircase to the West door and, at long last, reached our destination.

It was very crowded with tourists. We got split up and each went our own way. The interior was awash with people. The rucksack got in the way. There was a babble of noise. Glitter and colour everywhere. The building strained to impress.

I went out and sat on the ground facing the main door, glad to be out of it all, feeling somewhat dejected. I had expected some sort of emotional climax. It hadn't happened. Soon, very soon, the others emerged and sat silently nearby. It was clear we were all disappointed. No-one spoke. Each face told the same story. We sat in a stunned line. This was wrong. Five hundred miles for this?

I was told, it seemed an awful long while ago now, that there were five special places on the way. I had unconsciously assumed that Santiago, the destination of the whole route, was one. It seemed not. I had found only four. So, either I had missed one, or the fifth was further on.

I turned to the subdued Claudio.

"We will walk on to Finisterre, "I said quietly.

He nodded as if he had known all along.

****

We stayed three days at Santiago, resting, just idling, rich with time. We took a cheap hotel room with a view over a spacious square, got up late, luxuriant with ease. Energy welled up in me like the water in the numerous fountains. I ran up staircases three steps at a time, paused at the top, convinced I could leap the cathedral if I could be bothered to do so.

Most of the time I wandered alone, following whim, definitely no guidebooks, allowing the lure of an alleyway, entering a building where the feel was right, emotive and intuitive tourism. It was good to roam at night, when the spirit of place was most apparent; deserted streets and plangent squares, shadowy and evocative, each nurturing a delicate sense of a sweet lack, a romantic parting, a dwelling in a pleasure of lost love, a memory of her softness in falsifying recollection; a yearning made beautiful, an aching beauty which inhibits escape. The temptation here is to succumb to a languid self-pity made ornamental. I see from my diary that I found it difficult to write straight, factual sentences; they wouldn't stay still but would swan off into poetic elaborations, mutant purple prose.

The feel of Santiago is hauntingly distinctive. It is a self-conscious melancholy, a lament made decorous, a loss performed. Arcades and shadows, Baroque decor, sunshine annealed through metallic cloud; Santiago is crisp with a soft centre, like a veneer of ice over deep snow, a lone rose on a treacherous surface.

It is supposed that St.James is buried here; maybe, maybe not. The uncertainty is part of the place. St.James is buried, is absent, yet perhaps, was never here. The very sense of his absence could itself be illusory. It is a lack tinged with doubt. After a while, the truth flits away among the colonnades, at night a cloaked figure in moonlight, masked in mother of pearl.

Santiago is a beautiful city, a beguiling city. It is a city of façades; of dramatic effects and theatrical props, a place dressed up, where people dress up. With its colonnades and squares, the plethora of churches and seminaries, it is a town of secrets, of masquerade. Here truth is a problem. A show of shadows and hidden streets, an embodiment of De Chirico where there is promise and expectation and the fulfilment lies around the corner, somewhere else. You could stage Romeo and Juliet here. It is a habitat for troubadours and minstrels, romantic poets and mystical composers. A charming place; spell-binding, enchanting, holding with its appeal, seductive, dangerous. Here a man could sleep well.

Unreal city.

City of Distractions.

It is a place of entertainment, some of it religious. There are excellent restaurants, many lively bars, concerts and an active cultural life. I kept bumping into people we had met briefly on the way. There were many reunions. Each brought a memory of some part of the way. It was like the journey flashing before the eyes with each meeting.

"It's over," said the city, "enjoy yourself, savour the memories." I didn't believe the sirens.

On the second day Claudio suggested that we visit a friend of his.

"I want to represent to you a musician, a composer."

"O.K. I'm easy, whatever you say."

We went in late afternoon, as the sun set over a watery day. It wasn't far, down a canyon of a street with the inevitable arcades either side and tall buildings above, to a noble door. Then through a dark hall, up cold, spiralling marble stairs to the top floor. The main room was bare and spacious, uncarpetted and uncurtained, little light slipped through the large windows shadowed by the building over the narrow street outside. Claudio introduced me to a slim, wistful man, Emilio, with hypnotic, green eyes.

"Do you have Spanish?" he asked, shaking my hand.

"No, well just a very little, and then only at the level of 'Me give fire-water, you give squaw'."

He grinned.

We sat in comfortable black chairs and Claudio and Emilio talked easily in whispers. I understood almost nothing as the soft talk lapped mesmerically around me. Emilio put on some of his music and I went and sat on the floor in a dark corner. The city seeped into me through the sounds, an invitation to romantic illusion. The music plashed around me like ripples on a deserted shore; a soft and lonely lilt, gentle and lost, with a tremulous, little-boy voice, singing querulously of the hopeless need of a love unfound; the song of a disguised lamb in a wolf-pack.

The room grew more shadowy as the sun set. Mandolins and antique guitars, propped up against the wall, withdrew into the dark. Loudspeakers became looming henges in a dim and Celtic mist, haunted by a fragile lament, deft and vulnerable as a lacy web of shades. The pauses in their hushed conversation grew longer. Only the darkness and the music spoke, music of the darkness but made sweet and alluring, a child's call out of some hidden place, frightened and meek, not comprehending, overlain by years of adult time, ignored.

"I'm in here too," it said, "don't hurt me."

The limpid, eventide mood was broken when a middle-aged woman arrived and was introduced: Gitta, from Mallorca. Emilio turned on a single, discreet light which focused our small group. She looked like a traditional housewife; domestic, neat. She had a receding face, as if the features were trying to retire into herself. She looked like an artist in pies and pastries, cakes and biscuits. She spoke gently, slowly, caressively, all her sounds beautiful, the words especially chosen. She related events and simultaneously enacted them. I understood little, but much of what she described appeared to be "muy preciosa", exquisitely beautiful. As she spoke her delicate hands sculpted things in the air. It was fascinating. Deft touches from her long, stroking fingers making sculptures of ethereal butter; musical compositions in gesture.

She looked at me with gentle compassion. No, she didn't look at me, she looked into me, or through me as if I were an image, a projection. She looked at something else, something beyond.

Something she saw within me caught her attention. A smile flickered, then she frowned and became distracted for a moment. Her eyes closed and her head bowed slightly, she seemed to concentrate herself. She spoke, obviously to me, in English: "Oh, too much, too much, you are too nervous. Too much to do. You must wait the time. You understand?"

I nodded.

"You are teacher now, but you are not a teacher. You are writer. Write. It will not be difficult for you. You have already written many books. You know how to do it. I see you in a long, white robe. You were in Ancient Greece, wrote many books there. Can do again. Easy for you. You can do it. You knew them. You knew, who is it? Socrates, Plato, Sophocles. You understand? You must wait the time and open up yourself."

She came out of this strange, other world she had been visiting, and smiled, concerned, came over to me and took my face in her two soft hands and kissed me tenderly on each cheek as if I were a sick child who had much to suffer but couldn't understand why. I've never been kissed so gently, like a brush of moths' wings. A blessing.

****

On the morning of the third day I arose in some discomfort. I had slept very badly. There was a tender lump by the anus, a pea-sized sore oozing blood. Piles. It must have been growing for some time but I hadn't noticed it till it hurt. My 'sore arse' taunts had turned full circle and got me in the end.

It was early. I dressed quickly and went off to find a chemist. Tired and in pain, I strode out, bandy, each step to one side, like a saddle-sore cowboy. I was halfway there before I realised I didn't know the Spanish for 'piles' and had no dictionary with me. Unlikely to find a suitable entry in a phrase book anyway. Never mind, I'd mime it. Shouldn't be difficult.

I lurked outside the chemist's shop gathering up the courage. Eventually, I approached. Through the glass door, I could see a nun, in full gear, buying some Swedish walking sandals. I funked it.

It was no good, I couldn't mime piles in front of a middle-aged nun.

I slunk back to the hotel and knocked on Claudio's door. He had just woken. I explained the problem.

"What you need is the balls of the cypress," he advised.

"I need more balls than I've got, that's for sure."

"The little balls, you know them?"

"I know what you mean."

"You put them in hot water, as hot as you can resist, and put the arse in the water. Then you wash with water very cold."

"I'm not sure I can find the balls of the cypress in Santiago."

"Of course not. That is for at home."

He began to rummage in his rucksack, produced a tiny funnel with a long neck, and waved it at me.

"It is inside or outside, the problem?"

"Outside."

"This is for inside, for the squirting. I have some paste. Here."

I took the tube and went off to do my penance.

Chapter 37

Last Rites

We decided to leave & move on towards Finisterre around mid-day. We took a final look at the cathedral. The day was cool and cloudy, promising rain. Crossing the impressive square in front of the cathedral for the last time, the city tried to call us back. A lone piper played Dvorak's 'Going Home' from the New World symphony, on the Galician bag-pipes. It was captivating. Having tried all else, the city played the card of pathos and sentimentality.

"Don't go," she whispered, seductively, "don't leave me."

Sweet traps bind tightest.

Claudio said he wanted to go and buy some fruit for the journey. Kes went with him. So I sat on a low wall to wait for them and to watch the world for a while. The Plaza de Obradora, in front of the cathedral, is one of the great architectural spaces in Europe. It keeps to its place, doesn't impose, despite the towering theatricality of the church. The square is a vast, flat stage for people to interact. On three sides, the buildings are low and, from a distance, modest. There's enough detail to interest the eye if it looks, but mostly it doesn't. The zigzag staircase and tiers of towers of the cathedral provide a way up and out for the eye so there is no sense of being enclosed. The whole aspires to landscape; three low, regular hills and a cliff face which doesn't dwarf.

The Camino comes into the square from a curving slope in one corner. I watched pilgrims arrive. The emotion of achievement takes place here. People arrived in small groups, hugged each other, stood like adventurers amid the tourists. The difference was startling; the tourists were unreal, locked into themselves; in the normal world, they went about their business from behind the shop-fronts of their faces. The pilgrims had all their doors open. They didn't care, they had lost the sense of being observed. You could see their feelings, they moved like vivid, alert animals, exotic with emotional colour amid troupes of grey, mobile statues.

A couple arrived that I recognised. I waved. I had met them briefly, I recalled, twice; twice in more than a month's walk. They had been sitting, having a beer outside a nondescript bar in one of the string of villages along the Rio Valcarce. He had waved and shouted, "Good Day, pilgrim," as we passed. And, they had walked below while I sat on the balcony of the half-built house at Fonfria, waiting for Kes. I'd called 'hello' and they had looked up, smiled and waved cheerfully. That was all. But here I was recognised. I'd made it and so had they. They came over. She was a fulsome young woman with blonde hair in ragged plaits, a pretty face with a child's nose and wide open eyes. She embraced me with great warmth. She tried to smile, but couldn't control her mouth which quivered and she broke into a laugh which explained everything. He caught the laugh and echoed it and embraced me too.

"Very good, very good," he said, much moved.

We embraced again and they moved away. She was close to tears. It was worth a dozen cathedrals.

Beside me, back on the low wall, sat a demure young lady reading a guide book in English. She must have witnessed our little reunion.

"Are you English?" I asked.

"Yes," she answered, with plain reluctance.

"I'm sorry to ask but I've met so few English. I've walked from France."

I felt I had to account for myself.

"Oh," she said.

She avoided my eyes.

"Doesn't it make you envious?" I asked.

"What?"

"These reunions, these greetings. You make friends quickly and deeply on the Way and you don't care who sees your feelings. You must feel out of it all."

She didn't reply and continued with her guide book, noting

periods of architecture and the meaning of heraldry.

After a while she said, "I must be getting along," and moved off, drifting like mist, to somewhere safer.

It was easy to distinguish the Pilgrims from the Tourists. You could spot them from a hundred yards away. It wasn't just the clothing or the rucksacks, the pilgrims had become fuller, more vibrant beings. More real.

There is a Hindi word 'Maya'. It is usually translated 'illusion'. I prefer to think of it as meaning 'distraction'. Here, in the Unreal City, the Tourists were trapped in the state of distraction, wandering around looking for something to catch the attention. Their faces showed a deep dissatisfaction. Nothing was quite enough. They were just passing the time. Experience was like pinball, just being amused & entertained. It had no purpose, and no meaning.

Maya is related to the Sanskrit word 'Samsara' : the world of things & process, of birth & death with nothing more than looking for distraction in between. Many fill their lives with anything that will hold the mind for a while. They are tourists through & through, all their life. What are they distracting themselves from? What deep thing, buried in themselves, are they systematically trying, like Oedipus, not to see?

The pilgrim is different. There is a destination.

Have you no Home to go to?

****

Marta came with us to the edge of town. We hugged farewell, and she went off to catch her train, and Claudio, Kes and myself, walked on.

"These days will be a bit difficult, " said Claudio, who had walked this section before, "there are no refuges. Last time I slept in a broken truck. It was cold, very cold."

We were glad to leave the noisy road and turn off up a country lane. By a wood we found an old yellow pointing into the trees. We followed it. There were many tracks and no more yellows and we soon got lost. It began to drizzle and then to rain quite heavily, the wind grew gusty. We paused in a saturated clearing to swiftly don our rain gear. Claudio wore a swirling cape. Rain dripped drearily off of trees and bracken. It was cold. I grew increasingly anxious while we wandered around for about an hour until we reached a cross-roads in a clearing, a place where three roads met.

Then something odd happened in my head. I found myself in a relaxed mood of warm intensity, energetic and calm. It was like being plugged in somehow. A sense of power thrilled through me, and with it came the sense of mental slippage I had felt in Rabanal, but here there was no quality of alienation or strangeness, and no fear. Self-consciousness slipped from me and I let it go. It went like a burden at long last shed. Something within me was dying and I was well rid of it, it was no loss but an immense gain. This was my world and I was at home in it. It was all a special place. I carried the special place with me. Let it rain, it was of no consequence whatsoever. It didn't matter that we were lost in a wood, that it rained, that it was cold, that sweat was making my arse hurt; nothing mattered. I had no worries about finding the way, or somewhere to stay, these things would be taken care of somehow, they weren't my business. I'd acquired trust. I walked along in a state of continual surprise. It was all so easy, so effortless, so simple.

It was a sort of total slippage, a landslide of the mind. It just fell away, slipped from me. I felt lightened, disengaged, unworried, confident. It was the same world yet utterly changed. Barriers had dropped. I had connected up, no longer radically different from the trees or the sky. We were all of a piece. It was as if everything was a manifestation of a single energy, here differentiated into a tree, there a fern, and part of this emergence was myself. We were all coming from the same place. I felt puzzled, indeed, astonished, and liberated from what were now experienced as trivial personal concerns.

I walked on in a sharpened, slightly euphoric, daze.

"You all right, Dad," said Kes.

"I'm feeling a bit odd."

"You <u>are</u> a bit odd."

"I feel ......"

I didn't know how I felt.

"I feel as if anything could happen, as if the rules have changed. If an elephant came around the corner now, I wouldn't be surprised."

"Your eyes have gone funny."

"What's wrong?" said Claudio, catching up.

"Dad's seeing elephants."

"Good, good," said Claudio.

We took a path at random and came out of the wood. We paused to make some coffee at a bus-shelter at the next village. It continued to rain heavily. There was an empty box of matches on the seat. It had a picture of an elephant on it. I wasn't surprised.

On through the village and down a path through fields. Then we came to a road. Down the road to our left was another village. We turned right. It felt utterly wrong. None of us had maps. We had to find the way as we went. Claudio had walked to Finisterre before and half remembered the route. He had a list of villages.

As we walked on, the sensation of wrongness grew ever stronger. I knew that the village behind us was the village he was looking for. I just knew. It was a fact. No doubt about it and yet I didn't trust this weird knowledge.

"I think we have to go back," said Claudio, "this does not seem to be the way."

"I was about to say that it felt all wrong this way," I said.

"Why didn't you say before?"

"It seemed silly."

We turned around. Of course, this village was the correct one. Something strange was happening.

I found it hard not to smile all the time, and felt I was smiling even when I wasn't. I touched the line of my mouth to check.

"Soon we get A Pena," said Claudio as the sun was setting on this damp day.

"A place?"

"Yes, a village."

"What does it mean?"

"In Galician it means 'a rock' but in Spanish 'sorrow.'"

"Same thing. So, soon we get sorrow," I said thoughtfully, "I've felt that all along."

"What do you mean?"

"I don't know what I mean. I think I know more than I know."

"This is the place," announced Claudio.

We walked through the straggling village to a small sports field. At one end was a little concrete building like a bunker. It looked grim.

"This is where I slept the last time."

Inside it was wet and dirty. Kes and I swapped glances of disbelief. Surely not here. It was just a small concrete hut with a roof, but open to the elements on the side which faced the field. Rain gusted in. There was little shelter; the chill, wet wind ruffled the surface of grimy puddles on the floor inside. Dull grey walls, seeping cracks. More tomb than room. Kes and I looked at it with a crestfallen lack of all enthusiasm. There was just about enough space for our sleeping bags. This was going to be a cold, uncomfortable night.

A couple of hundred yards away was a lone house.

"I will go to the house," said Claudio, "to tell them we are here and nothing to be worried about. Just some pilgrims here for one night and not to fear."

Off he went.

This was the worst place of the entire trip.

I began to open my rucksack.

"Well," I said, trying to make the best of it, "it's what there is. We'd better get unpacked."

Our flimsy sleeping-bags would be totally inadequate. Even fully clothed, in the bags, we'd be cold. Probably wet too.

"Put all your clothes on, Kes. Everything. Several layers, dirty stuff too, wear your washing. At least it will keep mosquitoes away.

Elephants too."

Kes was clearly reluctant to get busy. He sat on the ground and lit a cigarette, coming to terms with the tough night ahead. I sat by him. He looked miserable.

"Cheer up, Kes. I have a strong feeling that it won't be as bad as it looks."

He said nothing, drew heavily on his cigarette.

"Come on, man, we've been through worse than this."

He was unmoved. We sat silently in the dark, rain slowly soaking in.

Claudio returned, beaming.

"I have found a place to stay. The people in the house say that it is impossible for anyone to stay here. They have offered us a store room. I have seen it. It is a good place."

We packed up quickly and followed him. It was a good place. An annex, entrance through the house, up concrete stairs to the first floor. Breeze block walls with a hole like a loading bay looking out to the crops, cosy further in, like a cave. The impression was overwhelmingly brown, the colour and feel of old books, the tan of worn leather; belts and straps, saddles and horses' tackle of all kinds hung and dangled, deeply stained hafts of wooden tools caught the light, glinting chestnut and tawny. Festoons of sun-dried herbs, feathery and fragile, cascaded from hefty nails in the walls. There was an autumnal savour of oregano. A palace compared to the bunker. It seemed we had a charmed life.

We moved in.

There was a bar up on the road and we went to have a drink and see if we might get some food. Claudio didn't hold out much hope.

"Beer," I said in Spanish, and then, in English "What do you want, Claudio?"

"I'm sorry, but I have not the pint glasses," said the barman, smiling, "you are English, no? I work many years in England."

He brought out his son to talk to us, and his wife. We asked her about the possibility of some food. She was apologetic, but there was nothing in the house. She would see what she could do. Half an hour later, she produced a small feast which overflowed our table.

It was like Fonfria. First we had nothing. We waited, and then had all we needed, and more.

"When we go back I expect there will be a beautiful princess in my sleeping-bag," I said with relish, swigging my wine.

"A frog, more like," said Kes.

"O.K. then I'll kiss the damn thing."

"Then it will turn into a prince," said Kes.

In a sense there was a princess. I slept like the unborn, as if enwombed, as if nurtured by sleep, deep and sweet.

Chapter 38

Mood Swings

I woke to the same foolish mood of contentment, dressed quickly, found the bathroom downstairs, and took a stroll outside, around the house. It was like a wander in the country of my mind. This was my place, all of it, I belonged here.

Tall, straggly spears of late maize flanked the building. A cage of wood and chicken wire held a bored dog. Beyond were fields with black figures, mostly women, tilling the earth, like visual punctuation.

The right thing to do was something which matched, married or counterpoised all these emanations. Living was a musical experience. Everything had inscape, spoke of approval. The world was well pleased with me. I felt cured.

Back inside, the farmer's wife had prepared breakfast for us and brought it up on a tray; bone china. She smiled greeting, which I warmly returned.

There was no hurry to leave. We lived amid a sense of great space, an ease of time. Each action, each sentence enfolded with its own pace; a slow grace.

That day's walk was entirely like that. Nothing much happened and it was full of incident. Mostly, Kes walked ahead with Claudio and I walked alone. There was no loneliness. The world scrolled through me rich and intricate; the constantly changing sky, the sheen of the road, the motion of water, the glory of pure colour, the this-ness of each tree, the exact shape of a house; a ripped cigarette packet by the road was a sculpture, a pile of horse-dung a work of art. I was in a dynamic gallery of unending creation aware that I was a contributing creator of all the fascinating and exquisite content, everywhere apparent. The day was quite magical. I felt humble and privileged, and grateful, and constantly astonished. I could find no ego, I was tender and vulnerable, without defence. I was God's fool.

I think I grinned a lot.

It was getting dark when we stopped for a drink in the bar at

Olveira. Three men in the bar had that brash chumminess which comes from extensive afternoon drinking. When they found out I was English, they spoke loudly, and at length on the skills of Manchester United. Claudio was very anxious about finding somewhere to stay and mentioned the problem to them.

"There is a house in the village," said one, "you can stay there. Just ask at the new house on the corner and you can get the key."

We went to the house. The door was opened by a thin, timid woman who obviously didn't like the look of us. She could scarcely talk to us at all through her fear. She said that there was indeed a house that pilgrims could use, her own old house, but she couldn't possibly give us the key without her husband's permission and he was at work, just recently gone off for the night shift.

We went back to the bar. So near, but it was too much to hope that our luck would hold. The jollies in the bar commiserated. Then one of them noticed, through the window, that the husband was just that moment passing. Claudio went out to speak to him and suddenly all was well. He gave his permission with expansive generosity and we returned to the new house and retrieved the key.

The old house was in grey stone with a green door. Inside it was dusty and a bit spooky. There was no electricity so we lit candles. The family had only half moved out. There was some old furniture, photographs of the children on the walls, odd objects left behind casually as if it were some Marie Celeste of a building; a bottle opener on a side-board, a speckled mirror, a pair of gloves, a few dirty plates, a teddy bear. One bedroom was full of dolls, sitting in a line like a phantom welcoming committee.

"I'm not sleeping in there," said Kes firmly.

I could feel what he meant.

"O.K. I'll take the haunted room," I said.

"Watch out for their steel teeth in the night," said Kes helpfully.

We hunted around in the garden for some wood and lit a fire in the wide, brick-lined grate.

The word that there were pilgrims in the house had got round the village. People arrived with gifts of food; a small churn of milk, some tomatoes, a bag of apples, a few oranges, bread. The villagers were curious and respectful. Pilgrims were rare here. We were celebrities. Quite a crowd gathered outside, the kids looked at us as if we were exotic and wondrous travellers.

Soon we had all we needed again.

I slept untroubled, like a baby.

****

I woke before the others and went down to the living-room to catch up on my diary.

I selected a nice, fat orange for breakfast and found myself staring at it, in my hand. I looked at it for some time wondering why it had caught my attention. Just an orange, nothing special. Then I realised that I couldn't see it. Don't get me wrong, there was nothing the matter with my eyes, nor the orange. It was there, rough and solid, filling my palm, but I couldn't see it, no-one could, it wasn't the sort of thing which could be seen. I could see the side of it facing me but the side which rested in my palm, that I could not see. I turned it around. Now I could see the side which had rested on my palm, but now, of course, I could no longer see the first side. I took it to the mirror and held it up before me. Now I could see both sides, one ahead in the mirror, and one facing me, but what I actually saw was two separate circles. I could put the two halves together in my mind, but only there, the orange was simply not the sort of thing which could be seen, not whole, in its entirety, as it existed, the entire globe. Neither could I see its insides. Doubtless its segments were neatly arranged within, making up its sphere, at this moment. I began to peel it, absorbed, seeking its message. I prised apart the segments and ate them slowly till there was only a pile of pieces of peel on the table.

The table couldn't be seen either, not the side not facing me, not its underside, not the grain of its wood which existed within it, now, and made it what it was. It existed whole, all sides and insides, but all

I could do would be to walk around it and see it in parts, take it apart and see its inner structure, and then it would be no more. I would have converted it to a series of experiences, taken its wholeness and made it into a linear sequence in time.

Similarly, I couldn't see the house I was in. I could see this room, at least from the perspective I got from my position, shadowy in the morning light. I could wander from room to room, convert it to a sequence, but that wasn't the whole of it, as it existed now. I could not see it all at once, front and back, roof from above, foundations buried beneath, all its intricate spaces, all its inner materials.

My battered and worn diary sat unopened on the table. There it was with all that had happened to me within it. It was all there, now, all at once. Yet the only way I could access its contents would be to go through it in a linear fashion, read it. Like any book, like the walk itself, like my life, all one thing yet gone through bit by bit, translated into time. What bound it together and made it one thing were the links across time, like the orange I shared above Zubiri and the orange I had just eaten, like the Taoist symbol on the wall in Pamplona and the church at Eunate split into sun and shade, like the thought of the symbolon or the Star of David.

I sat quietly on a chair in the corner among the shadows. I sat a long time, thinking, while the others appeared, ate, packed and eventually told me that they were ready to go.

****

Mostly road through a wide, open landscape until we reached a lone house, the Bar Casteliño, four-square and simple, like a massive child's toy building brick with windows, by the roadside. We went in.

Claudio scanned the menu, made some appreciative noises, and ordered for us all. Soon, there arrived a plate of prawns decoratively arranged in a circular pattern in a pink sauce. Pretty. Kes and Claudio tucked in with relish.

"Delicious," said Claudio, appreciatively, waving a prawn on a tooth-pick at me, "try one."

I couldn't. It might have been a plate of vomit. I stared at it. What was the matter with me?

An image flashed before the inner eye, more vivid than dreams. It took over, imposed itself. A deep icon of my own true self, my totem. I was a huge and absurd mouse, up on two legs and pretending to be human. The mouse had no courage, no resilience. Life could pat this ridiculous creature and claw it as it wished. I could be played with and batted around the place, finished off with one cruel and casual stroke at a whim.

Other images came and went like a swift slide show: a wretched child in a flimsy pink dress, sobbing out her misery in a dark coal-shed, alone and freezing in a world of cruelty and impotence which she didn't understand; a fuzzy-minded tramp, outside of all human warmth, chilled to the heart under a cold and dripping bridge trying to light a damp fag-end; a young widow draped in a black dress pierced with stars, long black hair, dark wet eyes, drooping over a grave; a piece of human meat in a road accident, stunned painless by lethal injury, greyly dying, consciousness filled with nausea; a cat, tortoise-shell fur stretched over bones, fangs in yellow gums in a gaping mouth, staring mad eyes with terrified pupils, neck pulling back in final spasm, a last pitiful gasp: 'pah'.

And more, intolerably, unbearably more: an entire planet of suffering.

This was the way the world was, not the slightest shadow of a doubt. It had always been there and I had taken little account of it. What had I ever done about it all except to keep it at bay by devious, habitual means. It would wipe out a gnat as flippantly as a child, a community, a species, all species. It killed everything that lived, that had ever lived, that ever would live. It didn't care, didn't notice, just went on about its business, world without end.

I began to cry, then to weep, and then to sob, uncontrollably. I tried to hold it back but it gusted through me. It hacked its way out like a gush of acid. I felt unclean, impure. A brush with virtue had bred worms. I felt maggoty. The grief I had been damming up so long ate its way out.

Slowly it began to recede, the sobs subsided. I could notice the bar, clean and bright, washed in sunlight, ordinary. Its normality offended me, didn't they know? I offended myself. I looked up. Claudio continued to eat in a studied way. Kes looked puzzled and embarrassed. No-one spoke. I sat silent for many minutes. Washed out.

Outside, Claudio consulted his list of places to be found in sequence, ignoring totally what had happened in the bar.

"Where to next?" I asked, trying to be normal, feeling drained.

"San Pedro. It's an important place on the way. We can take good water there," he said gently, scanning me to see if I was all right.

"A village?" I managed to ask. It didn't seem to matter very much.

"No, a church."

It was helpful to be moving. Down the road, left following a sign for Cee, then a footpath into the landscape once more, through sparse groves of eucalyptus and their healing scent.

The path cut through a clinker of fragments of beautiful green stones quite different from any other rock I'd seen, each a deep and satin olive as if concentrating verdant Galicia, approaching blue. Serpentine maybe, or perhaps Olivine. Was the village we had stayed in, Olveira, named after this outcrop? The place of the green stone, a substance sacred in Celtic mythology, hardest matter showing the signs of nature's fertility.

Miles more, wordless.

A dirt road took us into a land of low, rounded hills covered with gorse. We appeared to be making for a hut and a radio mast on the horizon.

"I don't remember this part," said Claudio, "I think this is not the way."

He stared around at the rolling hills looking for some landmark he could recognise. He looked worried.

"I'm sure we are wrong here. We will climb this hill and look for the way."

There was no path. We each took our own route up the hill, treading on the low spiky plants. At the top we sat and waited patiently while Claudio stood anxiously scanning the whole panorama. From here I could see there were tracks all over the place. A chill wind blew softly. On the horizon was a slight gap in the hills, that was the way, I knew it. It just felt different when I looked in that direction. I waited quietly for him to lead us that way.

"It's no good. I can see nothing I can recognise. We are lost. We cannot search for yellows. Very few on this part. You must tell us the way, Michael."

"Me! I don't know the way, Claudio. I've never been here before."

He waved his arm vaguely, "Regard the area. You must use your intuition."

"But I don't trust my intuition."

"No, but I do."

He sat down and started to make some coffee, ignoring me.

I stood up and turned myself around facing each direction trying to feel what was the right way. It was all different now my decision was for three people. I walked up and down nervously. The feeling towards the niche on the horizon was just the same. There was nothing like it in any other direction. I sat and drank my coffee.

"Well, Michael?"

"We go that way down the hill to that track, turn right, then left at the cross-roads. The church is up there."

Down at the cross-roads was a yellow marker, pointing left. We soon reached the church. There was a fountain and good water. What on earth was going on?

We took a long break. Kes seemed wary of me, wouldn't look me in the eye. When I asked him if something was wrong, he said he was tired and took a nap.

Chapter 39

Battling Ego

Metalled road down-hill to a busy main road at the end of which was the sea. I stopped suddenly, catching sight of it, deep blue, white boats just specks. It felt like a gateway, an opening. I could feel it pull. Claudio said something but the words were just noises. I stood stunned, something in me expanded to the sea, filled the huge space of the vista. He spoke again.

"What?"

"Food."

"What?"

"We can get food here."

He gestured towards a supermarket over the road.

"Oh, right."

Claudio and Kes went shopping. I sat on a low wall on the street corner starring at the sea. I wanted to run towards it. I grew impatient, resentful of the delay. Why were they taking so long? This was it, the end of the whole thing, in my grasp, almost, just over there, the Sea! I was randy for it. Why buy food? Who needed food? It was completely irrelevant. What a time to stop! I paced about, my eyes drawn to that sweet, magnetic blue, mesmerised.

Claudio crossed the road, full plastic carrier bags in each hand, grinning like an imbecile. Kes had several bags also. What was he playing at? We could eat for a week on that lot. Miles to go yet. Think of the weight.

"Open your rucksack," Claudio said, returning, "we have much food. We must share the load."

He smiled warmly. It was a treat.

It was mostly tins, very heavy. I opened my bag and stuffed as many tins in as I could.

"We have lots of good things."

Claudio beamed at me. I could have throttled him. I wanted to get on. Now.

"I have forgotten cigarettes," he said, tutting, "I will go to the garage."

My legs itched with the imperative to get going. So close. I walked up and down, up and down. I could see Claudio chatting to the garage attendant. It felt like a plot to frustrate me. How long? I could think of nothing else. Kes ignored me.

At last Claudio returned, waving a packet of cigarettes cheerfully, and we moved off. The rucksack was very heavy with all those tins. I resented them. Couldn't we buy food when we got there, in Finisterre itself?

Claudio ambled along. A stroll. I tried to match the pace but it was too much. I couldn't control the energy. I cut loose, speeded up, left them behind, swept past a sign, 14 kilometres to Finisterre, about ten miles. I didn't look back.

Soon I found an efficient rhythm, fast but easy. I pounded on, reached the sea-side, turned right, along a street, down to the beach, up away from the coast, through a wood, along a road. The path undulated up and down. I took no notice of the surroundings. An urgent energy took over, driving the legs, running the body, usurping the mind with its own insistent desire; do your own thing, only you matters, get what you want, go for it, get it, get it, now, now, walk on, walk on, that's it. The others faded into insignificance. They didn't matter, they didn't understand. Only I of the three of us had walked every single step of the way, this was my trip, it was for me. They were auxiliaries. The purpose of the whole thing was to get me to see the sunset, this day, tonight. I wanted it, it was an obsession, all other thoughts and feelings were subsidiaries, functions of the dominating need. Claudio and Kes were nothing. I put them out of my mind.

I crossed a beach where the going was easier and again became unhappy with my pace. Being able to go a little faster on the hard-packed sand made me aware that the weight of the pack was slowing me down. This was not to be tolerated. With all the will I had left, I stopped and opened the rucksack. Tins of food were thrust down the sides like bombs, heavy tins, slowing me down, like my best friend and my own son. I took them out and dumped them on the beach, feeling something like glee. They wouldn't get in my way, I'd sussed their game, they couldn't fool me. I was wise to their tricks. It was a triumph. A strong man makes sacrifices, must be ruthless. I swiftly and efficiently closed up the bag, every movement slick and tight. I zipped it with decisive resolution.

As I strode away, a child caught me up, the tins in her hands.

"You've forgotten these, Señor," she said politely, with beseeching eyes.

"No," I said firmly, smiling knowingly at her, "they are not mine."

She backed off as if from a wolf. I watched her for three seconds, a long time, turned and rushed on, free, fast and lithe. Cunning. They weren't going to catch me that way. Oh, no.

The sun began to set ahead of me. I increased my pace, began to sweat. Long straight road. On and on. Edge of Finisterre, at last. Trivial streets. I found the small main square by instinct. Mobile cabin with two young girls inside idly chatting. Information. I rushed up to them, demented. The sky was darkening.

"The sun!" I shouted. I put one finger in my mouth and flicked it out with a plop.

"Where?"

They consulted each other, slowly, so slowly. End of a long day. One said something about a light-house, pointed to a road, five kilometres. Five kilometres! Too far. I'd never make it. My mind gunned through calculations, couldn't walk it in time, impossible, switched to alternatives, bus, taxi, hitch, speed, need a sport's car. The girls returned to their chatting. My eyes swept the empty square seeing failure. I sat on the kerb, desolate. The great wave of force rose up within me, crested, toppled and crashed in a spread of peace. I began to come to my senses.

Now I recalled the startled eyes of the girls in the cabin as a raving idiot charged at them. I heard my absurd demands. I grinned. I laughed aloud. I guffawed.

I rose to my feet, discovered my limbs were aching, went back to the cabin, asked, calmly, for the refuge. They directed me to a cheap hotel. I found it and took a room for three, wearily climbed the stairs, shed my rucksack, and sat in a wicker chair to think. Shadows thickened around me as I tried to sort it out. What had happened?

Gradually it clarified. I thought I could make some sense of this outburst. It seemed to me it was the ego's last ditch attempt to assert itself, proclaim its lying reality, take over and make itself. Hounded almost out of existence, it turned upon me in desperation and fearful energy, propounded itself, cancelled out all else, like a trapped beast it showed its teeth and snarled. It fastened on a desire and pumped it up. Here it happened to be the aim of seeing the sunset, but anything would have done. The ego could have used whatever was available. It had to re-affirm itself; assert the very fact that it existed, against the world, using people.

Alone in the darkening room, I sighed, got up, and went out to walk back down the way to find my son and my blood brother.

****

We used both stoves to cook our meal, late, in the hotel room.

"I have the need of more oil," said Claudio tetchily, "if there was the sardines then we have the oil."

He grumbled on. I squirmed with shame.

"Stir this, " he ordered irritably, as if to a child.

I stirred the pot as I was bidden.

He went off to try and beg some oil.

I stirred my pot.

Kes sat on a bed, thoughtful.

Nothing was said for a long time. I needed to make my peace.

"Well, Kes all over now."

"I suppose so."

"You don't sound convinced. No more walking, we've done it."

Claudio returned.

"The rice will be not right. I cannot get the oil."

Kes still looked as if he were mulling over something.

"What do you think of it all, man," I said quietly.

Claudio bowed down to his rice, tutting.

"The Way?" said Kes.

"Yes."

"I don't know."

"Too soon, eh?"

"No, it's not that," he said slowly, " the person who starts the walk is not the same person who finishes. It changes things. To find out what I think of it, I'd have to do it again."

I nodded in agreement.

I thought this was a pretty nifty remark from Kes and, as usual, got out my notebook from my breast pocket to jot it down. Once I'd recorded it, a few other thoughts arrived and I scribbled away, forgetting my duties.

"Stir the pot!" shouted Claudio."

"O.K. O.K."

I stirred.

"What do you write?"

"Oh, just a thought, about Oedipus. You know about Oedipus?"

"Yes."

"It means 'swollen foot.' He limped, like Hephaestus."

" 'Claudio' means 'Oedipus' in Spanish."

"What!"

" 'Claudio' means 'the one who limps'."

✳✳

Morning was rich with creamy light. Out on the balcony the world opened to sea and sky. The sun blazed. 'Finisterre' means the end of the earth, of course, but it wasn't the end of everything, beyond the earth was a thrilling expanse of living essence of blue. Compact white fishing boats bobbed gently nearby like souls, or the vessels for souls. The sun ruled in splendour.

We waited all day in calm patience.

Finisterre doesn't look out to the open sea. It is part way down a narrow cape and faces a wide bay with mountains across the water. There remained one last short walk down the cape to a vista across the great space.

Come late afternoon we washed and tidied ourselves as if for some job interview, some test, and strolled out feeling lightened without the rucksacks.

"I think this way," said Claudio, turning off the road up a sloping path, "one last church, San Guillermo."

We climbed steadily up the dirt track.

"It is not here," muttered Claudio, his troubled gaze sweeping the hills. We climbed some more, zigzagging into modest mountains. The sun began to sink and we couldn't see the water beneath.

"We must have passed it," he said turning off the path into dense, spiky gorse, first calf-high, then knee high, then waist high. Kes almost disappeared. We spread out and searched the hillside, the tough and malicious needles catching in our clothes, scratching the flesh. We battled through like fleas on a hedgehog.

"Here!" shouted Kes to my left.

I laboured across to him to find a hollow on a saddle of earth with ancient, almost buried, stones. Not a church but the weathered remains of a small hermitage, not recognisable as a building at all, just a shelf with half a stone hut. It felt secret and venerable. Up on a col on this narrowing cape, it had ocean either side of it, immense and endless, two horizons each dropping to an unknown end. Here was a centre of a circle with an unseen circumference. The eyes of the long dead hermit would face each day an expanse of sea ahead and a fathomless depth of soul within, behind those eyes, out on a limb at the end of the world.

"For every thousand people that reaches Santiago, only one goes on to Finisterre; for every thousand that reaches Finisterre, only one finds this place," said Claudio quietly.

Prominent on one side of the shelf was a stone coffin, lidless, inviting.

"It is the Stone of Fertility," said Claudio seeing me look at it, "young women who want babies come here and lay on the stone."

"Alone?"

"Yes."

"Powerful stone," I said, laying myself full length like a compass needle, my head pointing West, my feet to the East. A white feather fell from my hat.

Claudio scanned the horizon where the swelling sun majestically sank, deepening into orange, imperceptibly losing its power.

"We must move on."

"Can't we watch from here?"

"No, we climb one last time."

We hacked through the gorse to a rising path and then up to a high point at the very end of the cape. Here were boulders with pilgrims already sitting on them facing West like a colony of mermaids. We each found a perch and climbed up to join the audience. It was windy on this exposed headland. As the sun descended, the wind freshened to a vigorous gale as if the elements were fleeing the death of their master.

I glanced over my shoulder to see that the moon had risen diametrically opposite to the sun, living white against the plush blue, cool and elegant like a Lady in Waiting.

I caught Claudio's eye and nodded towards the rising moon.

"Moon in Pisces," he shouted above the gale.

He smiled as if he had a secret.

"And sun in Virgo," he added.

"You mean I'm sitting in the middle of my own astrological chart?"

"Yes, the most important features of it."

"Does that mean that this is a special event for me?"

"It is important for all of us, but, perhaps, specially special for you."

It felt very odd. The bloated sun, magnificently red now, a

massive ember, sank ever closer to the water beneath. It seemed eager to reach its death; a stupendous ruler processing with dignity out of the vast hall of his domain, while, behind me, I could feel another presence, an alternate respectful power, ennobled with imminent loss, serene. As one fell into the lightened blue, the other rose out of a darkening depth of deepest azure. Stars appeared around her like a retinue.

"Is it a full moon, Claudio?"

He glanced up.

"No, one more day. If we had taken one day longer ....."

The sense of excitement settled. We all grew quiet, each sitting on our own stone, sharing the sun's demise. All around it, the sky played a fanfare of red as its monarch departed, a tremendous russet halo marked his passing. Above us it faded into blue, ever deepening Eastwards.

The tip of his robe touched the sea, still he sank and merged, sank further, painting the sea with his glory, until the last radiant glimmer was extinguished like a candle and the gale blew cold. Still we sat as the ruddy sky faded further, blue seeping in, washing it lilac and purple, violet, cooling it towards inevitable, purest indigo.

People began to leave, each abandoning their rock in silence. Claudio and Kes left too. I sat still. Movement felt inappropriate, vulgar, as if I hadn't yet been given permission. I could feel the moon behind me, rising as if up my spine, proud and demure, till she settled in to my mind, bringing peace.

At last, the final Special Place.

I walked alone off the mountain. A barn owl floated spectrally by through the twilight. The landscape held an immense, intimate secret close, very close to consciousness. I could feel her aching to tell me. A blue truth ready to flow over me, into me, through me, offering drowning, a soft and loving engulfment.   I wanted her.

Chapter 40

Post- Camino Blues

In the morning I began my journey. Yes, began, the sense was powerful that the entire walk had functioned to bring me to a start. Perhaps all apparent endings are like that. Finisterre is, at best, halfway, maybe just another way station. From now on there would be a long downhill section, back into the cave of mundane life, past the fire, to take my place on the benches and there to try to talk to people who could not understand, who would judge me crazy, feet off the ground, head among the stars, in cloud-cuckoo land. Some kinda nut.

The world around me felt like a mirage.

Bus to Santiago, then buying train tickets for London. More friends from the Way had reached Santiago in our absence. Some of them, with Claudio, came to see us off.

"Don't forget the transit of Pluto," said Claudio, looking worried, "it is a time of opportunity. Go with the changes."

Our train began to pull out.

"Remember," he shouted, "don't stand against the things. It will break you."

****

The so-called express crawled along, stopping frequently, sometimes at deserted halts with one house and a startled cow. We were alone in the hot carriage. Kes fell asleep. I tried to write, caught up on my diary. Then, all at once, the train began to charge. It speeded up to a rollicking pace, swaying alarmingly at slight bends, bumping up and down at small irregularities in the track. Then it hit a long, straight section and went hell for leather. Suddenly it hit fire. Both sides of the carriage roiled with flames, close to the track, as the train plunged through a forest fire. It careered through a vigorous, crackling blaze as the tinder-dry trees burnt with turbulent energy. It raced on for several minutes until it rushed out of the heat like a cork out of a champagne bottle, and slowed down, back to its former desultory pace.

The driver must have seen the fire ahead down the track and gone for it. Very Spanish. It could never have happened in England. There the driver would have stopped well behind the flames and telephoned for help. Imagine a driver that didn't. A reprimand at least, maybe he would lose his job. He'd be breathalysed, some explanation sought as to why he had done such a foolish, dangerous thing. It would make the national newspapers. Not here. Here it would not require a report. When, later, I commented to the other travellers, they brushed it off. Nothing special, it often happened in Galicia.

Some years ago, I recall the governor of the Cricketers up at Mill Green telling me a story about an experience he had had in the war. An old Royal Navy man, he had been stationed for a while at Malta. Many other nations also kept their fleets there. Apparently there was a creek where warships were moored. There were two bays suitable down this creek. All the other nations used the first creek. The second was difficult for big ships to get into. It was narrow, awkward, rocky and shallow. Ships could get in, but it was tricky. Go in slightly wrong and it would rip out the bottom of the ship. This was where the British navy moored their ships. The tradition was to place the ship exactly right and then order full speed astern. They backed in, fast and backwards. No tentative creeping along but an all or nothing dash. Thus the captain showed his mettle. The crews were proud, and very loyal. I don't know how true this story is, but it doesn't matter, it represents an attitude. This old chap in the pub remembered it full forty years later.

The point of all this is that spiritual progress involves taking risks. It can't be done in a cosy way noting, and abiding by, safety regulations. In order to get anywhere the status quo has to be challenged. The surface mind has to be undermined, identity put under stress. The gamble is with the mind itself. I've already recorded here my trouble with what the guys in white coats would probably call 'mood-swings.'

Only there, deep in, behind the dragons, and the murkier monsters, lies the treasure, hanging in our cave, on our inner tree, at the end of the rainbow. It doesn't look or feel like treasure. We don't want to know.

You have to have a certain panache to plunge through that fire, climb that tree, examine that bitter fruit. It requires a courage, a heroism, a stupidity, a faith.

****

Back home my old self was waiting for me to put it on again. It no longer fitted. I couldn't get used to the absurdities, the constrictions, I'd grown out of my social clothes. I found it hard to take seriously what others thought was obviously important.

Work is a service. It is always serving something. However we are employed, it contributes to some end. Whatever the intellect may fabricate, the heart always knows, somewhere in there, what it is our work serves. If it doesn't serve what our deepest feelings know we should serve, then the mind has to find some way to keep that betrayal from full and open consciousness. The mind's energies swirl around that truth to avoid confronting it. We use the energy we are given to protect ourselves. That knot of self-betrayal shrinks and hardens, becomes a stone in the soul. We develop self-defensive ploys to sustain the avoidance. The swirl around the stone itself thickens to hide the condensing stone within. More energy being taken to hold up the whole dynamic structure, maintaining the tricks while the stone concentrates and solidifies ever more, deep within. There are many betrayals, many stones.

We deeply know that we should serve the energy itself. We shouldn't divert it into these damaging functions, that is a sort of greed, a sort of fear. A malaise and discontent forms within us. We know the malaise is the message, that something is profoundly wrong and needs to be put right; a task which involves releasing the force bound up in our own inauthentic selves. We haven't the courage.

When we act according to the energy we receive, the energy

flows freely. Events conspire to help us. We become fittingly creative, the stones yield their locked up power; they become green and blossom.

There is no morality other than that we should use the energy we are given according to its nature. This is the proper service, the true work. This is absolute.

****

Travelling in to town was a dispiriting experience. I'd walk to the station at the Essex end, early September sun still quietly powerful, life flickering through all and everything in light and colour and breeze and bird-calls. And then, as the train grew closer to the city a weight coalesced in the head and seeped downwards like cement, fixing the muscles, taking their energy, sloughing viscous down till, by the time I reached the terminus, I'd become transformed to an urban thing, a putty-man, sparkless, made into a grey convict, all drably uniform, all the way through.

London was intolerable. The noise of the city was overbearing. I had not realised before how disruptive was the discordant din of town life. The traffic above all, not just its racket but its rhythm, or lack of it. The irregular intrusion of starting and stopping engines, squeals of braking cutting in, a sear of horn, a banshee of police siren, all destroyed some inner music. I just couldn't stand it.

Normality had become insane. Too many people, too many masks showing plainly that something behind judged their lives as missing the point, without knowing what the point was. I grieved for them, yet my attempts to speak of what mattered were fended off like attacks. I could see, when I looked into people's eyes, that my glance went deep and hit home, but they took the wound with all the others and went on with a sort of irrelevant heroism. Often, when I spoke of the walk, a wistful look would come into their eyes. "Oh, I'd love to do something like that," they would say, and I'd begin to offer practical details about how to get going, and the barriers would rise up before me. Some day, some year, some time. Not now, not soon. No (sighing) can't be done.

The first weekend back I escaped to the Norfolk coast for the wide spaces of sea and sky, like a desperate trip to see a lover.

On the Sunday night, after the first week's work, back in Ingatestone I sorted out Kes, as kin in a crazy world, and took him for a drink in the Community Club.

"No more beer and wine, Kes," I said, handing him his blackcurrant and lemonade.

"Too right. No more of lots of things."

"You too, eh?"

"I can't get back into school."

"I know what you mean."

"They want me to pay attention to all this stuff that doesn't matter. The teachers don't know anything and they want me to treat them as if they did."

He gazed unhappily into his drink.

"Not much different from my end. I'm obliged to teach the stuff that I don't think matters. I feel as if I'm betraying them. It isn't honest."

We drank gloomily.

"What do you see in your beer, Dad?"

He smiled wryly.

I grinned back and gazed into the froth. Feelings welled up swiftly and clearly.

"Well," I felt embarrassed, "it sounds a silly word to use but the truth is that I see joy. I see joy, Kes, and something else."

I put down my glass.

"I see pain, terrible pain."

****

Monday morning I reluctantly caught the train into London, as usual. I walked towards the college from the terminus, as usual. I'd got about three-quarters of the way down Paul Street, just to the point where it opens out into a broad cross-roads, when things went radically weird.

I was thinking about a sculpture I'd just passed on a sheer, vertical wall. It showed two men, more than life-size, naked bronze glinting in the September sun, apparently climbing the side of the building. The uppermost stretched upwards with one hand, using the other hand to reach down to help the one below. The lowest stretched one hand up to his fellow and the other downwards, apparently to passers by, like me, in the street below. An invitation. A ladder.

Although I had seen the sculpture hundreds of times before, this time it struck deep and as I reached the cross-roads it unlocked and unleashed something within. Something burst. A gush of energy fountained up and flooded through me. It wiped me out. An infinitesimal flicker of fear as the tidal wave hit, but the rush was so warm, and tender, and loving that it unpacked the fear and I became liberated into what it was made of: an ocean of pure energy, an ocean made of oceans. I dizzied with the spin of it and clutched at railings nearby.

The world turned surreal. It was simply obvious, in a way which it would be absurd to question, that feelings were the realest things. The energy out of which everything was made had felt quality. The exact kind of felt quality made the thing what it was. Water arose within me and I drowned. It penetrated all and extended indefinitely. Within me bubbles of grief and guilt, like black grapes, full and over-ripe, fell as dark snow, each bursting with its offering, merging and fermenting instantly. Every bit of my psyche was giving up its ghost, as if every synapse, every neurone, every regret and failure, every betrayal and negligence, every leaden meanness curved out of itself, unfurled in slow-motion elegance as pain became beauty; each unwound like a fern, like a crest, like an inflorescence, like a released watch-spring, million upon million in orchestrated mirroring, they opened out to reveal others opening out within themselves, like hands in benediction, like a welling of compassionate tears, like blood-red roses opening in a field of snow, like butterfly wings, like an igniting flame, each dying in their gift of their own last gasp: 'pah',

'pah', 'pah'. Stones were flowering with a soft music like myriads of rain-drops plashing into dust.

The willful restriction called 'time' gave up the effort. It paused, as if on the very edge of death, hesitated, and abandoned the tedious and unnecessary business of going on. Time itself opened out. The space between the seconds slipped its diaphanous veils. They fell away. Time elegantly slowed, and melted. There was a vast expanse of time as it gave itself.

I lost track of what was me and what wasn't. Everything appeared, no, was, undoubtedly was, made of Love. I was in Love as factually as I was in the street. And the street and the Love were scarcely distinguishable. Matter was mother and lover. I was in her and she in me. I shared her knowledge. Not anything separate from this being, not something else apart which I might look over, contemplate, consider, perhaps reject. The knowledge was nothing other than what I was and could not be rejected. I knew things, inexpressible things, impossible things; stuff which just could not fit into stupid pigeon-holes called words and concepts. Their inadequacy was pathetic. Opposites involved each other. Logic wouldn't work. Language was made of childish building blocks, it couldn't cope.

It went on and on, incredibly rich and whole. It was hard to take, such aching compassion, so much of it. Everything was alive, made of consciousness, carressive, light-soft and sun-like. I think I would have glowed in the dark.

And it passed. It must have taken maybe a second or two. A glimpse, a vista. It hadn't felt strange. It wasn't news. I had somehow known it was there all along. I had known it always, known it by its absence. I had been yearning for what I already had but had perversely refused to admit. It was as if I had lived all my life in some small, parochial market-town, and then one day, one ordinary day, I'd turned a corner and seen the cathedral for the first time. There it was resplendent in spring sunshine, soaring and magnificent, pinnacled and towering and glowing with golden light, transcendently real. It had been there all along, of course, yet I had been systematically avoiding it unwittingly, going about my trivial business, taking this or that deviant path, chosen unknowingly to miss it, slowly mapping its presence by the pattern of my avoidance. At any time I could have turned aside, away from my usual routes, my practised haunts, down some apparently insignificant alleyway, allowed myself to get lost, and find what I needed, waiting patiently to be found, always there, like the sea. And now there it was, in the space I had made by going around it, intricate and superbly structured, manifest in its coherent wholeness, taking my breath away. No longer possible to deny.

I walked on, a bit shaky, radiating euphoria though I felt gutted, washed out, washed through.

I reached the park in front of the college where the usual sad bunch of battered and bruised alcoholics were assembled by their usual bench. As I passed, one of them raised his can of strong lager in a toast towards me and jerked up a stubby thumb.

"Keep the faith, Bruv, " he shouted, out of the blue.

Strong in my mind came the image, and the feel, of a sweet spring, pure water trickling from rock, from stones, in the high mountains, then flowing down, easy and exuberant through lush pastures, straight and true, uncontaminated, unpolluted. I let it sing through me, made no attempt to steal it, fashioned no obstacle, diverted no current to swirl in pointless eddies. I let it alone.

I looked up at the name of the laundry just over the road from the college. 'Feel Clean' it said in black letters on white. I did. For the first time in my life I felt clean.

I walked on, up the steps of the Doric portico of the college with its echo of the Greek temple, passed between its columns and went in.

I was single-minded. All I wanted to do was to find out what people needed and give it to them, if I possibly could.

In this state I walked into my philosophy class.

I don't think any of us knew quite what had hit us.

17602651R00199

Printed in Great Britain
by Amazon